TE MAHI KETE

TE MAHI KETE

MĀORI FLAXWORK FOR BEGINNERS

MICK PENDERGRAST

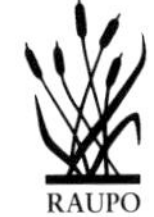

A RAUPO BOOK
Published by the Penguin Group
Penguin Group (NZ), 67 Apollo Drive, Rosedale,
North Shore 0632, New Zealand (a division of Pearson New Zealand Ltd)
Penguin Group (USA) Inc., 375 Hudson Street,
New York, New York 10014, USA
Penguin Group (Canada), 90 Eglinton Avenue East, Suite 700, Toronto,
Ontario, M4P 2Y3, Canada (a division of Pearson Penguin Canada Inc.)
Penguin Books Ltd, 80 Strand, London, WC2R 0RL, England
Penguin Ireland, 25 St Stephen's Green,
Dublin 2, Ireland (a division of Penguin Books Ltd)
Penguin Group (Australia), 250 Camberwell Road, Camberwell,
Victoria 3124, Australia (a division of Pearson Australia Group Pty Ltd)
Penguin Books India Pvt Ltd, 11, Community Centre,
Panchsheel Park, New Delhi – 110 017, India
Penguin Books (South Africa) (Pty) Ltd, 24 Sturdee Avenue,
Rosebank, Johannesburg 2196, South Africa

Penguin Books Ltd, Registered Offices: 80 Strand, London, WC2R 0RL, England

Originally published by Reed Books, 1975
Revised, 1986
Reprinted, 1991
New edition, 2000
Reprinted, 2002, 2003, 2005, 2006
This edition published by Penguin Group (NZ), 2008
7 9 10 8

Text designed by Sharon Whitaker
Printed in China through Asia Pacific

ISBN: 9780143011033

A catalogue record for this book is available from the National Library of New Zealand.

www.penguin.co.nz

Contents

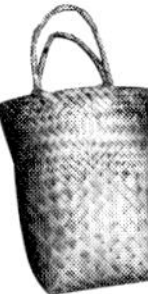

Acknowledgements

For this new edition I continue to appreciate the help and generosity received from the following people who gave so freely, and with so much love and kindness, their patience, time and knowledge and without whose help and encouragement my whole life may have taken a different direction: Kara Waenga of Te Whanau-a-Apanui; Te Turi (Julie) Ranginui of Ngāti Tuwharetoa and Waiarua; Raukawa Nora Hurihanganui of Ngāi Tahu; Vi Williams of Ngāti Porou; Makere Maangi-Matiu of Te Whanau-a-Apanui; Cathie Penetito; and the late Makingaroa and Moana Richmond of Ngāi Tai; Ramari Waiariki of Te Whanau-a-Apanui; Heneriata Rerekohu Gage of Ngāti Porou and Te Whanau-a-Apanui; Lucy Peta of Te Whanau-a-Apanui; Waranganuioterangi Maangi-Matiu of Te Whanau-a-Apanui. Katarina Konui and Peter Hallet, both of Ngāti Tuwharetoa, kindly posed for the photographs.

It is twenty-five years since this *Te Mahi Kete* was first published and unfortunately many of the friends and informants acknowledged above are now no longer with us. I recall them with sadness and loss but also great love for the warmth, enthusiasm and generosity with which the experts shared their knowledge and the learners their frustrations and achievements.

For the first edition I wrote:

> It has been sometimes said that Māori weavers and artists are jealous of their knowledge and reluctant to part with it but it has been my experience that the opposite is true. I have found them proud that others are interested in the crafts of their ancestors, and pleased to pass on their knowledge to those prepared to make a genuine effort in time and concentration. I cannot blame them for discouraging those who expect to learn the skills without effort.

Since then and through the publication throes of later books, I have found no reason to alter this opinion.

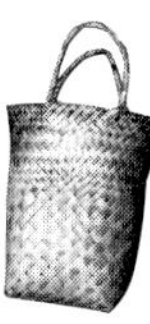

Foreword

Aitia te wahine ō te pā harakeke

This Māori proverb means 'Marry the woman who is always at the flax bush, for she is an expert flax worker and an industrious person'.

In former times the Māori male would no doubt look for these qualities when he was choosing a wife. She would plait his kete, his rourou (food basket), his flax sandals, weave his korowai (cloak), and probably prepare the flax fibre for his aho (fishing line). She would pass on her skill to his daughters and grand-daughters.

Today men, as well as women, wish to make kete from flax. But because instructors of this craft are few and far between, would-be learners are deprived of this important aspect of art.

This book by Mick Pendergrast now brings kete plaiting right into your home. The simple instructions and the numerous illustrations will definitely fulfil the needs of those wishing to pursue this interesting art.

Tenā koe, Mick. Ko tāu rourou, ko tāku rourou ka ora te manuhiri.

Roka Paora
Te Kaha

INTRODUCTION

The Polynesian ancestors of the New Zealand Māori were already raranga experts when they first arrived in Aotearoa/New Zealand. However the climate in the new land was much cooler and the plants that were the basis of basket and mat making in the tropical homelands, did not grow in the harsher conditions. Therefore the immigrants were forced to search for alternative materials. These were eventually discovered and although the new plants proved to be satisfactory alternatives, they were different enough to force some changes of technique. New food gathering methods changed the functions of some baskets and new forms of basket developed to fill these needs. Although New Zealand Māori baskets still retain many similarities to those of tropical Polynesia, they are unlikely to be confused.

Kete continue to be made and are used by New Zealanders of all races, and have become something of a New Zealand icon.

People with a family elder who is expert in the art are privileged in that they have the opportunity of learning the techniques and traditions in the traditional manner, handed down within the family. Others less fortunate have a better chance of finding a teacher today, as many schools and polytechs run courses with competent teachers. For those who are unable to attend one of these courses I hope this book will continue to be of value.

The technique normally used in Māori basketry is raranga, plaiting. A weaving technique sometimes called finger weaving because there is no loom, is used for cloak making and is known as whatu, or whatu kakahu. Whiri, braiding, is the method used for making a long narrow braid. In Māori there is no confusion between the terms raranga, whatu and whiri.

While there is a basic technique for making kete that is common throughout the country, individual workers have often developed their own variations and preferences within the main framework. For this publication I have endeavoured to find a method that, while simple enough for a beginner, produces a finished product that is both attractive and useful. I settled on a technique in which the working strips are added in pairs for the initial commencement braid. Although experts seldom use this method, it has advantages for beginners who are working without a teacher. Because the strips are added in pairs to the commencement braid, the beginner may avoid some confusion by remembering that one of each pair goes to the right (and becomes a dextral) and the

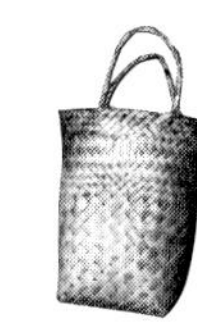

other goes to the left (and becomes a sinistral). The double cast-on causes the strips to be closer together, so the first rows of plaiting are tight.

Instructions are given for two kete of this type. The first and simplest, which was evolved by Kara Waenga of Cape Runaway is a flat satchel with shoulder straps. It is described in chapter 3, A simple satchel kit with shoulder strap. The skills used in the construction are used again in making the second kete. This is a little more difficult, with four corners at the base, instead of two, making an almost flat bottom. Because its shape suggests a bucket I have called it the bucket kit and it is described in chapter 4.

The more common commencement method used by most kete makers is described on page 77.

In this edition, a new section has been added on the making of a plaited hat. It uses skills that have mostly already been practised in the sections on making kete. See chapter 5, Making a hat, page 80.

There are also sections on the plant itself, on the cultivation, gathering and preparation of it, and on traditions relating to it. At the end there is a short glossary of a few words that readers may not be familiar with.

1 TRADITIONS RELATING TO FLAX AND PLAITING

A new craft carries with it the fascination of learning new customs and traditions. Experts in flax crafts observe a number of customs both during the gathering and preparation of the flax itself and in the plaiting or weaving of the finished article. Some of these observances date from far in the past, while others will be seen to have post-European and some very recent origins.

Whether the tradition be old or new, however, students of Māori craft get more satisfaction from their handiwork if they have learnt and practised the customs associated with it. In the case of basketry, none of these customs are troublesome to carry out. I hope that you will find your new skills all the more enjoyable for having absorbed a little of the culture from which they sprang. Often too, a tradition will have a very rational basis: where possible I have given the reason for its observance.

Since *Te Mahi Kete* was first published changes have taken place in the observance of traditions and tapu relating to the fibre arts. Some older experts still maintain those that have always been important within their own family, hapu and/or tribal area. Others, especially those who have grown up divorced from their traditional background may observe few or perhaps none of them. I am disappointed when I occasionally see the rough and careless treatment of the materials, see them thrown around and tramped on. I remain convinced that the care that the elders of the past took to lay out their prepared strips in neat piles, one set ready for the right hand and another for the left, and the careful and methodical way they dealt with each process was reflected in the final results.

The placing of bundles of waste flax leaves around the base of the plant has been questioned (see overleaf). The dampness of the decaying leaves may attract insects harmful to the plant. I originally recorded this practice in the eastern Bay of Plenty where the sea winds and friable soil probable counter the insect problem. Flax does break down quite quickly into fine black soil so it may be worth composting it separately and then returning the resulting compost to the plant.

All around the world education and a more scientific understanding of the functions of the body have released many women from prohibitions relating to the menstrual cycle. I know older weavers who still teach their students to adhere to the old rules and not approach the flax plant or the art during that period. I am sure many younger women will view it differently, perhaps as a primal part of their female identity and function.

I have also become aware of a few customs new to me. At one time weavers took particular care to remove loose fibre from the surface of the completed kete so it could be given away in its most perfect form. Today some kete makers leave the loose fibres in place. The person who receives the kete will remove them and in doing so become part of the actual making process and thereby closely associated with the maker/giver. When Eddie Maxwell gives a basket as a gift he makes sure that it is not empty, even if it contains only a token gift such as a small bar of chocolate or a piece of fruit. Perhaps this reflects an old tradition when a gift of produce, seafood or a special delicacy would normally be presented in the appropriate container, usually a kete. This attractive custom has been adopted by a number of kete makers.

The customs listed below are those published in the first edition of *Te Mahi Kete* and collected from the 1950's to the early 1970's. Individual flax workers will decide which are personally relevant.

1. Cutting flax. Flax should not be cut from the plant at night or in the rain. The fact is that rain, along with frost and cold weather, makes the leaves hard and difficult to work with if they are cut at these times, because of their extra moisture content.
   The young shoot (rito) and the leaf on each side of it must not be cut. The reason for this is obvious: the plant will be severely weakened by such overcutting.
   The leaf is not at its best when the plant is in flower. So late summer and autumn are generally considered the best times to cut.
2. Burning flax. Flax must not be burned. Scraps of unwanted leaf should be gathered and tied into a bundle to be placed under the plant or somewhere where they will rot.
3. Children. Most weavers discourage children from touching, playing with or stepping over either the flax being used or the leftover pieces. An admirable tradition, as anyone who has had to pick it up afterwards, or untangle it from a lawnmower, will know.
4. Eating while working. The majority of plaiters, and cloak weavers too, do not eat while working.
   The connections between food and tapu are many and complex, but modern flax-weavers should bear in mind that their best work will probably result if their attention is undivided.
5. Women. Women with their mate wahine (menstrual periods) do not go to the flax plant.
   Another destroyer of tapu. Nor should anyone, especially women and in particular menstruating women, step over the flax leaves or strips.
6. Perseverance. A kete, once started, must be completed. If it is not, then the weaver will not make progress in the art.
   This appears to relate to the fact that if students are not keen enough to stick to the work until it is finished, they are probably not interested enough to practise the skills until they are properly mastered.
7. Selling your work. Some weavers do not favour the selling of baskets. Others make them especially for sale.
   A point in favour of selling the kits is that this is the only channel through which some who wish to own a kete can come by one. A restriction on selling them puts a restriction on those who can own one.
8. Your first kete. It is usual for the first article of any new craft to be given away (or sometimes buried).
   Unsightly as the first effort may be, it is a valued gift to an expert weaver, who sees not its unshapeliness, but the effort and concentration that have gone into it. To receive a first kete from a learner is taken as a compliment by an experienced weaver. Teachers often receive their pupils' first efforts.

2 The Flax Plant

The swordlike leaf of the New Zealand flax must be well known to all New Zealanders. It has a very wide distribution throughout the country and needs no introduction here. Flax is a member of the lily family and in spite of its common name is not related to the flax family at all, but was popularly called flax because of a similarity between its fibre and that of real flax.

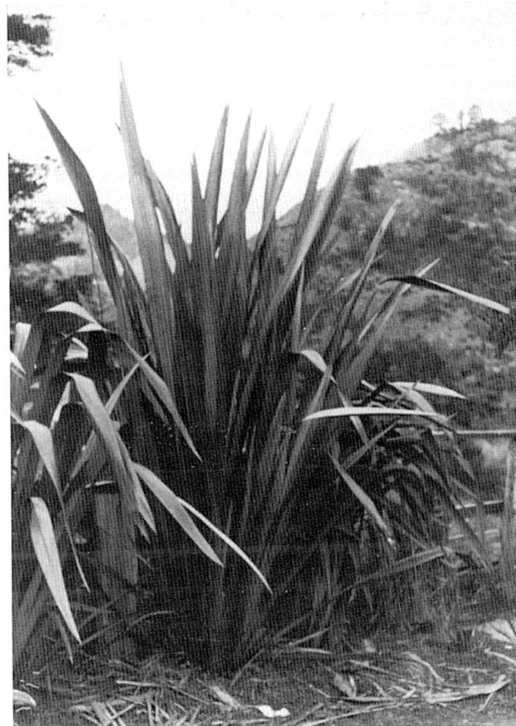

Fig. 1. *Phormium tenax* plant with stiff upright leaves, too hard for kete making.

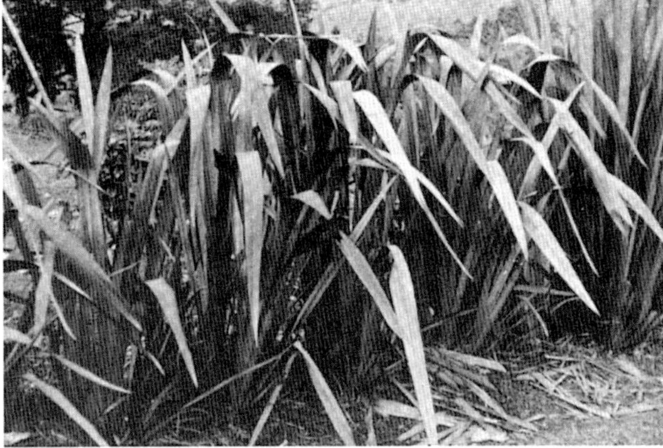

Fig. 2. *Phormium tenax* with softer drooping leaves suitable for kete making.

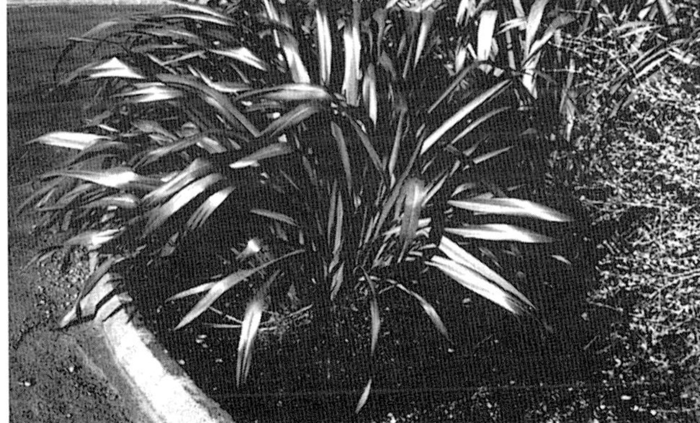

Fig. 3. *Phormium cookianum*, or mountain flax, usually a smaller plant seldom used for kete making.

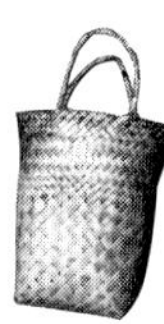

There are two species: *Phormium tenax* (figs. 1 & 2), the plant so much a part of any New Zealand swamp scene although, in fact, it is not at its best in swamps and will grow in a wide range of soil types and climates; and *Phormium cookianum* (fig. 3), which is generally smaller and has softer, more drooping leaves. Within the two species there are infinite varieties and sometimes it is not easy to decide to which species a given variety belongs until it is more closely examined. The twisted seed pods of *P. cookianum* are a simple way of telling the two apart. *P. cookianum* generally has a yellow or lime green flower while *P. tenax* flowers are usually orange or red. The leaves of *P. cookianum*, when held between the fingers, usually feel thinner and softer and have less fibre than *P. tenax*.

Phormium tenax is the plant used for kete making although *Phormium cookianum* can be used and Te Rangihiroa states that the Nga Rauru people of south Taranaki, where *P. tenax* was plentiful, imported and cultivated it for baskets, mats and burden carriers because of the softness of its leaves.

The Māori cultivated, and still do, a large number of varieties of *Phormium tenax* or harakeke, valued for special properties. Plants with soft, white, silky fibres are esteemed for cloak making, those with strong, long-lasting fibre for fishing gear. Plants with leaves that are soft and easily manipulated are in demand for kete making and some varieties with harder leaves are used for heavy-duty work-baskets and mat making.

The beginner is advised to spend some time looking at the various plants in his or her area and in examining them closely before selecting the leaves to be used. Experience will prove the best teacher here. As a general guide, the softer the leaf feels to the hand and the thinner and more flexible it is the better, for these leaves are much easier to work with. Leaves of this type often, but not always, droop down at the tips (fig. 2). Sometimes plants with stiff, hard leaves (fig. 1) become much softer and more workable when cultivated and kept trimmed.

It is a good idea to begin a collection of suitable plants. Some can be collected in swamps or along the roadside and others obtained from people who cultivate their own varieties. The usual method of propagation is to dig up an individual fan. The leaves should all be cut back except the central shoot or rito (see fig. 4). These fans can be planted singly or in groups of three with the roots or more correctly the rhizomes pointing outwards. This is the traditional method as used by the late Mrs Marara Maihi.

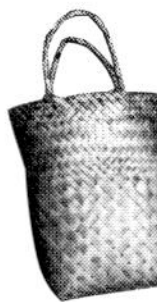

Flax plants grow best in rich garden soil but will also do reasonably well in swampy areas or on dry clay banks. The fact that in their natural habitat they are more common in swampy areas is probably due to the fact that in better soil they will be smothered by taller vegetation and that the young seedlings take a considerable time to become established and during that time are apt to be overgrown and killed by more robust plants.

The cutting of flax at night or in the rain is regarded as a bad omen and with experience it is soon found that leaves cut at these times are much harder to work, probably because there is so much moisture in the leaves. Leaves cut on dull, wet or cold days are better left for a time before being used. In winter they can be loosely tied in a bundle and kept for up to a week in a shed, by which time the leaves will have lost a lot of their excess moisture and be much softer to the touch and easier to work with. In the summer an hour or so in the sun makes them softer but leaving them too long causes them to roll up and become hard and brittle.

Spare leaves and scraps should be gathered up and tied in a bundle, which can be placed beneath the growing plants to decay. A great, almost ritual respect is shown for the plant and the leaves and strips at all times. Most experts have a great aversion to the burning of scraps or leaves of flax, and also to allowing them to be used for indiscriminate play by children. Perhaps this tradition grew up from a desire for general tidiness, but in these days of motor mowers, which quickly get tangled and clogged with fibre, it is still an admirable rule that should be practised by all.

Below are listed the various processes for the harvesting and preparation of the leaves that I have found to be both simple and practical. They are given in the order in which they are performed.

Selection

If there is a local flax worker in the area it is a good idea to ask advice on where suitable flax grows. If there is not, test some different plants by cutting a leaf and splitting a strip about 1.5 cm wide from it. Run the back of the knife along the underside of the strip. This is explained in more detail in the section on scraping (see fig. 11). If the knife runs along freely, softening the strip as it goes, the plant is probably suitable, but if the strip is so hard that the knife makes horizontal cracks across the strip and will not soften it evenly, it will be much harder to work with. Softening the leaf in the sun may make some difference. Stiff upright leaves are usually harder to work with.

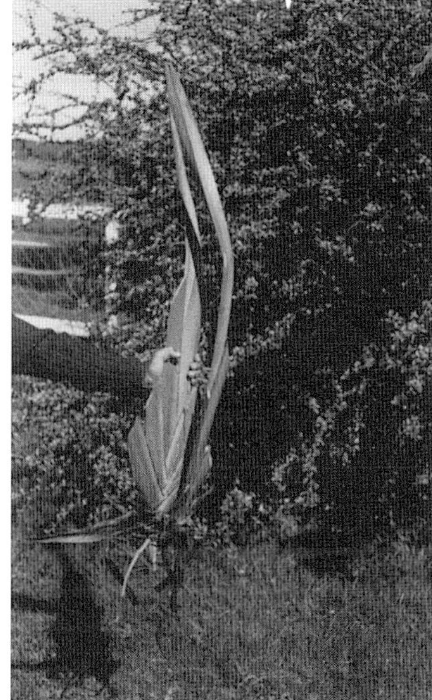

Fig. 4. A flax plant prepared for planting.

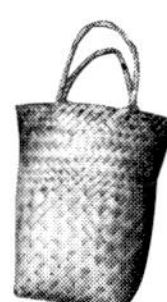

Cutting

Once the plant to be used has been chosen the leaves are cut. The leaves of the flax grow in a fan-like formation and on each fan the young central shoot called the rito (marked 1 in fig. 5) should always be left on the plant for new growth. One leaf on each side of the rito (marked 2 in fig. 5) is also left on the plant for the same reason. So the three central (and youngest) leaves are never cut.

The next leaves outside these (marked 3 and 4 in fig. 5) are the ones used for plaiting. From two to six will be taken from each fan. They are cut with the downward motion of a sharp knife as near as possible to where they join the fan. The old leaves outside and below these should also be cut to encourage and leave room for new growth and make future cutting easier. When a cultivated plant has been cut over, all the leaves except the three central ones on each fan (see fig. 6) will have been removed and the plant is left until new growth has taken place. Leaves cut from the plant at subsequent cuttings are nearly always softer and more pliant; they often dry out to a better colour, too.

If the three central leaves are cut the plant quickly weakens, and if two such cuttings are made it is usually sufficient to kill the plant.

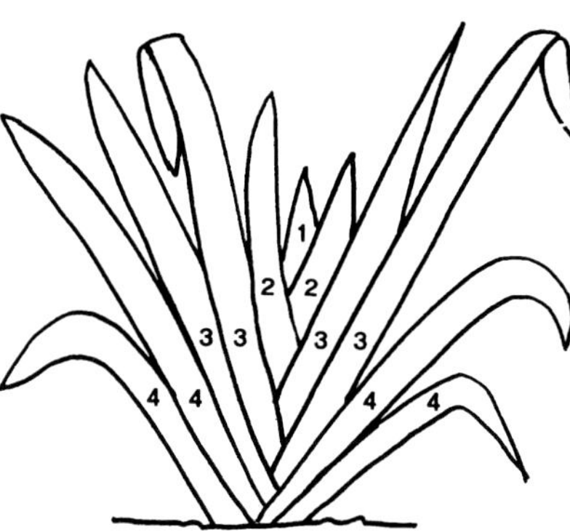

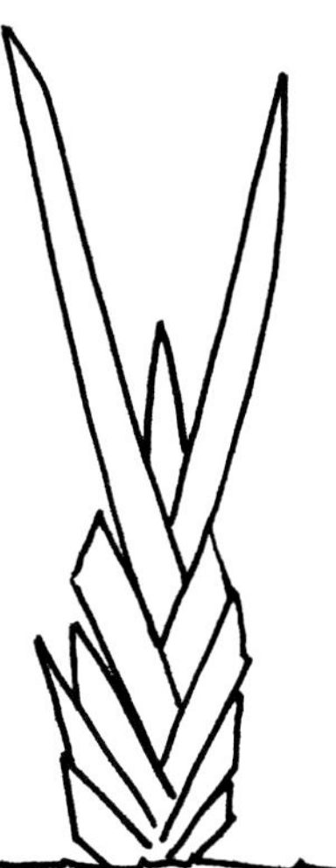

Fig. 5

Fig. 6

Splitting

The leaves are next split into strips ready to begin plaiting. If the hard butt at the base of the leaf is very long some of it can be cut off for easier handling but at least 20 cm of butt must be left on the leaf. For the kete we are making, 48 strips about 1.5 cm wide will be needed.

The two sections or halves of the leaf shown in fig. 7a are pressed together as shown in fig. 7b. The splits are made with the thumbnail about half way along the length of the leaf. First push the thumbnail through the double thickness of the leaf near the midrib, making a split about 10 cm long (see fig. 7b). Repeat this, dividing the leaf into strips 1.5 cm wide and working towards the outer side of the leaf. There will usually be about 3 or 4 splits depending on the width of the leaf (see fig. 7c). The outer edge of the leaf must not be included in the width of a strip as it will be found to be of uneven width and much thinner.

The first finger of the right hand is now threaded through the splits as in fig. 7d and then drawn towards the tip of the leaf splitting it into strips (see fig. 7e).

The strips are now split towards the butt of the leaf, but only as far as the place where the two sides of the leaf join together in the hard butt (see fig. 7f).

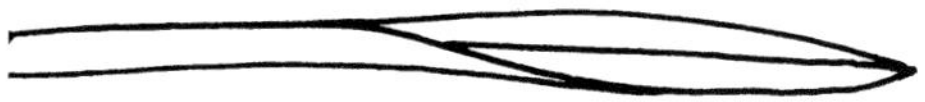

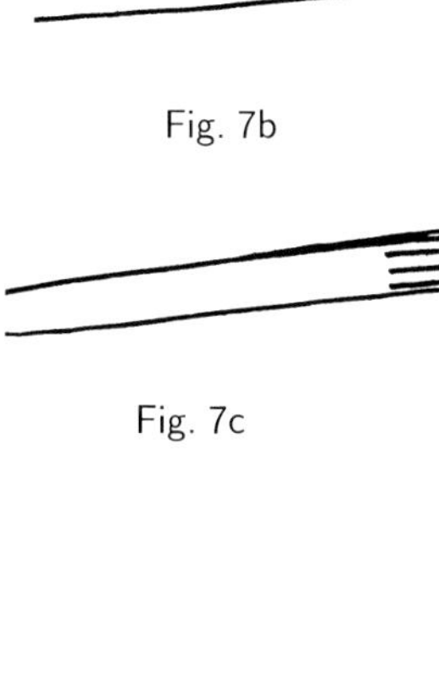

Fig. 7a

Fig. 7b

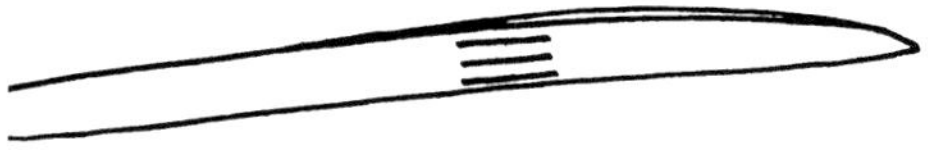

Fig. 7c

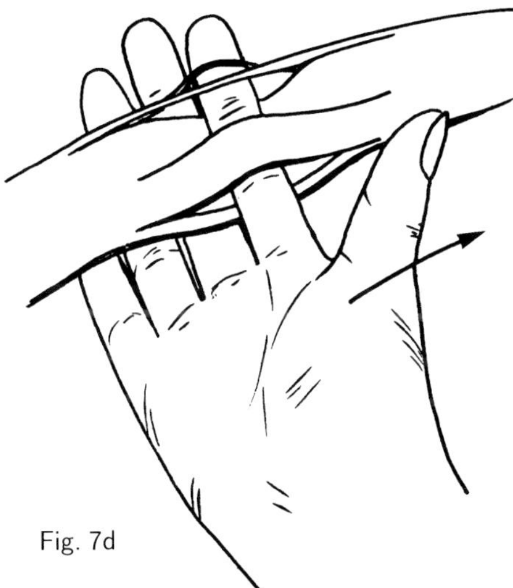

Fig. 7d

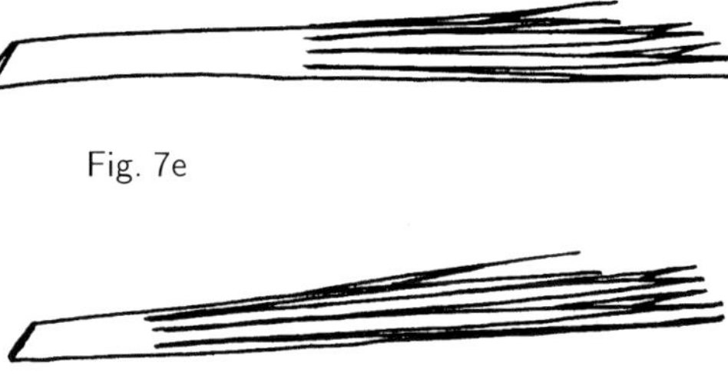

Fig. 7e

Fig. 7f

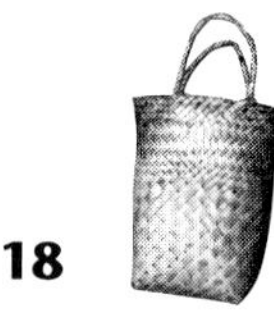

Tearing the strips off the leaf

The strips are now torn away from the butt of the leaf in such a manner as to leave a tuft of fibre at the butt end of each strip.

Take the butt end of the split leaf in the left hand and fold one of the split strips back at the point where it joins the butt of the leaf as shown in fig. 8.

Hold the leaf so that the butt end points towards you and fold one strip back as in fig. 9.

Place the thumb of the left hand very firmly on the strip where it is folded.

With the right hand pull sharply on the strip in the direction indicated by the arrow. This takes some practice. During the movement the leaf must be held very firmly between the left thumb and the rest of the hand. The strip should tear free from the leaf where it was held down by the thumb at the point where the strip joined the hard butt. The strip should have a tuft of fibre at the end that was torn off the butt of the leaf (see fig. 10).

Some types of flax tear off more easily than others, but this is a difficult movement to master and needs considerable practice. If a lot of green leaf material is left on the tuft it can be scraped off with a knife in the same way shown for scraping the strip in fig. 11.

Tear the next strip away from the butt of the leaf in the same way and then turn the leaf over and do the same to the strips on the other side.

The butt, midrib and outer edges of the leaf are waste material and should be put in a heap ready to be bundled up and put beneath the growing flax plant.

Bundle the strips up with all the tufted butt ends even and cut off the thin pointed end with a sharp pair of scissors, leaving the strips about 70 to 80 cm long. This disposes of unneeded length and tattered ends.

> **Note:** Some types of flax are so hard or the fibre in them is so strong that it is not possible to tear the strips away in the above manner. A method for dealing with this type of flax is described in Appendix 6. Some beginners would find this method easier to master than the more orthodox way described above.

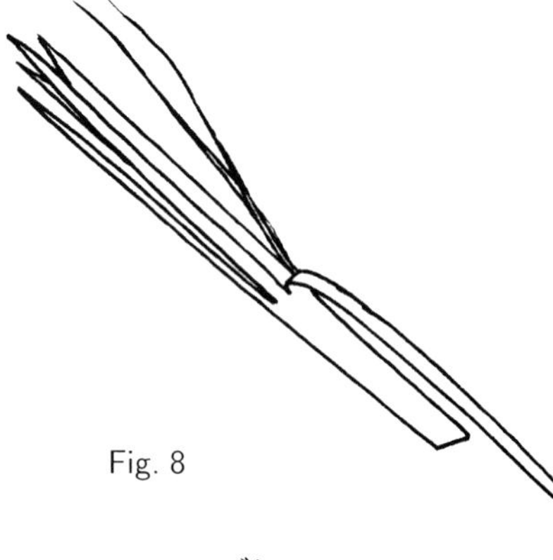

Fig. 8

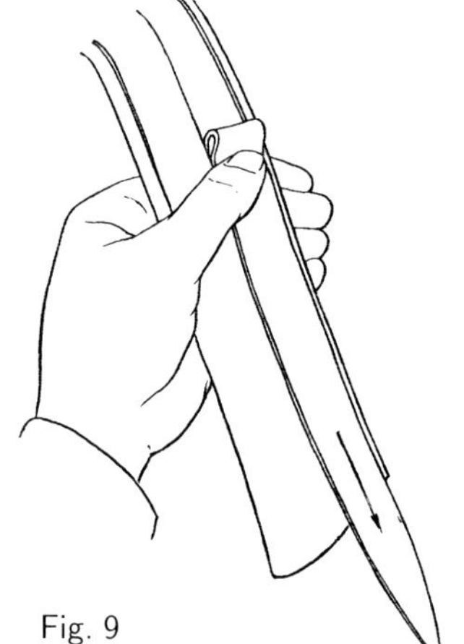

Fig. 9

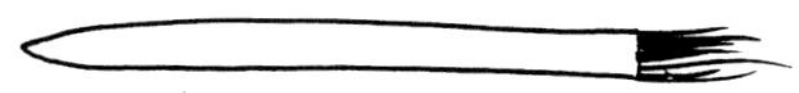

Fig. 10

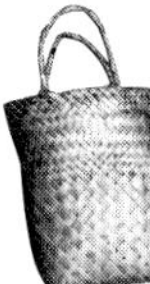

Scraping

The strips of flax are now ready for scraping. This is done to soften the strips and make them more flexible for plaiting; it also helps the flax to dry a better colour and prevents the strips from rolling and shrinking as much as they otherwise would as they dry.

The back (dull side) of the strip of flax is held firmly against the back of the blade of a knife with the thumb as shown. The strip is pulled between the thumb of the right hand and the back of the knife in the direction indicated by the arrow. It is probably easier for the beginner to scrape from the centre of the strip to the tip and then reverse the strip and scrape from the centre to the butt end.

The strip is now turned over and treated in the same way on the other side. The strips should now feel much softer.

This process was traditionally carried out with a mussel or other shell and some weavers still prefer to use the shell.

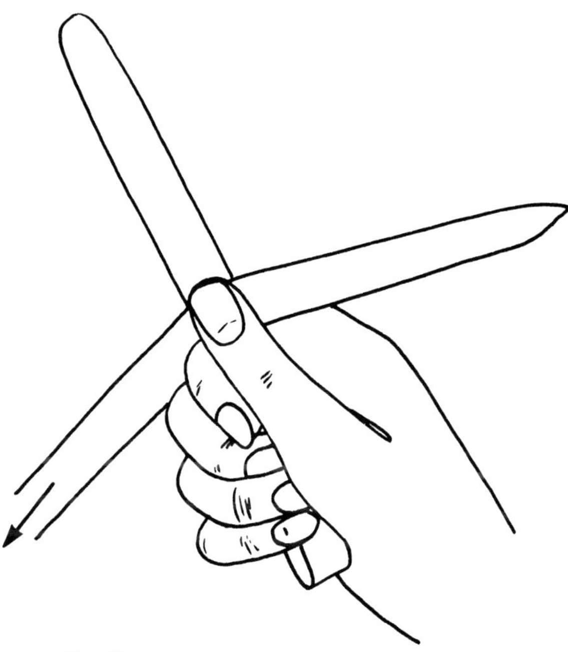

Fig. 11

3 A Simple Satchel Kit with Shoulder Strap

Fig. 12

Note: The commencement shown here with the strips cast on in pairs is not the commonest one, but is simpler for the beginner. The method of casting on single strips is shown on page 77.

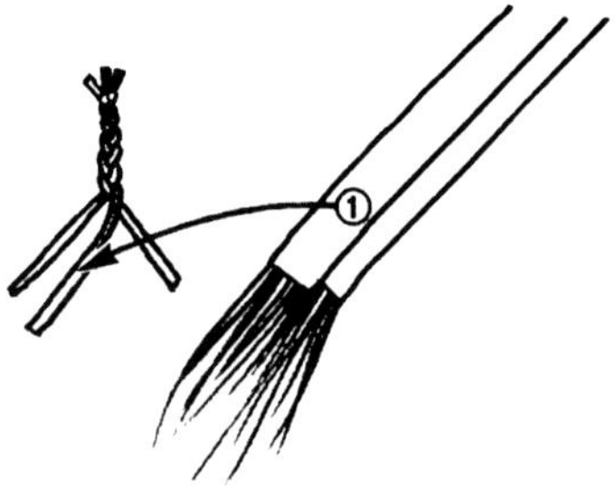

The base plait

The first step is to braid the fibre tufts at the end of each strip of flax together into a three-ply braid (whiri), so that the 48 strips that are to make the kete are joined together. This must be very firmly braided.

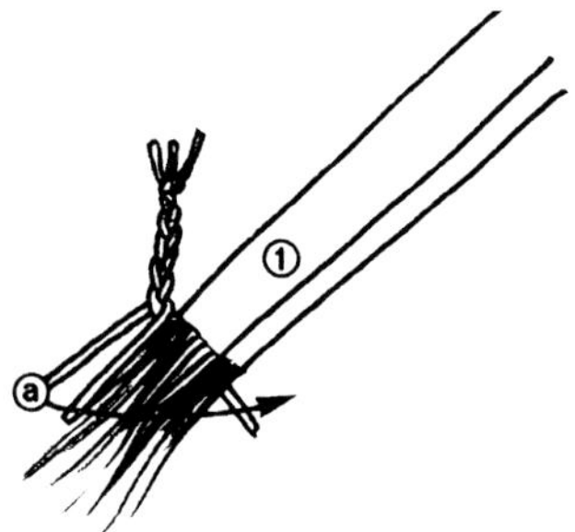

Fig. 13

You will need to know how to do the three-ply braid. For those who are not familiar with it, it is described in the section on making the handles for the satchel kete (figs. 136–140, page 50).

The strips are joined in pairs from alternate sides of the central braid. There must always be an even number of strips. When the first pair is attached to the right-hand side of the central braid the final pair will be on the left-hand side.
To begin take three narrow strips about 0.5 cm wide, tie them together, and make a short three-ply braid. (See fig. 12.) This is the beginning of the three-ply braid that will continue along the base of the kete.

Take two of the prepared strips of flax (marked 1 in fig. 12) and lay them on top of each other with the shiny sides up. These double strips will be referred to as 'pair 1', 'pair 2', etc. in the following directions and will be labelled simply as '1' in the diagrams.

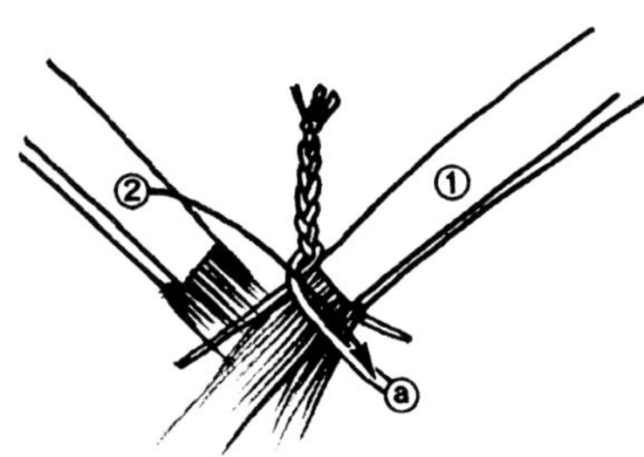

Fig. 14

Pair 1 is placed so that the fibre tufts cover the final strip in the three-ply braid. The fibre tufts point to the left and towards the worker. The leaf tips point to the right and away from the worker (fig. 13).

The narrow strip (a) from the left-hand side of the narrow three-ply braid is brought across the tufts of pair 1, which has just been added. This will hold them in place.

> **Note:** The numerals that label the strips in each diagram are for that diagram only. In the following diagram the same numerals will apply to a new set of strips. The strips must be braided very firmly.

Pair 2 of the prepared strips of flax is now laid on the narrow strip (a) from the three-ply braid, to lie as shown in fig. 15. This time the leaf tips point to the left and away from the worker and the fibre tufts lie across the tufts of pair 1.

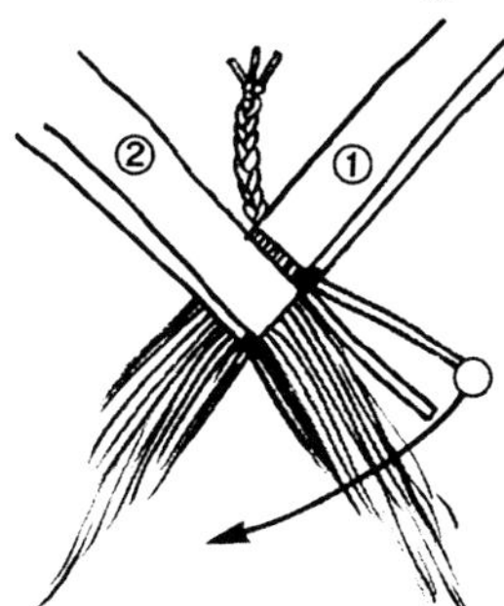

Fig. 15

Take the narrow strip that lies to the right of the three-ply braid and bring it across the tufts of pair 2 to hold them in place as in fig. 16.

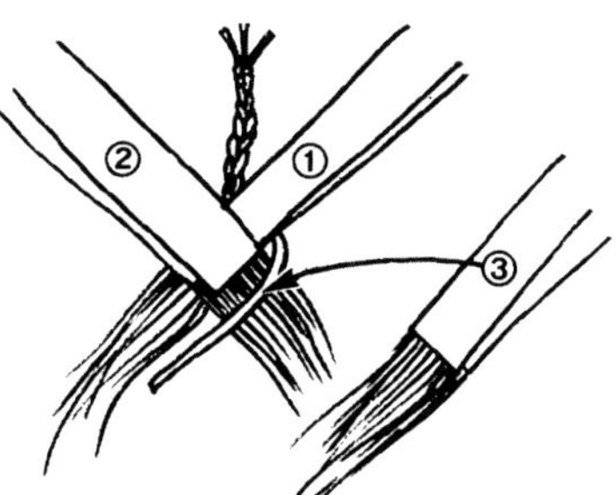

Fig. 16

Pair 3 is placed on the narrow strip, parallel to pair 1 to lie in the position shown in fig. 17.

The tufts of pair 1 and the narrow strip of the three-ply braid are now brought across the tufts of pair 3, as shown by the arrow to the position shown in fig. 18.

Pair 4 is now laid on the tufts of pair 1. The work should now resemble fig. 19.

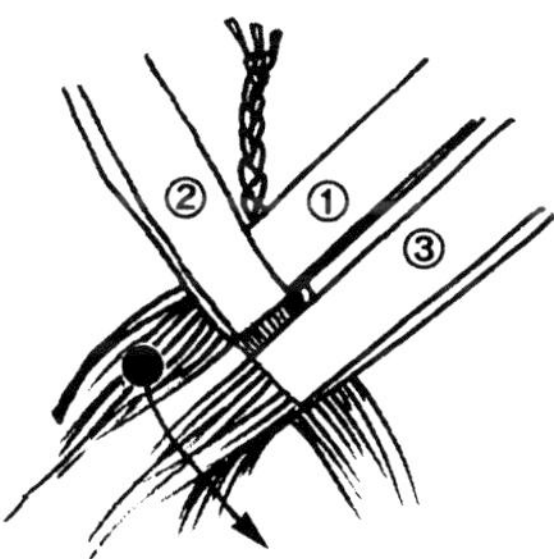

Fig. 17

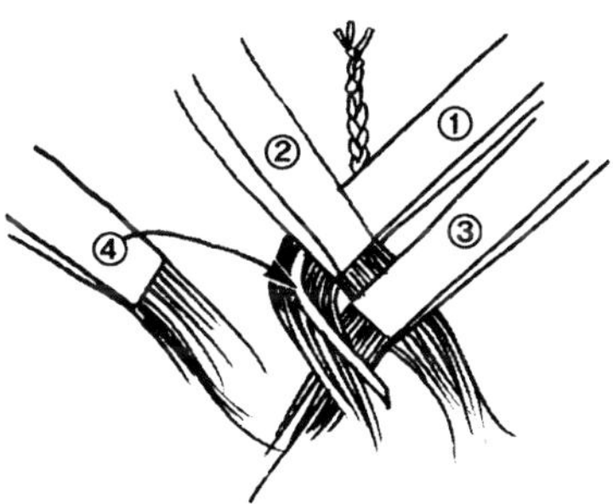

Fig. 18

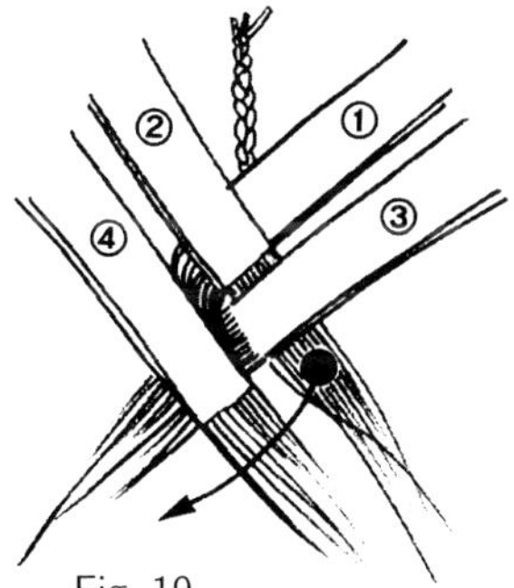

Fig. 19

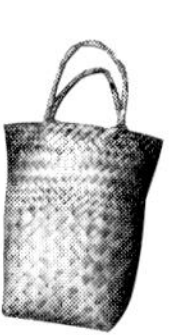

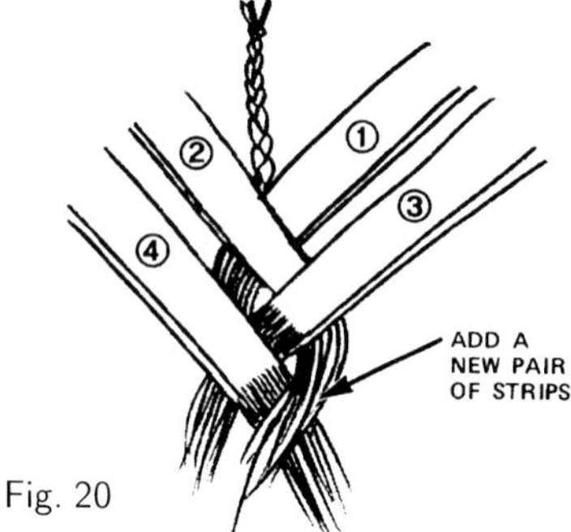

Fig. 20

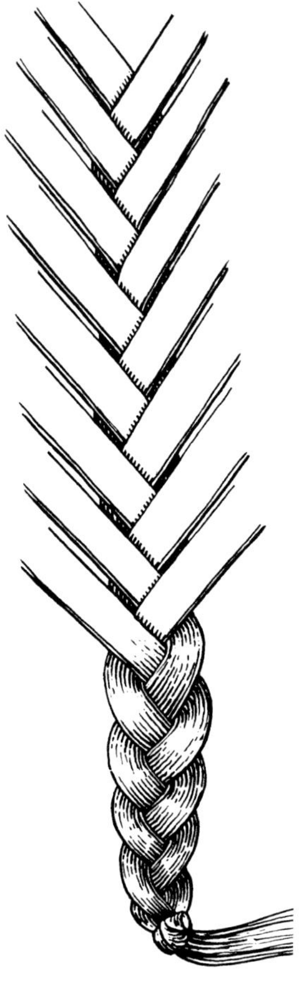
Fig. 21

The tufts of pair 2, on the right of the work, are brought across the tufts of pair 4, as shown by the arrow. The work will now resemble fig. 20.

A new pair of strips is now laid on the tufts of pair 2 in fig. 20. The tufts on the left are brought across as in fig. 17 and a new pair placed on them as in fig. 18. Bring the tufts over from the right (fig. 19). Add a new pair on the right (fig. 20).

Continue this sequence using figs. 17–20 until all 48 strips have been added (as in fig. 21).

The final pair will be on the left. There will be twelve pairs on each side of the braid. If there are not, a mistake has been made and the work should be undone and started again.

The three-ply braid is continued until all the fibre from the tufts at the ends of the strips is gathered into the braid. Tie the end in an overhand knot (see Appendix 1) and cut off the fibre protruding from the knot (fig. 21).

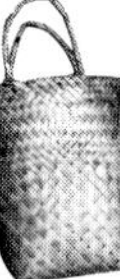

Plaiting the base triangles

The next step is to plait the strips on either side of the whiri or base braid into a triangle (see fig. 48 on page 29).

Turn the kete around so that it lies crossways in front of you. The base braid is underneath and cannot be seen. The end of the three-ply braid protrudes to the left (see fig. 22).

The top strip from the pair of strips labelled 1 is folded back towards the worker as indicated by the arrow in fig. 23 to lie in the position shown in fig. 24. The dull side of the strip is uppermost.

The remaining strip from pair 1 is moved to the left indicated by the arrow in fig. 25 to lie in the position shown in fig. 26. It lies at a right angle to the other strip of the pair that is on the opposite side of the base braid.
In this movement the surface of the strip is not changed. That is, the shiny side remains uppermost.

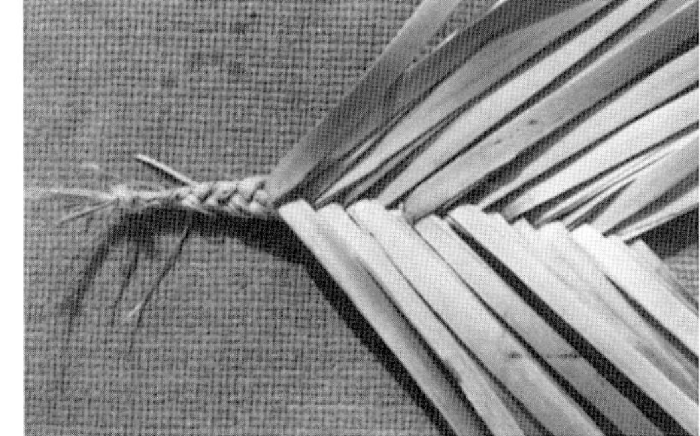

Fig. 22

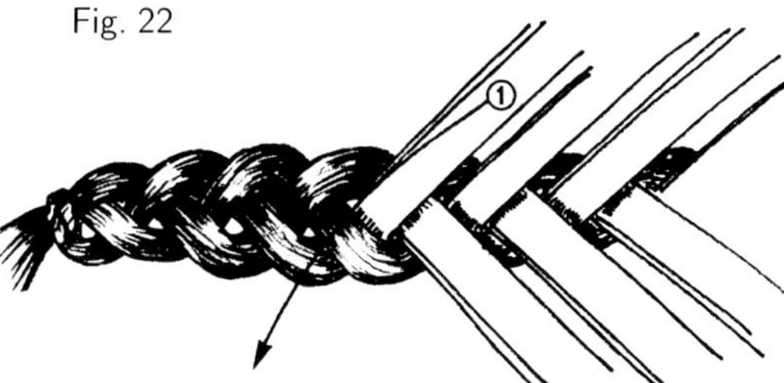

Fig. 23

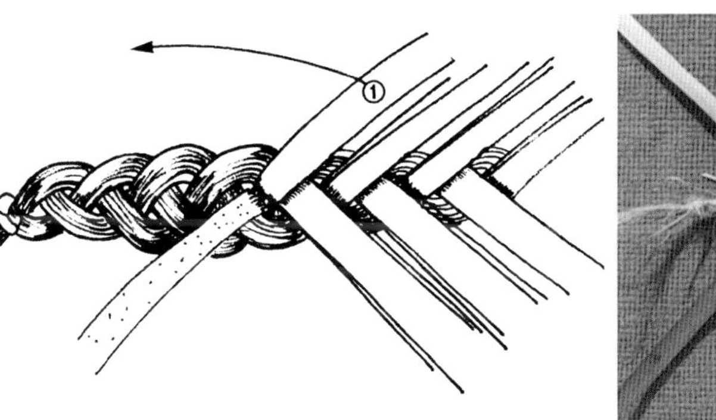

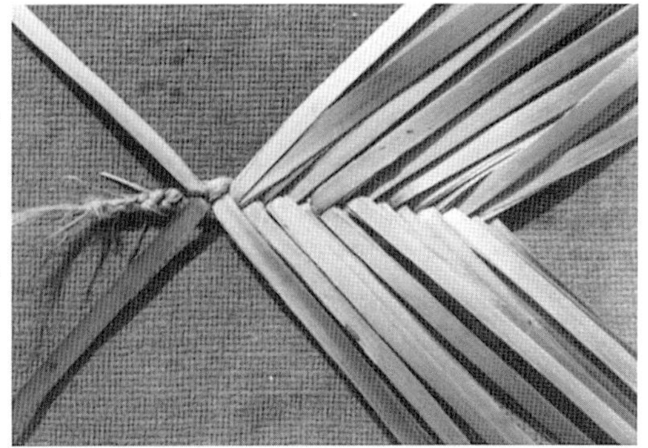

Fig. 24

Fig. 25

Fig. 26

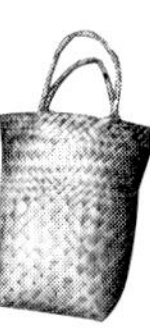

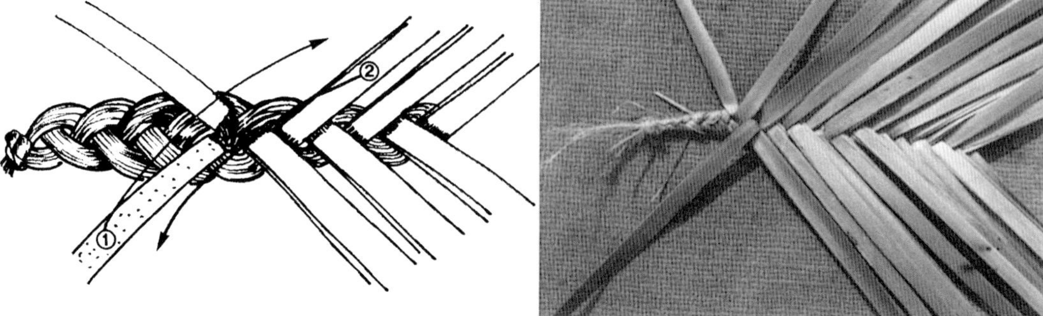

Fig. 27

Fig. 28

Strip 1 in fig. 27 is moved back to its original position as indicated by the arrow to lie in the position shown in fig. 28.

The top strip of the pair labelled 2 in fig. 27 is folded back towards the worker as indicated by the arrow to lie in the position shown in fig. 28. The dull side is uppermost.

Strip 1 in fig. 29 is moved to the left as indicated by the arrow to lie in the position shown in fig. 30. The shiny side remains uppermost.

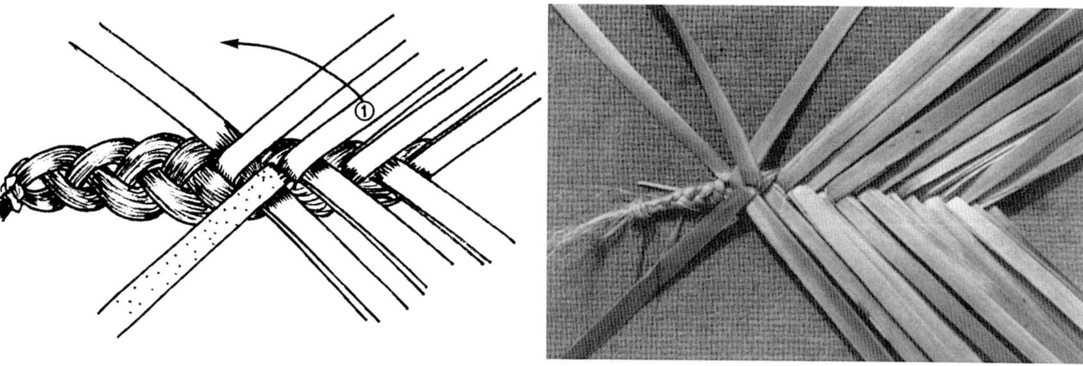

Fig. 29

Fig. 30

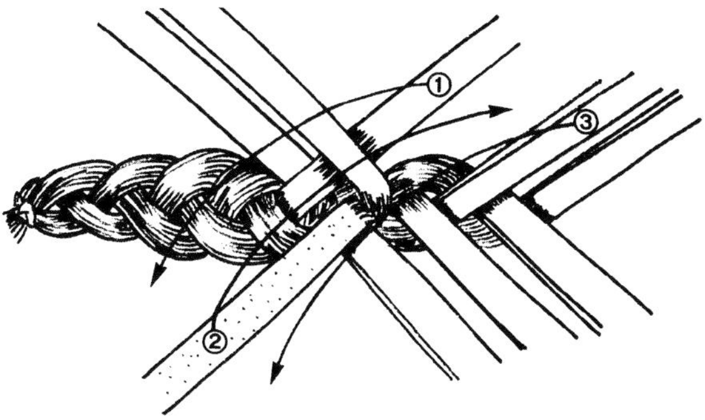

Fig. 31

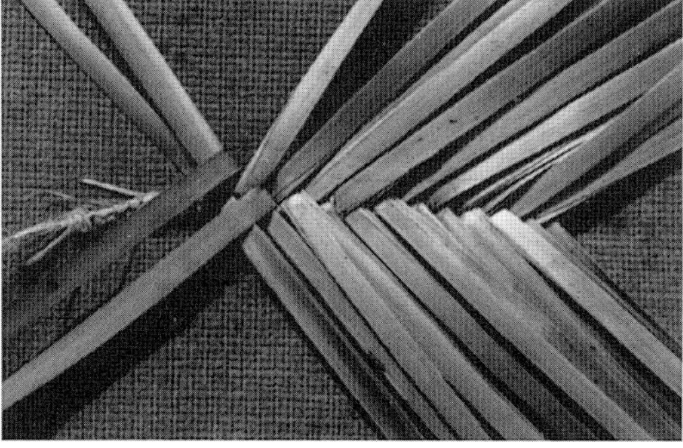
Fig. 32

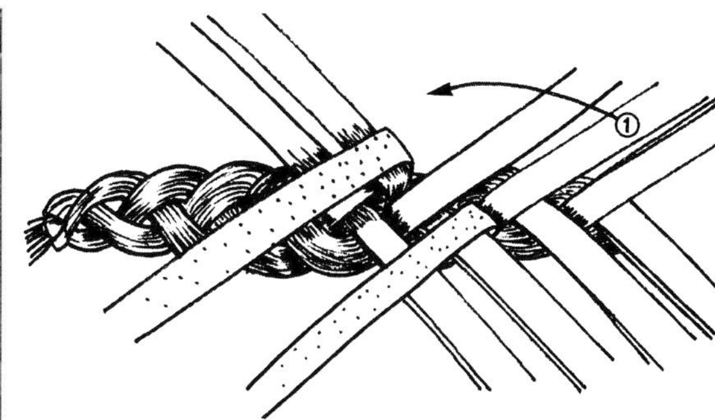

Fig. 33

Strip 1 (fig. 31) is folded back towards the worker as indicated by the arrow to lie in the position shown in fig. 32. The dull side is uppermost.

Strip 2 is moved back to its original position as indicated by the arrow in fig. 31 to lie in the position shown in fig. 32.
The top strip of the pair labelled 3 is folded back towards the worker as indicated by the arrow to lie in the position shown in fig. 32. The dull side will be uppermost.
The work should now resemble fig. 32.

Strip 1 in fig. 33 is moved to the left as shown by the arrow to lie in the position shown in fig. 34. The shiny side remains uppermost.

Following the arrows (fig. 35):
Strip 1 is moved back to its original position.
Strip 2 is folded towards the worker.
Strip 3 is moved back to its original position.
The top strip of the pair labelled 4 is folded towards the worker. The dull side will be uppermost.

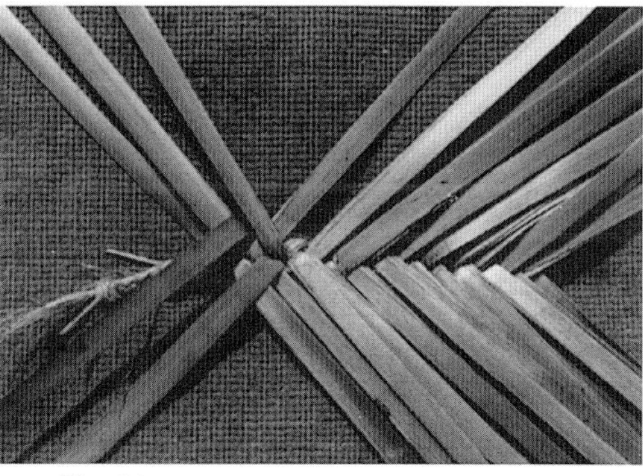
Fig. 34

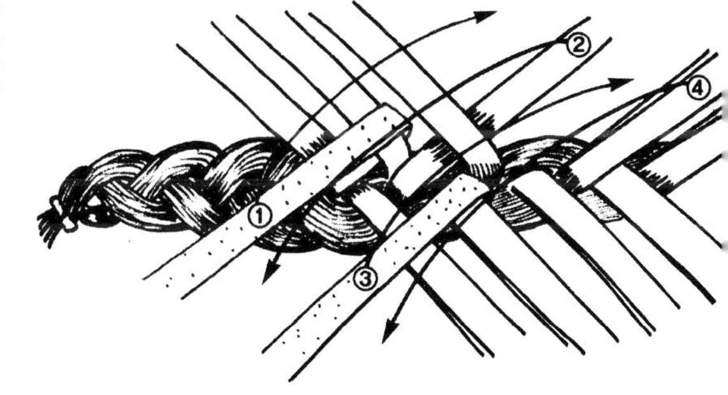

Fig. 35

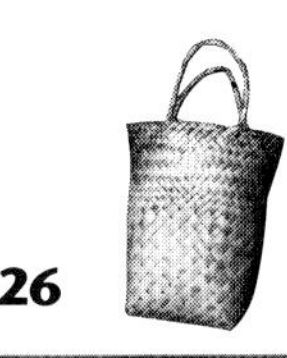

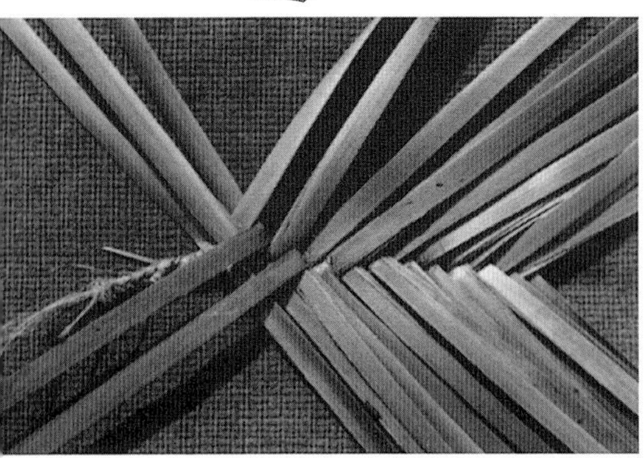

Fig. 36

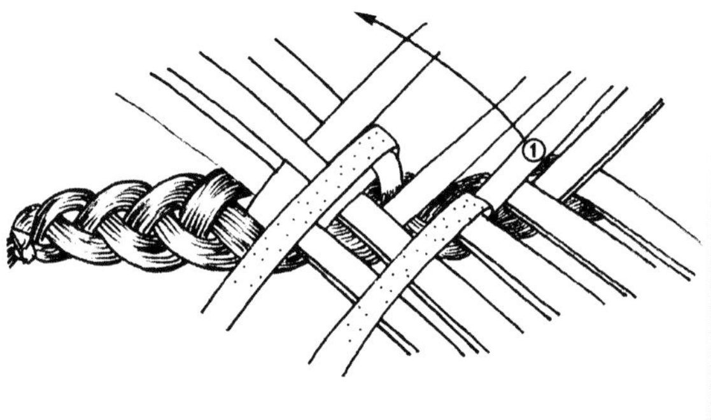

Fig. 37

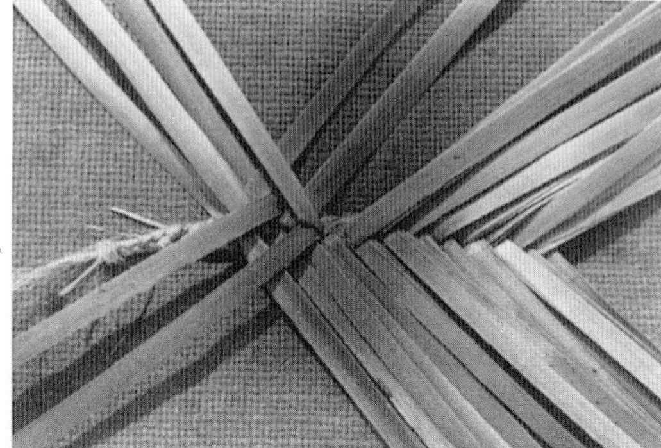

Fig. 38

The work should now resemble fig. 36.

Strip 1 in figure 37 is moved to the left as indicated by the arrow to lie in the position shown in fig. 38.

Following the arrows (fig. 39):
Strip 1 is folded towards the worker.
Strip 2 is moved back to its original position.
Strip 3 is folded towards the worker.
Strip 4 is moved back to its original position.
The top strip of the pair labelled 5 is folded back towards the worker.
The work should now resemble fig. 40.

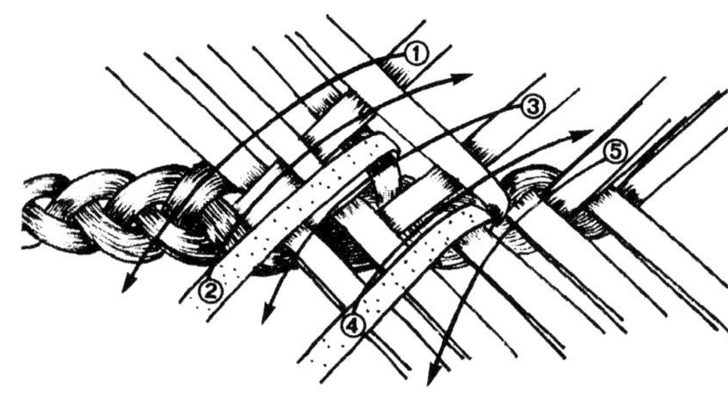

Fig. 39

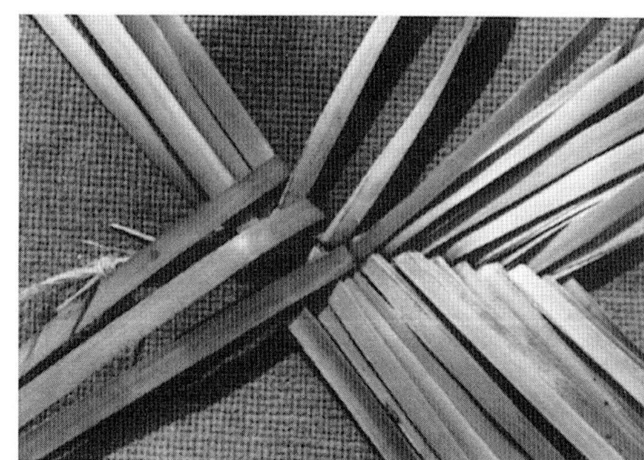

Fig. 40

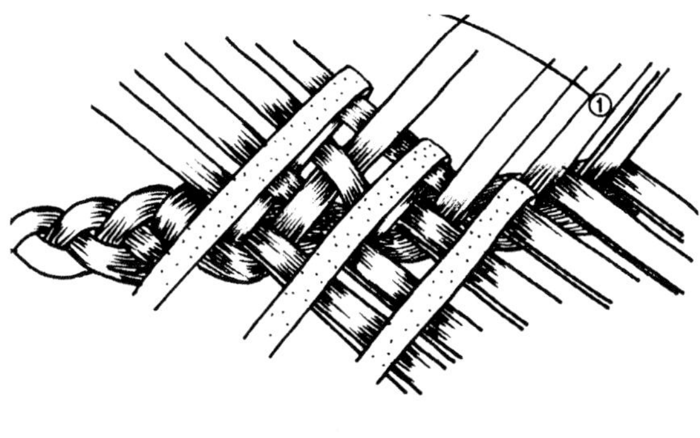

Fig. 41

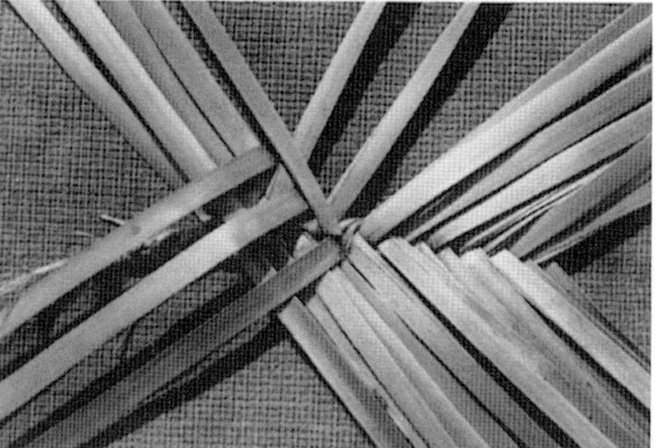

Fig. 42

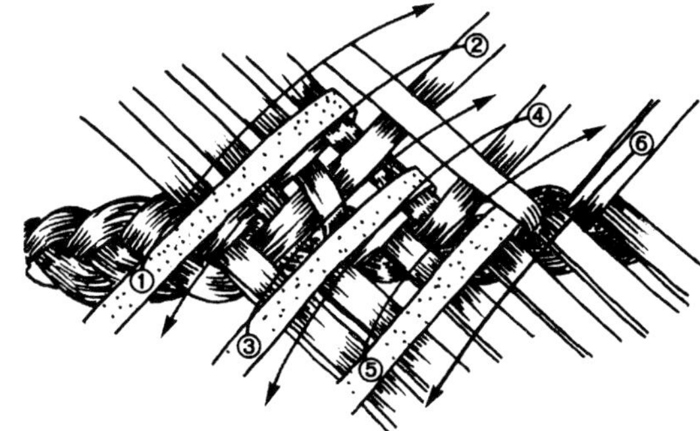

Fig. 43

Strip 1 is moved to the left as indicated by the arrow in fig. 41 to lie in the position shown in fig. 42. The shiny surface remains uppermost.

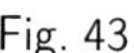

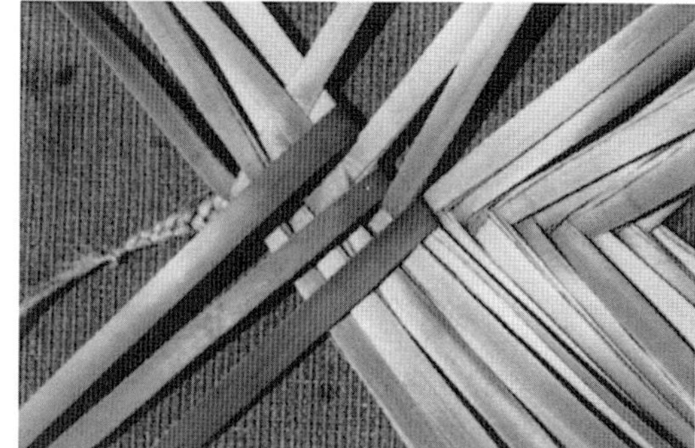

Fig. 44

Following the arrows (fig. 43):
Strip 1 is moved back to its original position.
Strip 2 is folded towards the worker.
Strip 3 is moved back to its original position.
Strip 4 is folded towards the worker.
Strip 5 is returned to its original position.
The top strip of the pair labelled 6 is folded back towards the worker.
The work should now resemble fig. 44.

Strip 1 in fig. 45 is moved to the left as indicated by the arrow to lie in the position shown in fig. 46. The shiny side remains uppermost.

Before the next movement fold strip 2 back into the plaited area to anchor the work, and prevent it from coming undone (see Appendix 2, page 90).

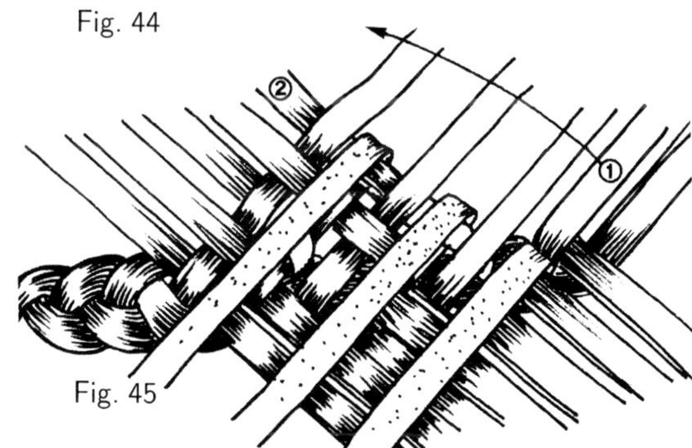

Fig. 45

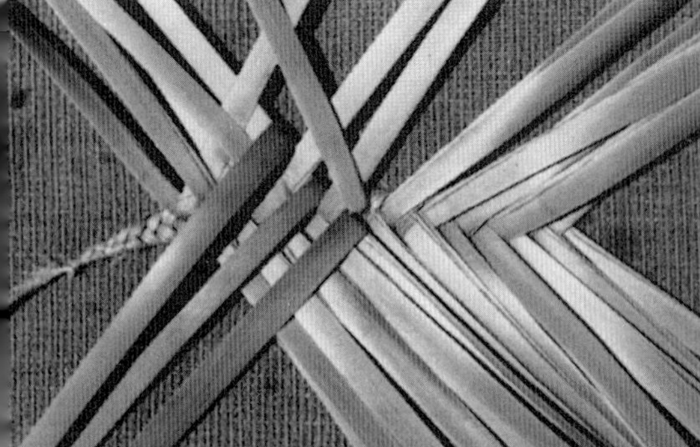

Fig. 46

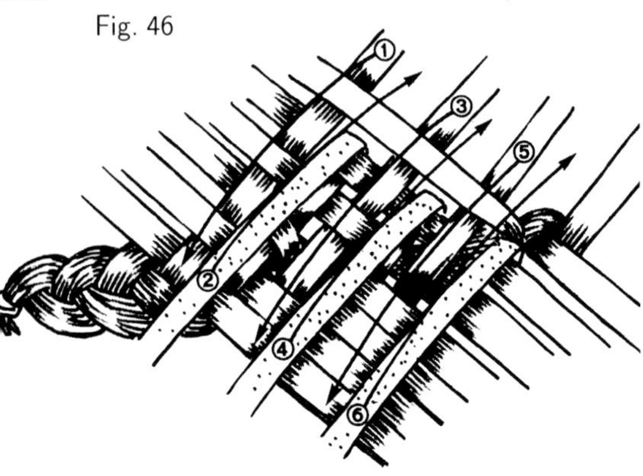

Fig. 47

Following the arrows (fig. 47):
Strip 1 is folded towards the worker.
Strip 2 is returned to its original position.
Strip 3 is folded towards the worker.
Strip 4 is returned to its original position.
Strip 5 is folded towards the worker.
Strip 6 is returned to its original position.

A sequence of movements becomes apparent. They are:
(a) Find the next pair of strips to the right of the plaited area.
(b) Fold the top strip of the pair towards the worker.
(c) Move the lower strip of the pair to the left, keeping the shiny side uppermost.
(d) Plait: that is, move all the strips that have previously been folded towards the worker back to their original position. Fold all the strips that come from beneath the work towards the worker.

This sequence is continued until all the strips on the far side of the base have been plaited into a triangle as shown in figs. 48 & 49.

Check the number of strips pointing to the left and right. There should be twelve in each direction. Anchor the work so that it will not come undone as shown in fig. 49. The method is shown in Appendix 2, page 90.

Take the four strips at each end of the plaited area and tie them in an overhand knot (Appendix 1). This prevents them getting across the three-ply braid and mixed with the strips on the other side, one of the great problems of the learner. The work should now resemble fig. 50.

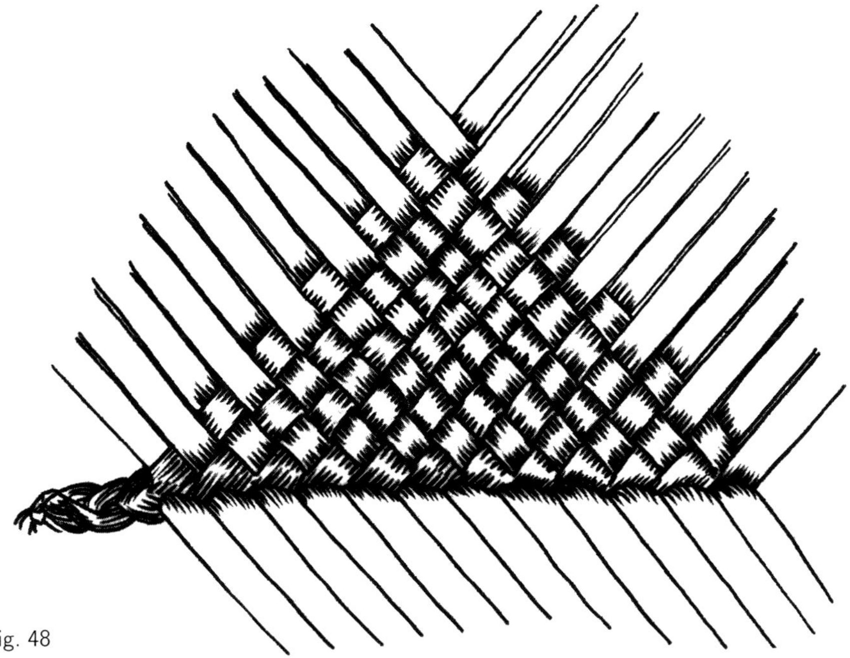

Fig. 48

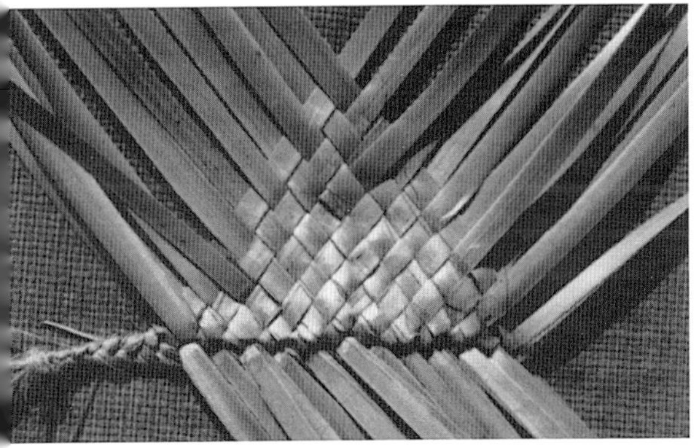

Fig. 49

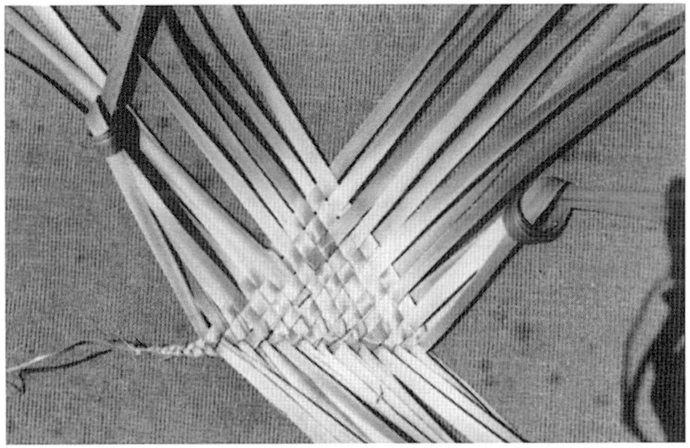

Fig. 50

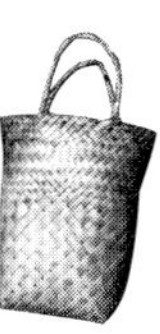

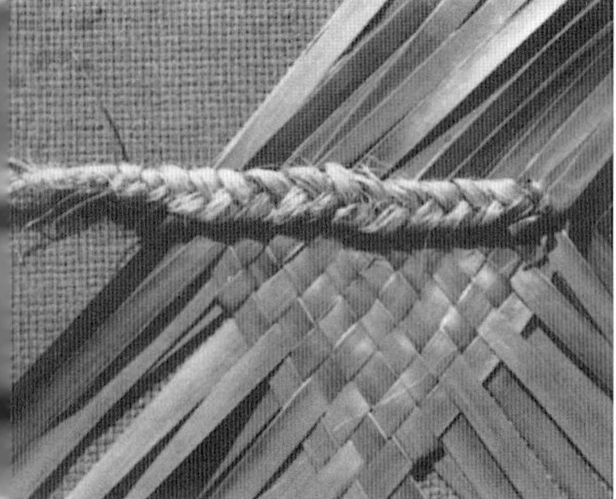

Fig. 51

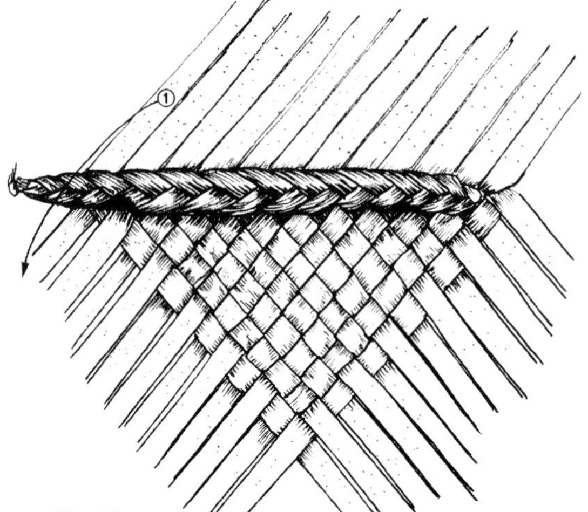

Fig. 52

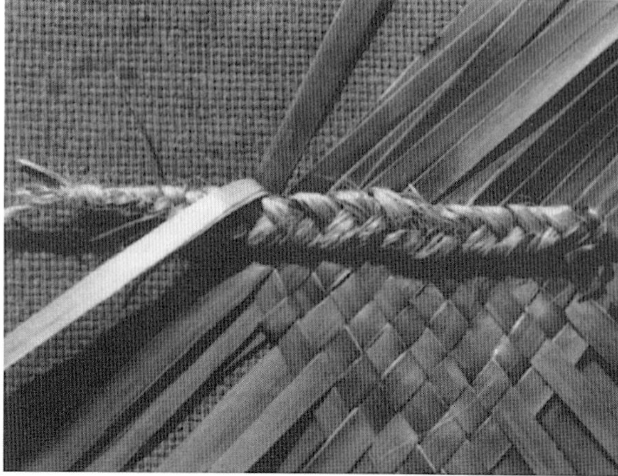

Fig. 53

Turn the work over so that the three-ply braid is uppermost. The plaited area should be towards the worker and the end of the three-ply braid protruding to the left (fig. 51).

The dull sides of the strips are uppermost, and the strips that are to be plaited are on the side away from the worker.

The strips on the other side of the three-ply braid are now plaited together in exactly the same manner as those on the first side. The work is partially covered by the three-ply braid and cannot always be well seen in the photos or in the work itself.

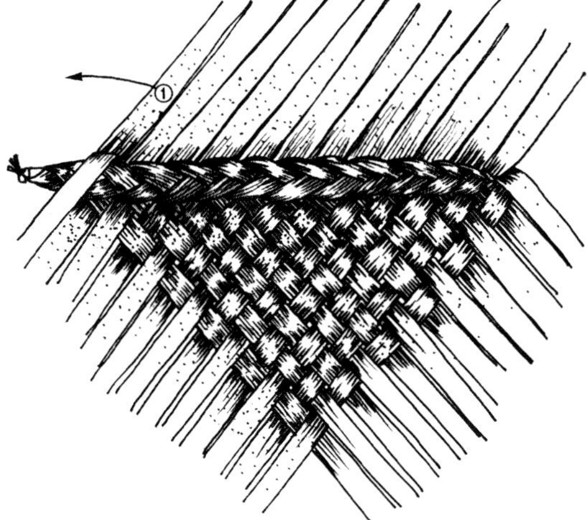

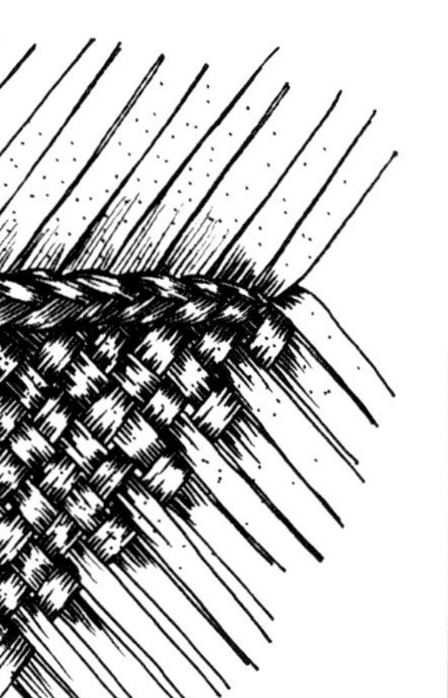

Fig. 54

The top strip of pair 1 is folded towards the worker as indicated by the arrow in fig. 52 to lie in the position shown in fig. 53.

Strip 1 is moved to the left (see arrow in fig. 54) to lie in the position shown in fig. 55.

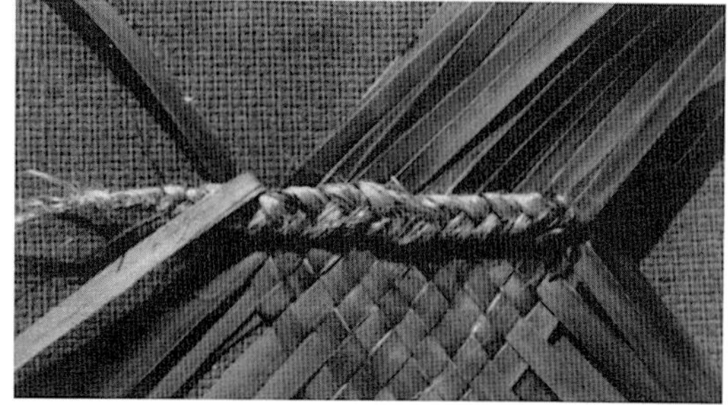

Fig. 55

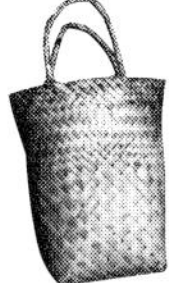

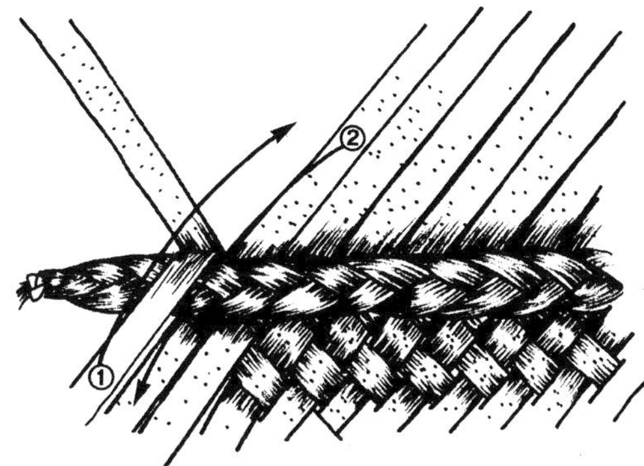

Fig. 56

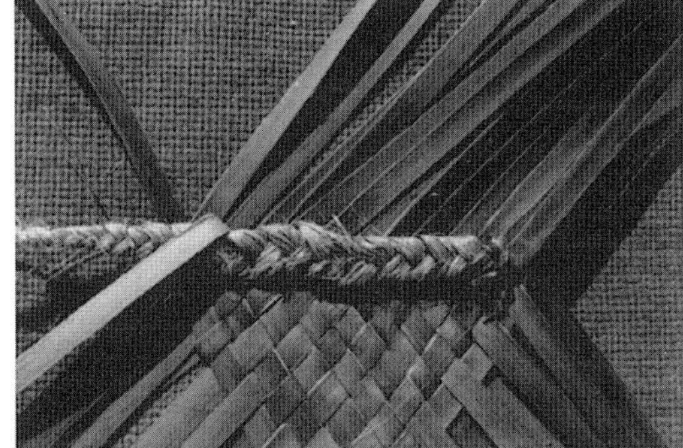

Fig. 57

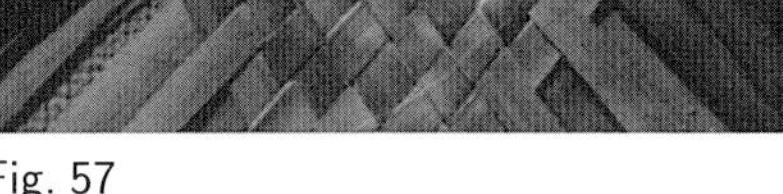

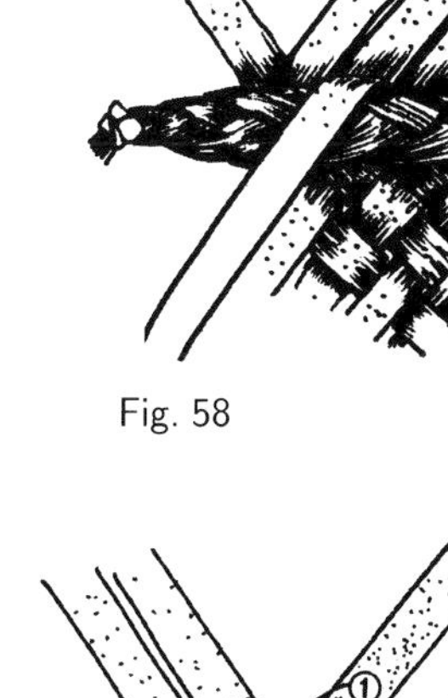

Fig. 58

Following the arrows (fig. 56):
Strip 1 is returned to its original position.
The top strip of the pair labelled 2 is folded towards the worker.
The work should now resemble fig. 57.

Strip 1 is moved to the left as indicated by the arrow in fig. 58 to lie in the position shown in fig. 59.

Following the arrows (fig. 60):
Strip 1 is folded towards the worker.
Strip 2 is returned to its original position.
The top strip of the pair labelled 3 is folded towards the worker.

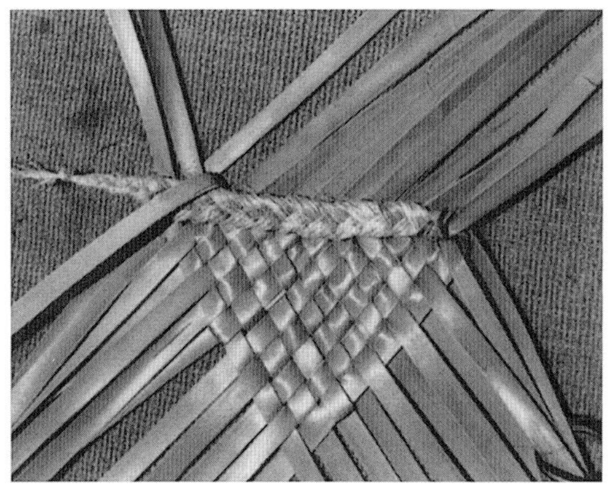

Fig. 59

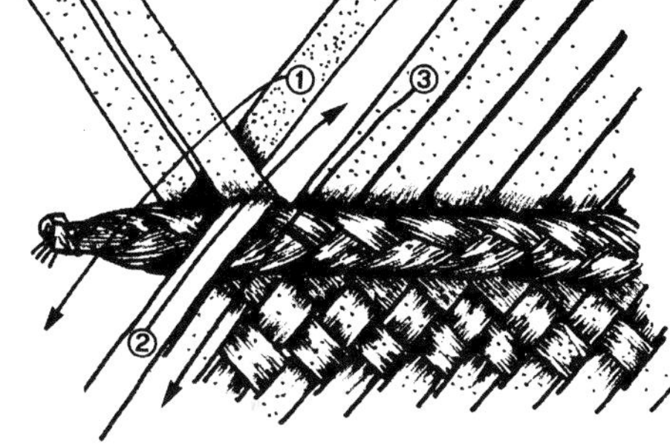

Fig. 60

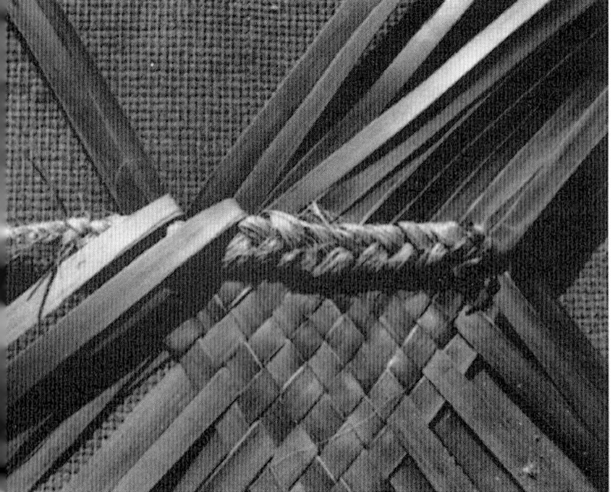

Fig. 61

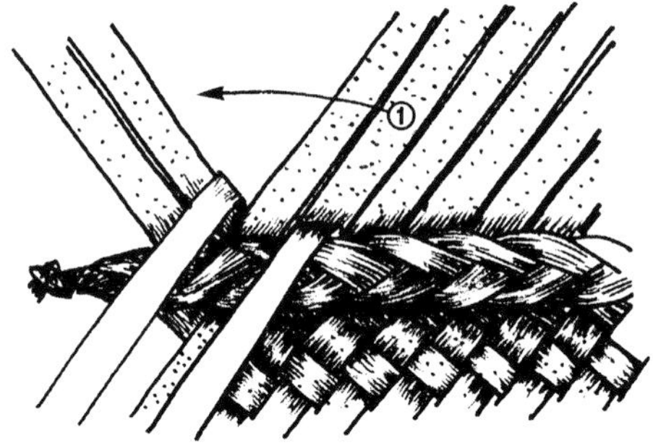

Fig. 62

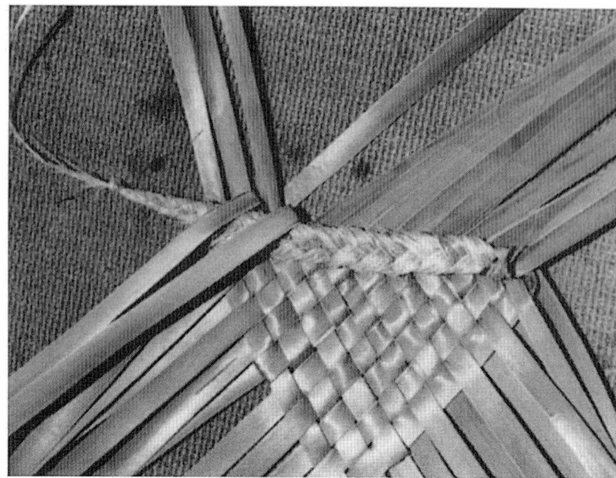

Fig. 63

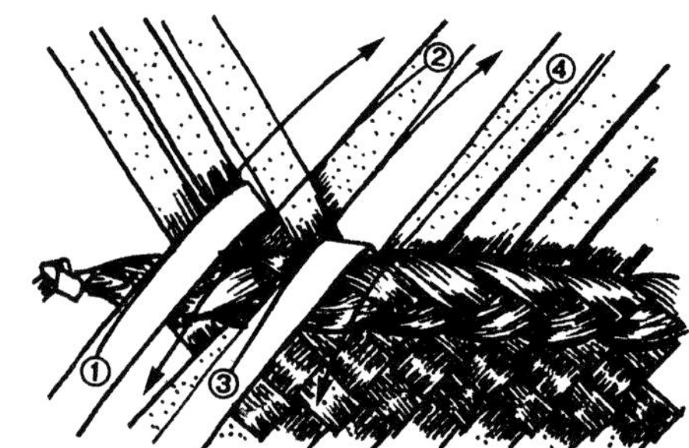

Fig. 64

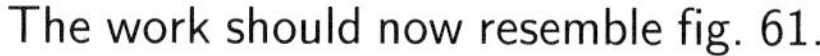

The work should now resemble fig. 61.

Strip 1 is moved to the left (see arrow in fig. 62) to lie in the position shown in fig. 63.

Following the arrows (fig. 64):
Strip 1 is returned to its original position.
Strip 2 is folded towards the worker.
Strip 3 is returned to its original position.
The top strip of the pair labelled 4 is folded towards the worker.

Strip 1 is moved to the left (fig. 65).

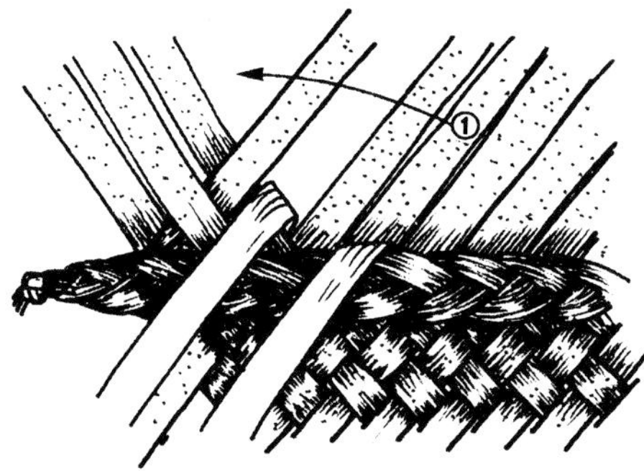

Fig. 65

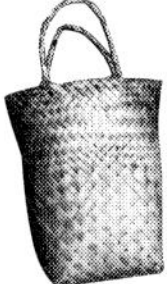

Following the arrows in fig. 66:
Strip 1 is folded towards the worker.
Strip 2 is returned to its original position.
Strip 3 is folded towards the worker.
Strip 4 is returned to its original position.
The top strip of the pair labelled 5 is folded towards the worker.

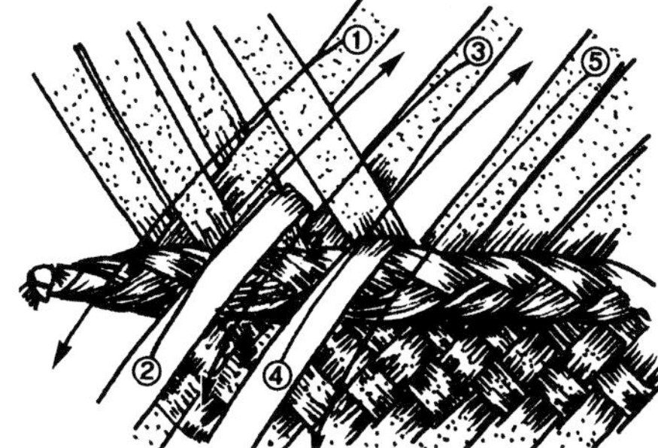

Fig. 66

Strip 1 is moved to the left (fig. 67).

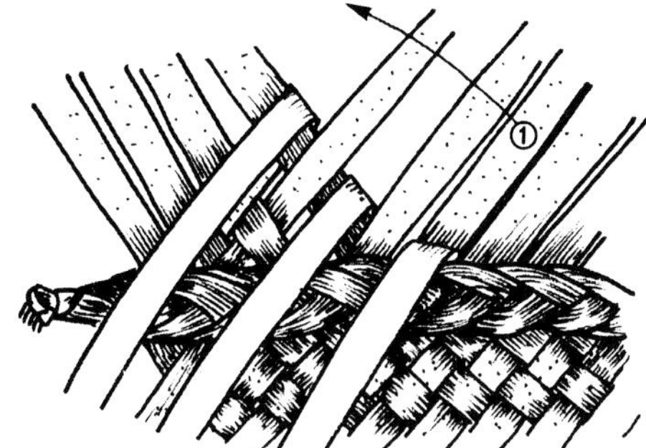

Fig. 67

Continue until the triangle has been completed. There should now be a plaited triangle on either side of the three-ply braid. Tuck strips back to anchor the work (see Appendix 2). Tie the four strips at each end of the plaited area in an overhand knot (see Appendix 1).

The work should now resemble fig. 68. There are twelve strips protruding on either side from the new triangle.

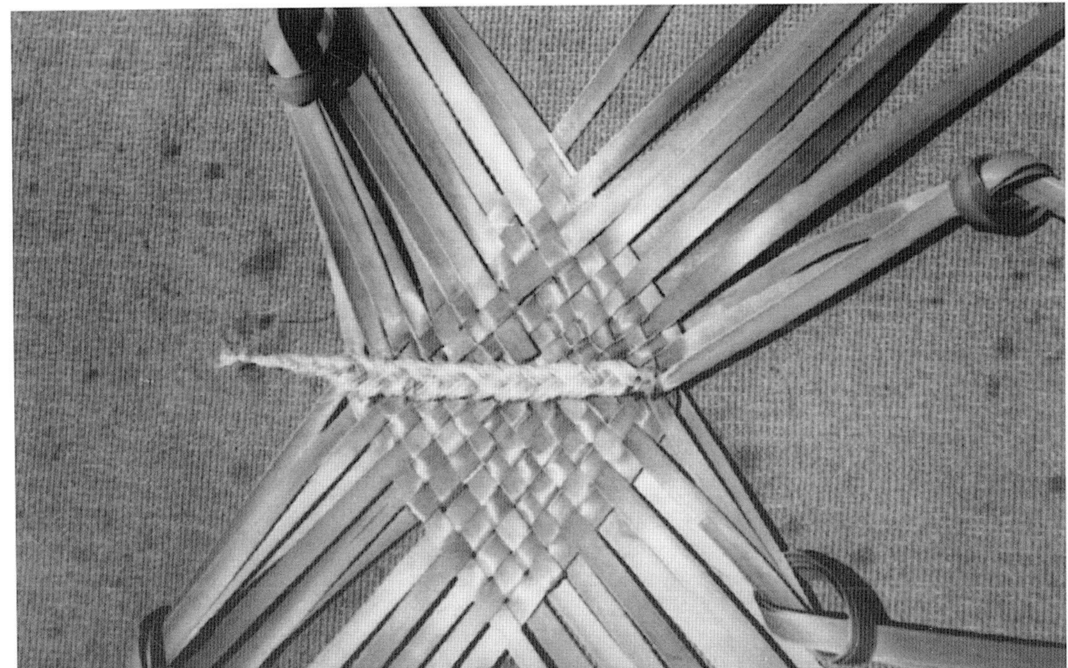

Fig. 68

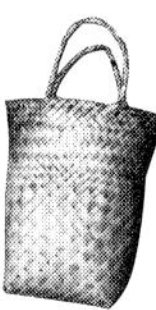

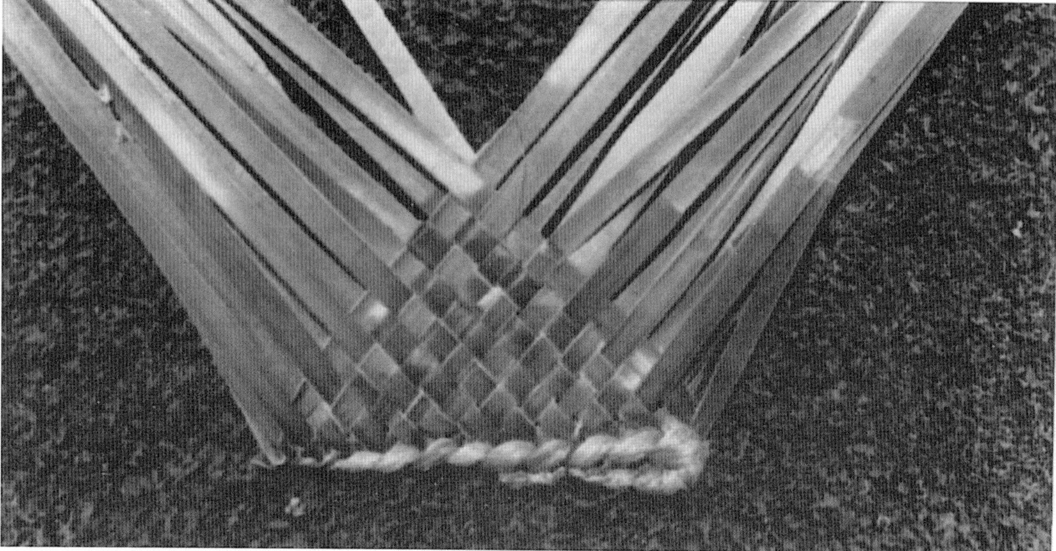

Fig. 69

The tail of the braid can now be folded back on itself and tied in position with a thin strip of scraped flax, as in fig. 69.

Plaiting the corners

The next step is to plait the corners of the kete.

Before beginning check again that there are twelve strips of flax protruding to the left and twelve to the right on either side of the three-ply braid along the base of the kete.

Fold the work along the base braid so that the three-ply braid is on the outside and the two plaited triangles are against each other, as in fig. 69. The whole kete will be plaited inside out, that is, with the three-ply braid on the outside of the work. When it is finished it will be turned the right way out. This makes the finishing braid at the top easier to do.

Note: In the diagrams following, the strips that have been brought from the right-hand side of the work and plaited into the left appear to have a curve in them. This shows them in a diagrammatic form. In the actual plaiting they are plaited as closely as they are anywhere else in the work, and the photos give their actual positions in the kete.

Hold the folded work so that the three-ply braid is uppermost and the corner that is to be plaited first is away from the worker. Untie the four strips that are tied in the overhand knot, on the left of the working corner. The two of these four strips that come from beneath the work (strips 1 and 2 in fig. 70) are folded back towards the worker as indicated by the arrows to the position shown in fig. 71.

Untie the overhand knot holding the four strips on the right-hand side of the work. Be very careful to see that each strip stays on the correct side of the braid until it is plaited into the work.

Strip 1 is brought from the right-hand side of the work as indicated by the arrow in fig. 72 to lie in the position shown in fig. 73. The dull side remains uppermost. Continue to take special care that the unplaited strips remain on the correct side of the base braid.

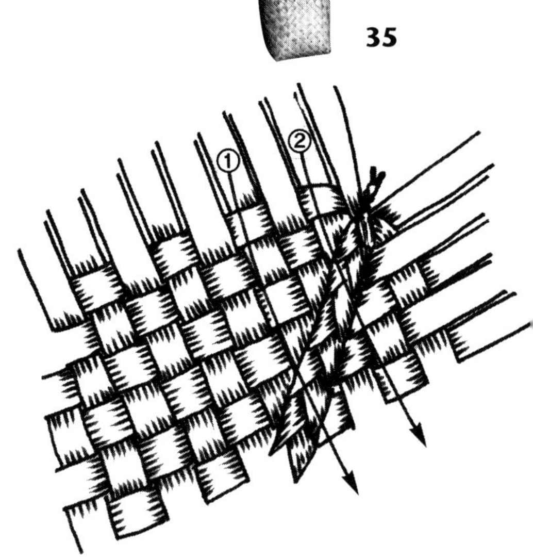

Fig. 70

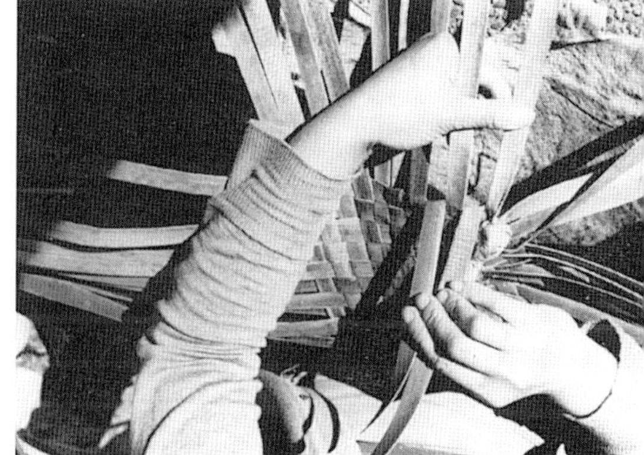
Fig. 71

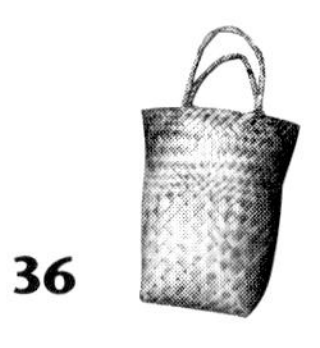

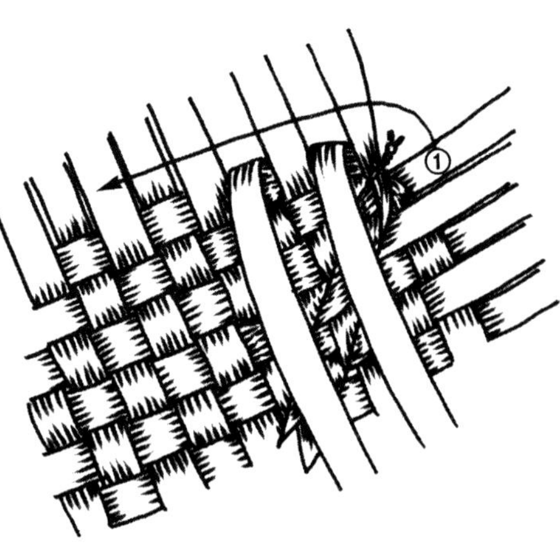

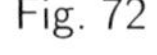
Fig. 72

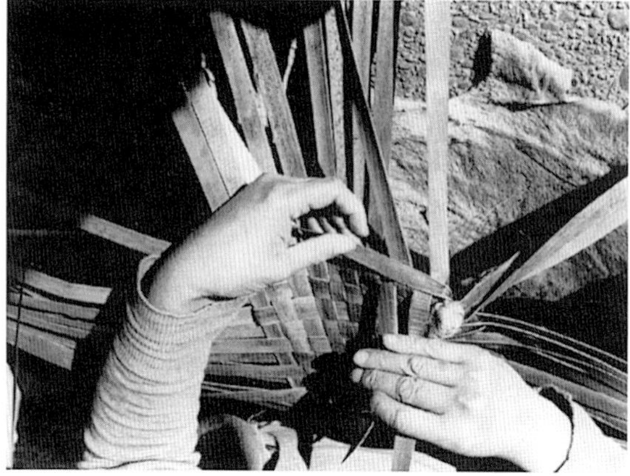

Fig. 73

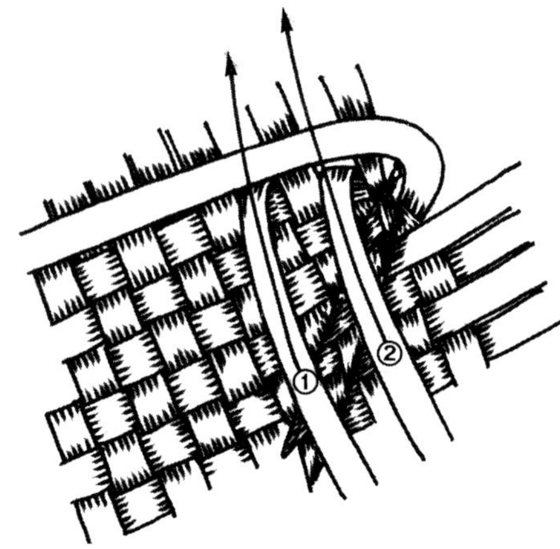

Fig. 74

Strips 1 and 2 are returned to their original positions (see arrows in fig. 74) to lie as in fig. 75.

Strips 1 and 2 are folded back to the positions shown in fig. 77.

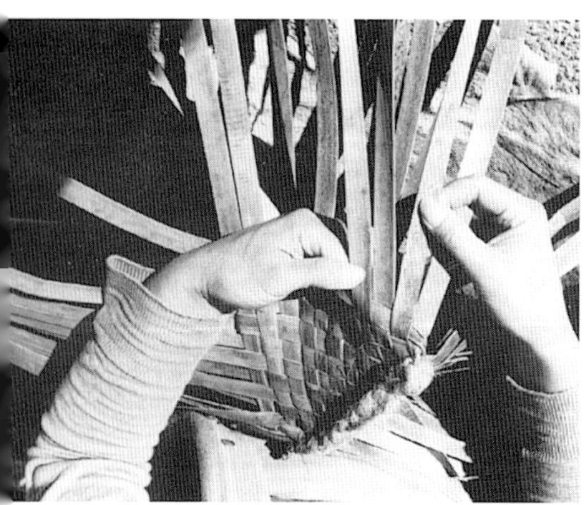

Fig. 75

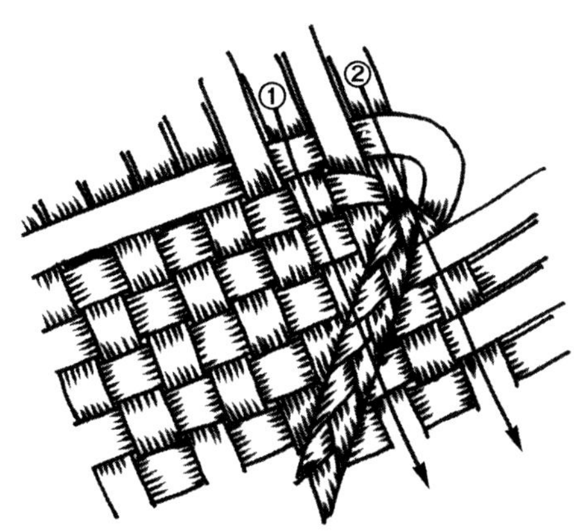

Fig. 76

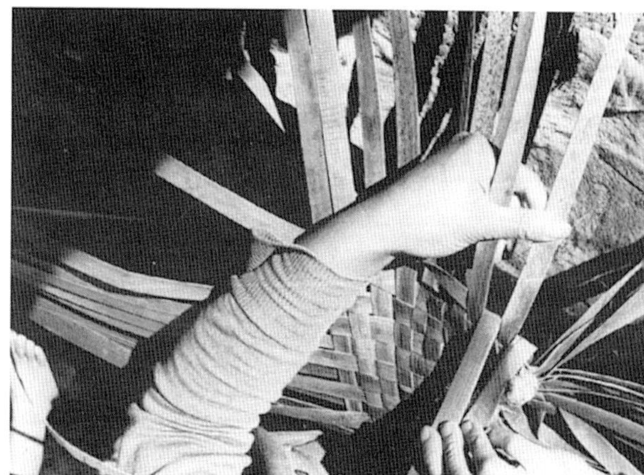

Fig. 77

Strip 1 is brought across from the right-hand side of the base braid (arrow) to lie in the position shown in fig. 79.

Strips 1 and 2 are returned to their original positions (arrows) to lie as in fig. 81.

Strips 1 and 2 are folded back to the positions shown in fig. 83.

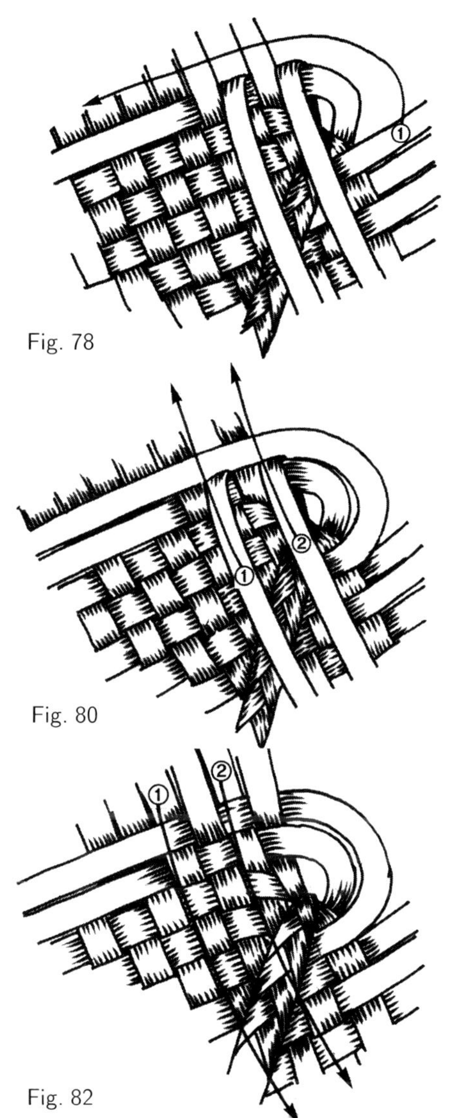

Fig. 78

Fig. 80

Fig. 82

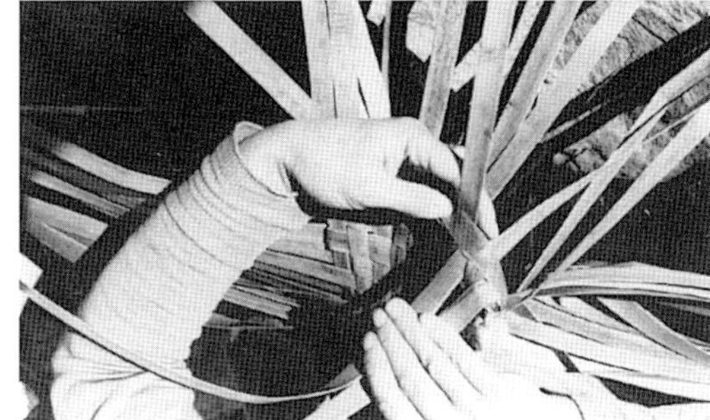
Fig. 79

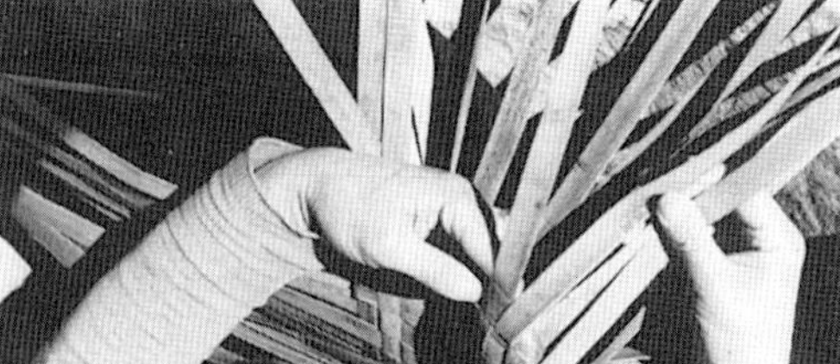
Fig. 81

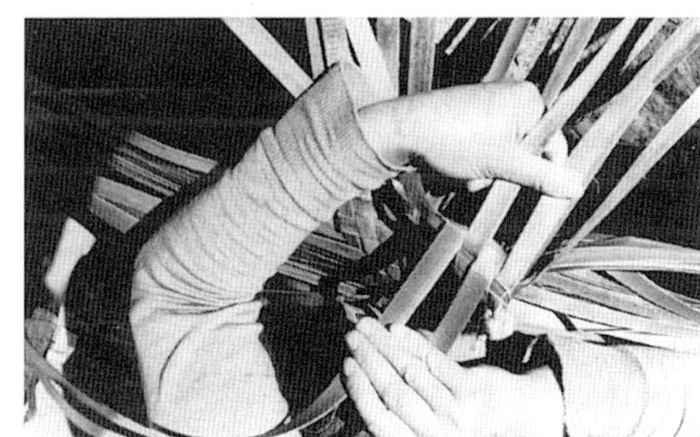
Fig. 83

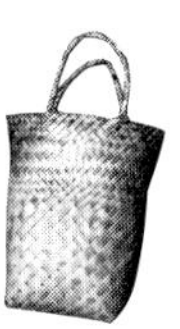

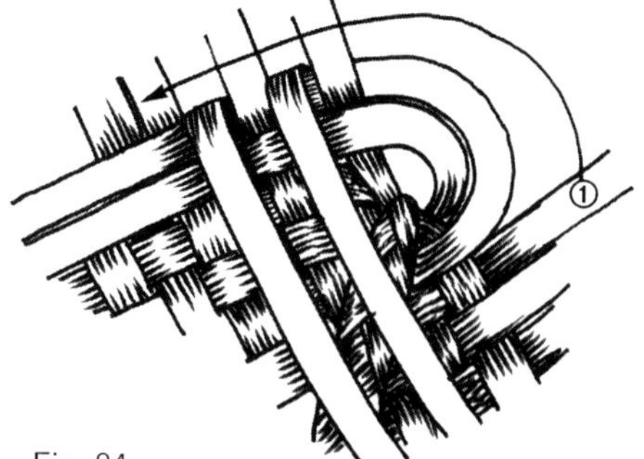

Fig. 84

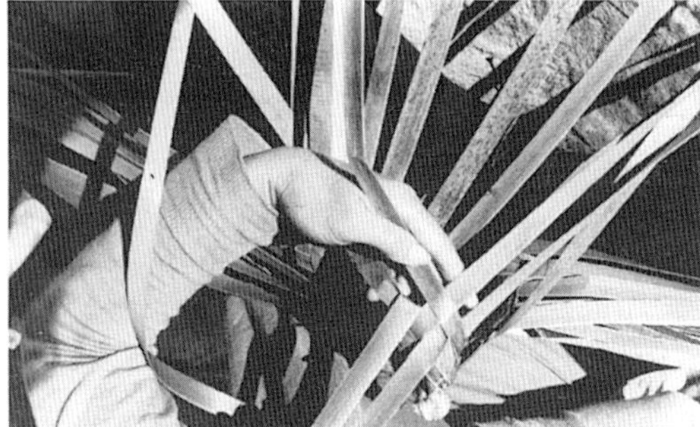

Fig. 85

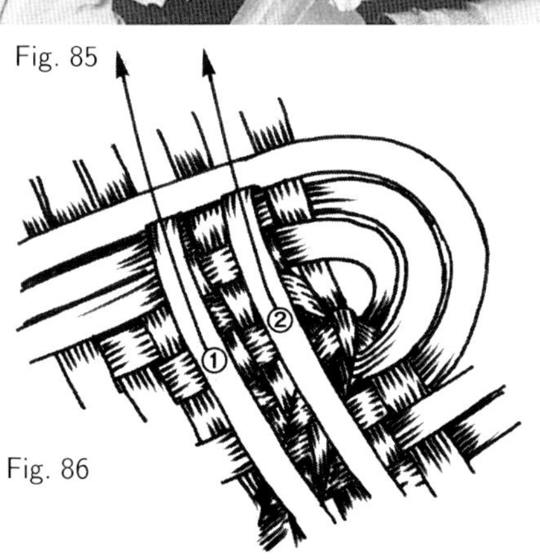

Fig. 86

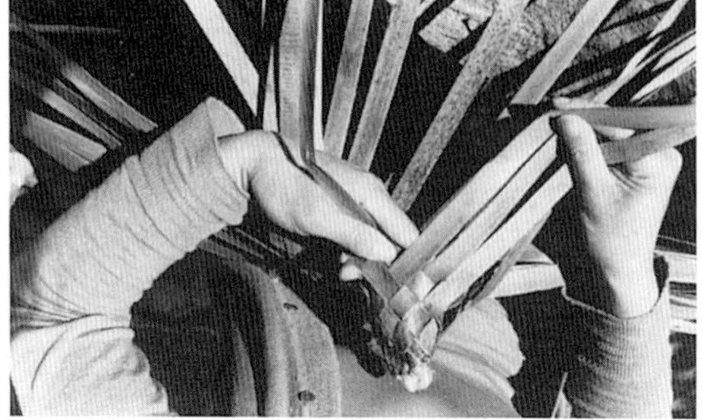

Fig. 87

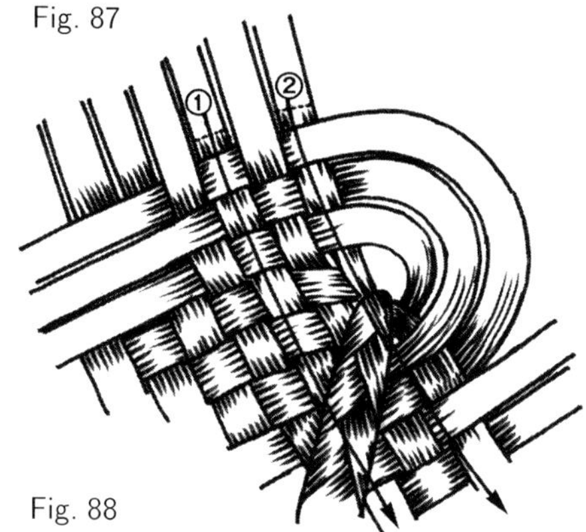

Fig. 88

Strip 1 is brought across from the right-hand side of the work (arrow) to lie in the position shown in fig. 85.

Strips 1 and 2 are returned to their original positions (arrows). The work should now resemble fig. 87.

Strips 1 and 2 are folded back (arrows) to the positions shown in fig. 89.

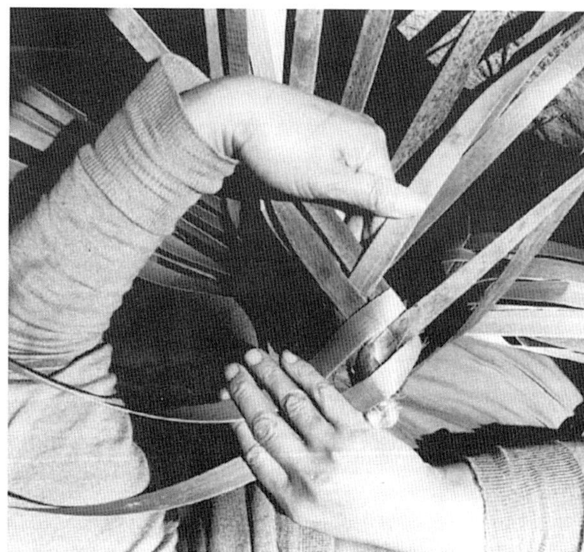

Fig. 89

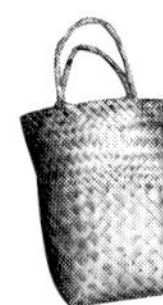

Strip 1 is brought across from the right-hand side of the base braid (arrow) to lie as in fig. 91.

Strips 1 and 2 (fig. 92) are returned to their original positions (arrows) to the positions shown in fig. 93.

Strips 3 and 4 are folded back, as indicated, to the positions in fig. 94.

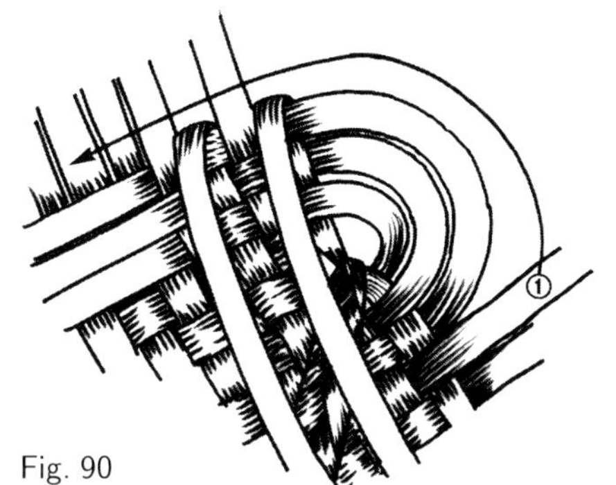

Fig. 90

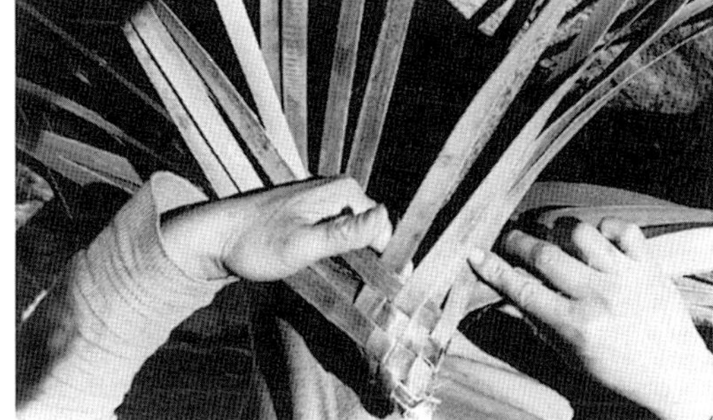

Fig. 93

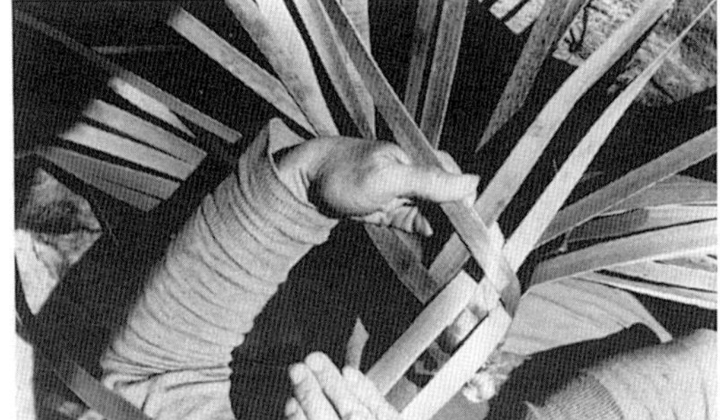

Fig. 91

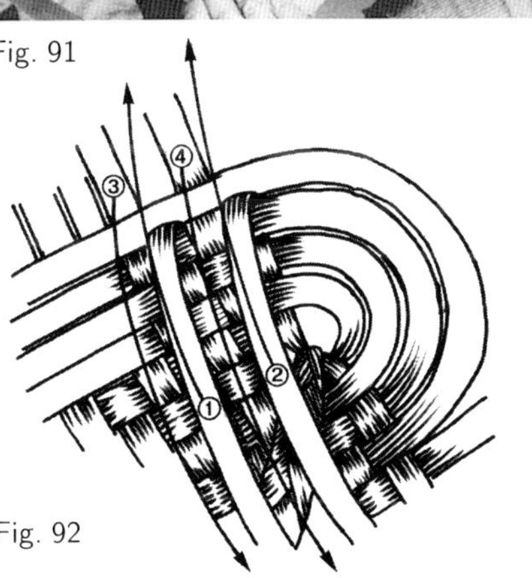

Fig. 92

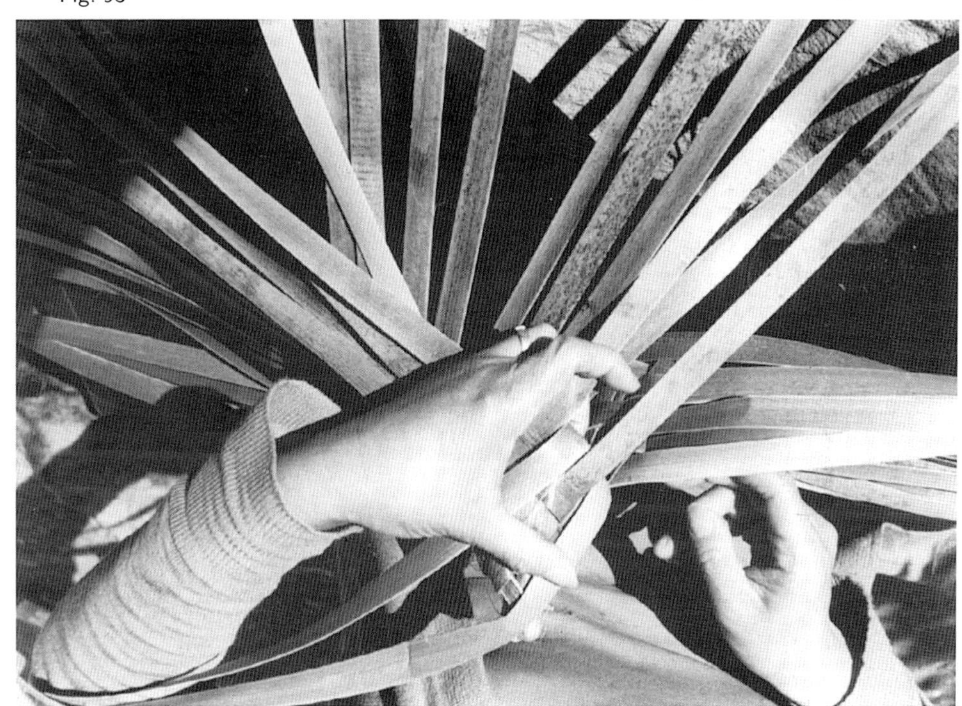

Fig. 94

Bring the next strip from the right-hand side of the base braid across to the position shown in fig. 95.

Return the folded strips to their original positions as shown. Fold the strip marked with a star (*) back from the left to anchor the work in position. Do this whenever work needs to be held in place (Appendix 2, page 90).

Repeat the movements in figs. 94–96 about three times until the top of the triangle is reached.

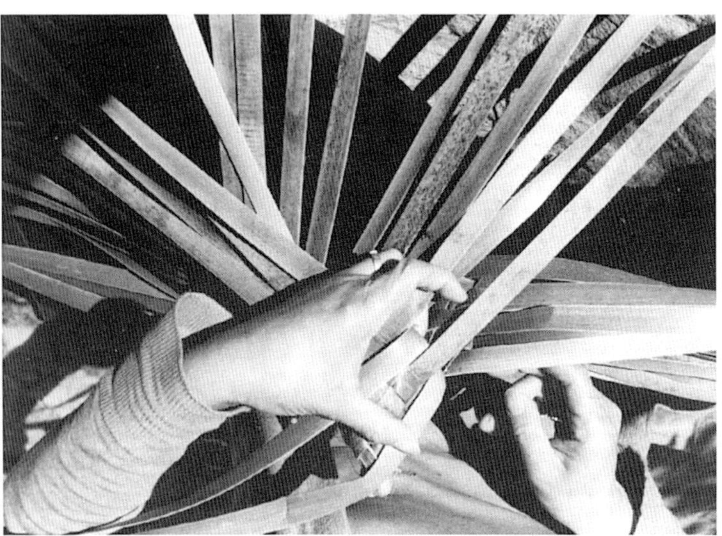

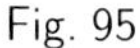
Fig. 95

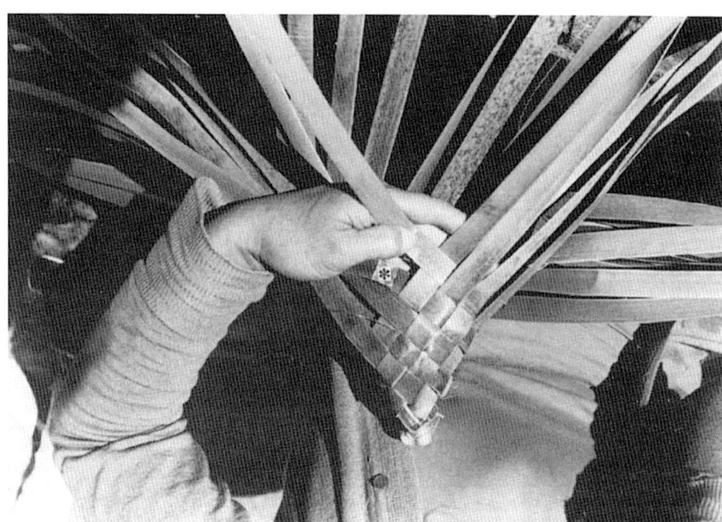

Fig. 96

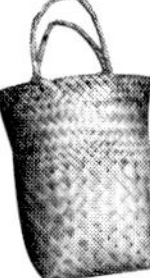

Filling the gaps between the corners and the base triangles

To the left of the plaiting you have just completed at the corner there will be a space. This is now plaited up until it is in line with the rest of the work.

Strips 1, 2 and 3 are folded back (arrows) to lie as in fig. 99.

Strip 1 is moved in the direction indicated (arrow) to lie as in fig. 101.

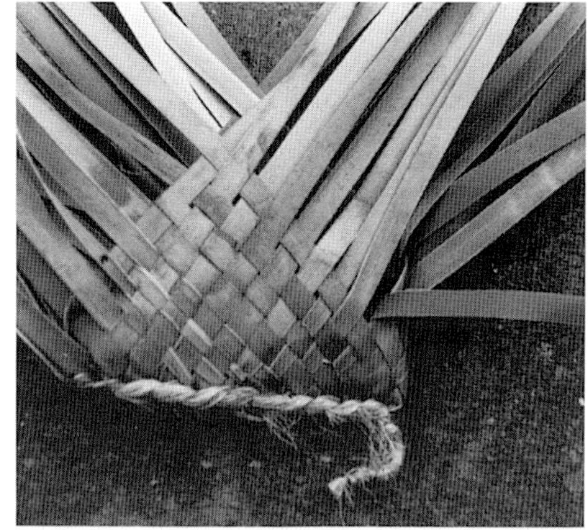

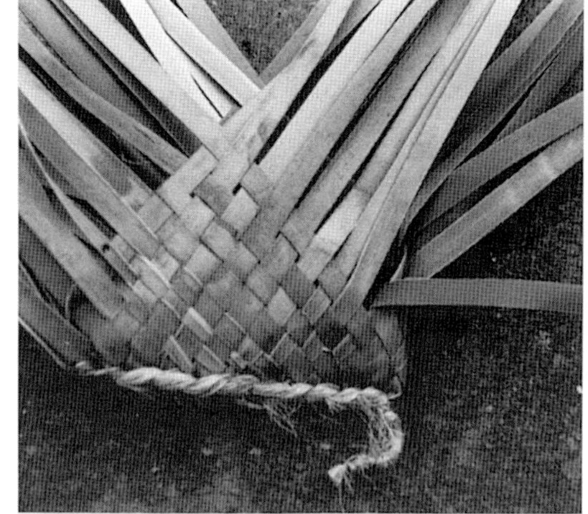

Fig. 97

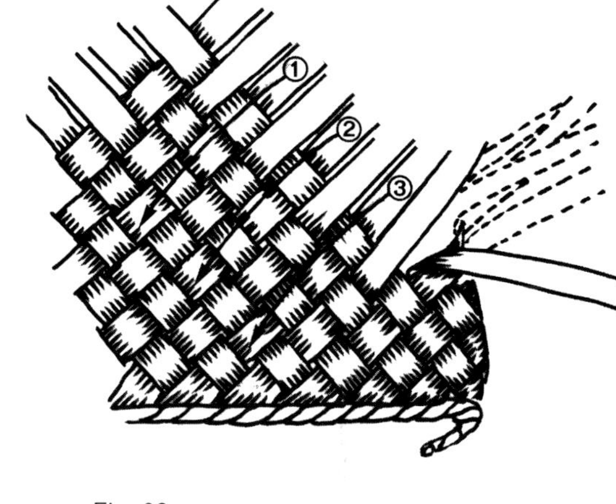

Fig. 98

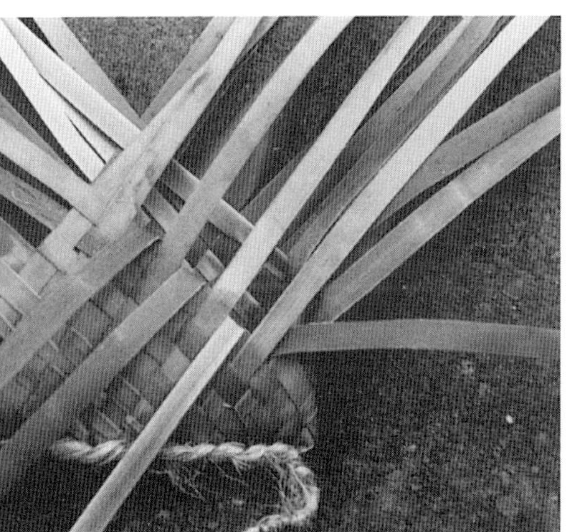

Fig. 99

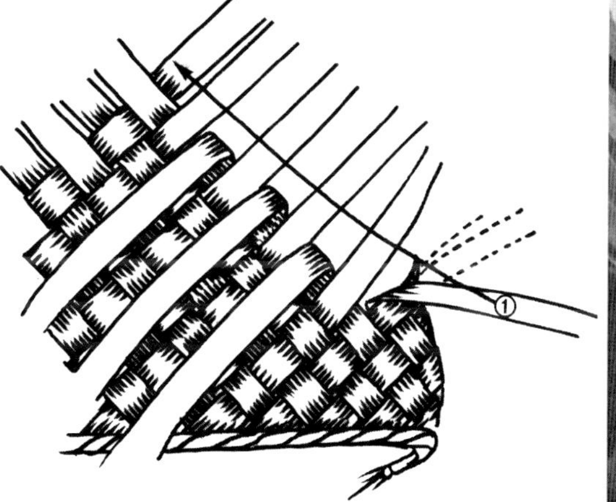

Fig. 100

Fig. 101

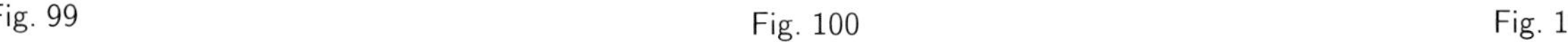

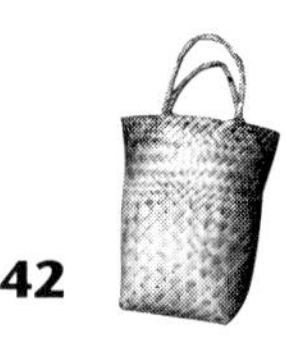

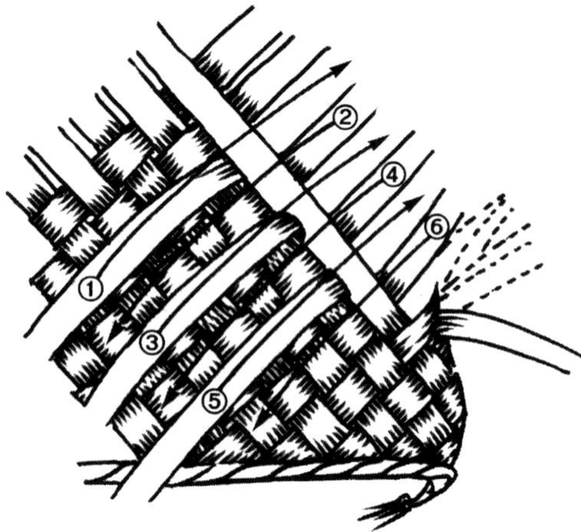

Fig. 102

Strips 1, 3 and 5 (fig. 102) are returned to their original positions and strips 2, 4 and 6 are folded back (arrows) to lie in the positions shown in fig. 103.

Pull on strips 2, 4 and 6 before working them. This helps to keep the work firm and close. Always pull on the strips that come from beneath the work before working them.

Strip 1 is moved in the direction indicated (arrow) to lie as in fig. 105.

Strips 1, 3 and 5 (fig. 106) are returned to their original positions and strips 2 and 4 are folded back as indicated by the arrows. The work should now resemble fig. 107.

Move strip 1 in the direction indicated by the arrow (fig. 108). Continue until the gap has been closed. If necessary anchor the work by folding a strip back through the plait (Appendix 2).

The corner at the other end is now worked in the same way, beginning with the movement shown in fig. 70.

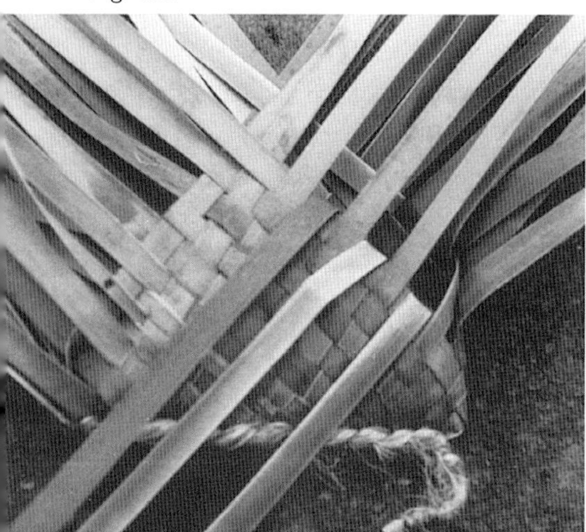

Fig. 103

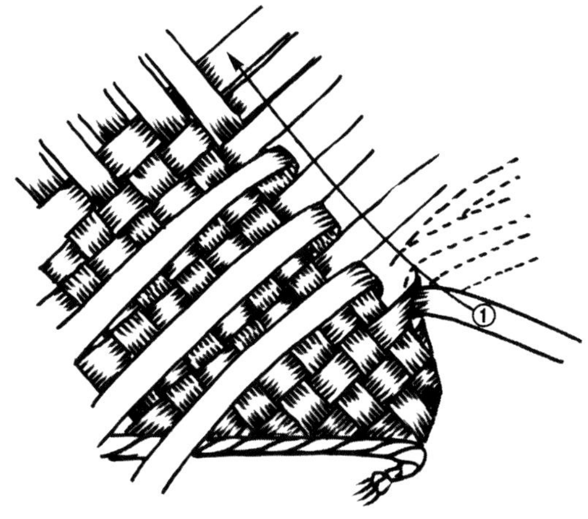

Fig. 104

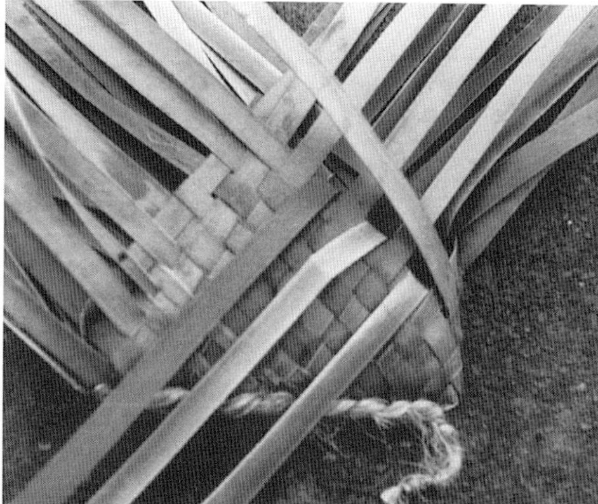

Fig. 105

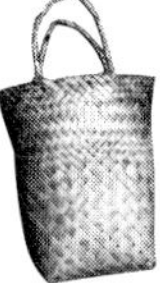

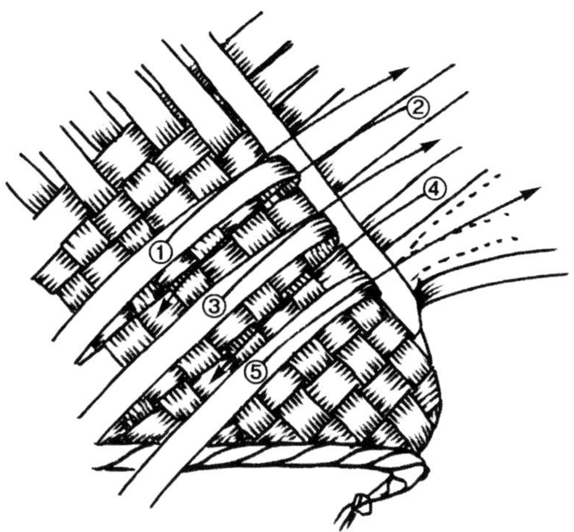

Fig. 106

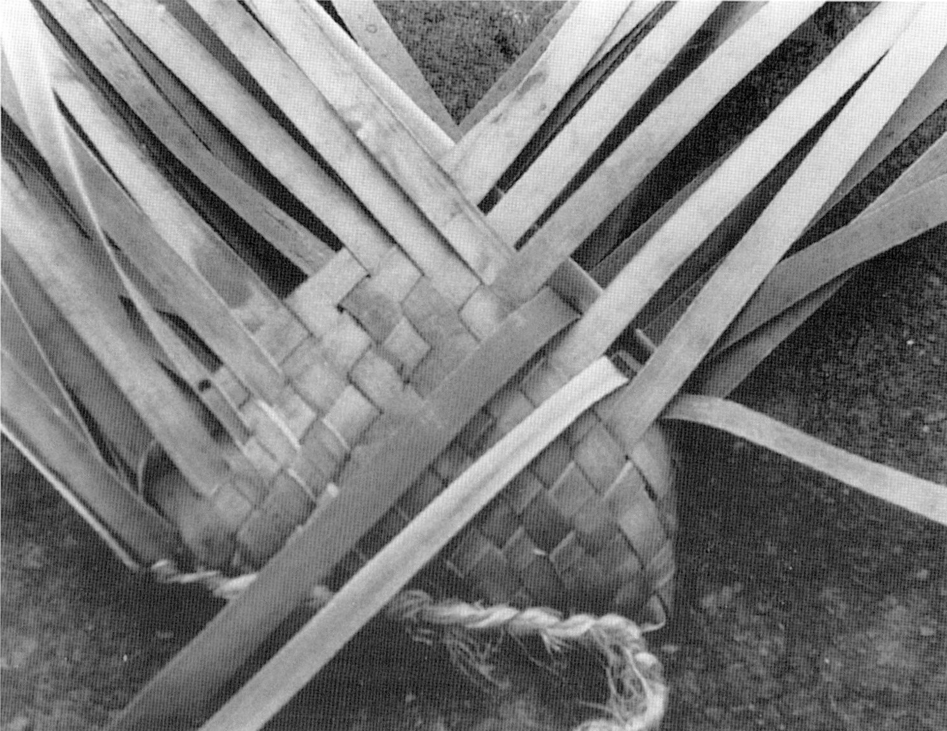

Fig. 107

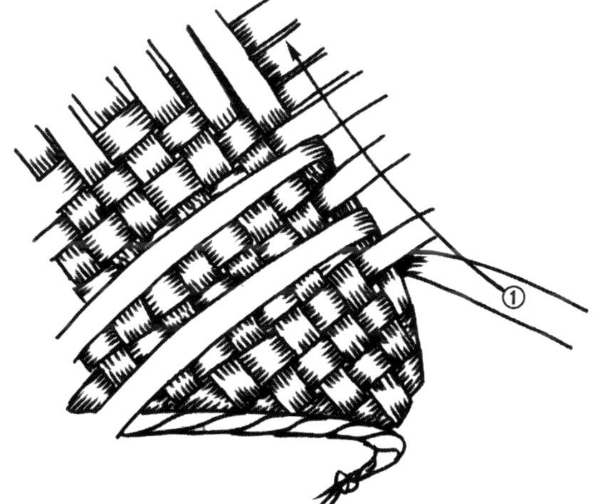

Fig. 108

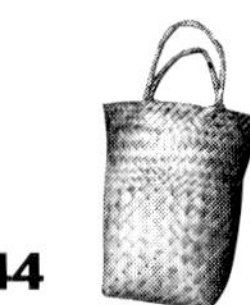

Plaiting the sides

The next step is to plait the sides to the desired height.

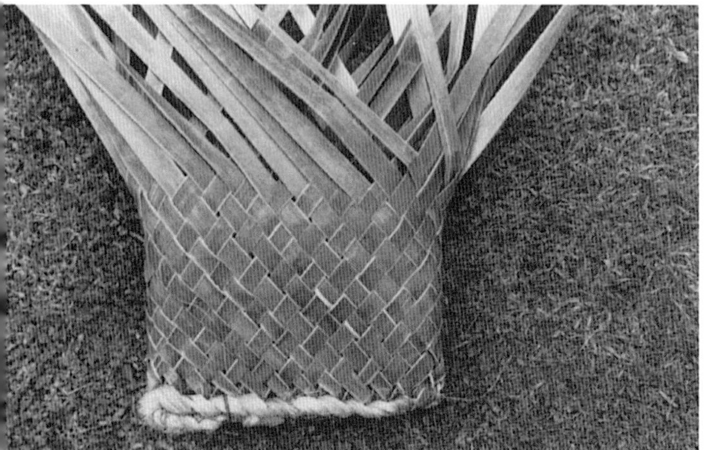

Fig. 109

Lift one of the strips *from underneath* the work at the position indicated by the arrow in fig. 110, so that it lies on top of the work as in fig. 111.

See Appendix 3 for notes on keeping the working edge even.

Lift the next strip to the right of it in the same way at the point indicated by the arrow, so that it lies on top of the work as shown in fig. 112.

Fold strip 1 back towards you, as indicated in fig. 112, to lie in the position shown in fig. 113.

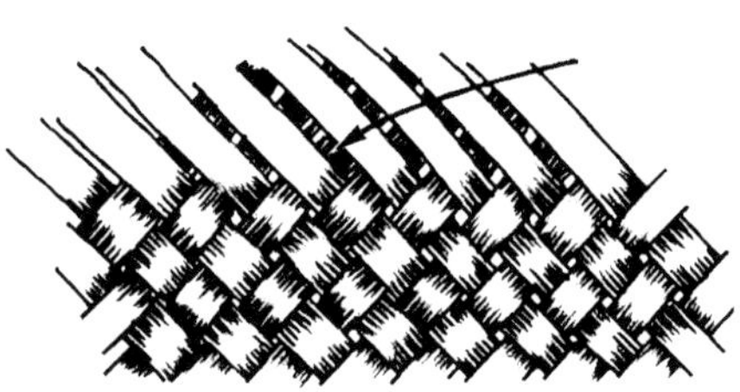

Fig. 110

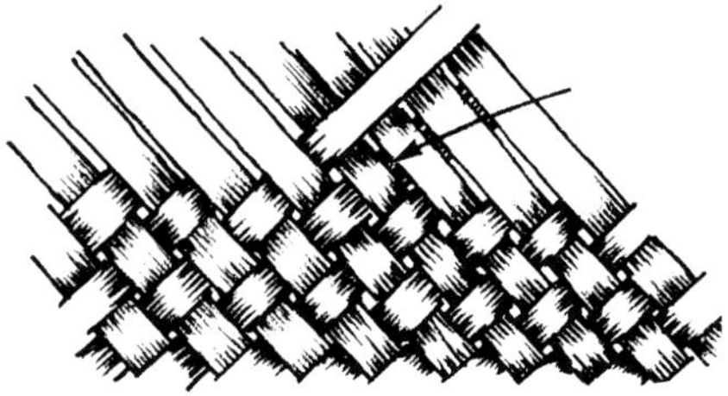

Fig. 111

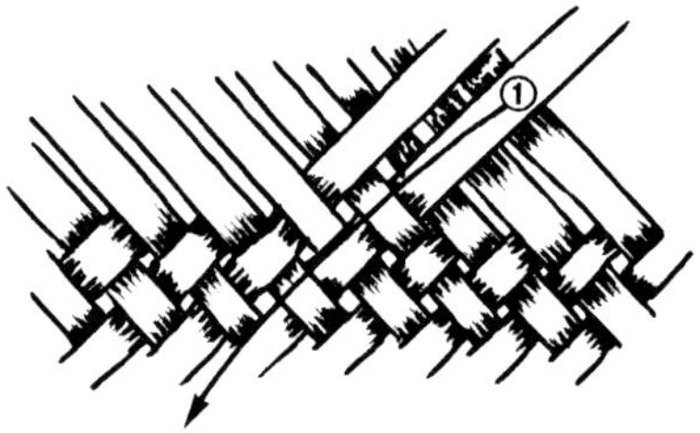

Fig. 112

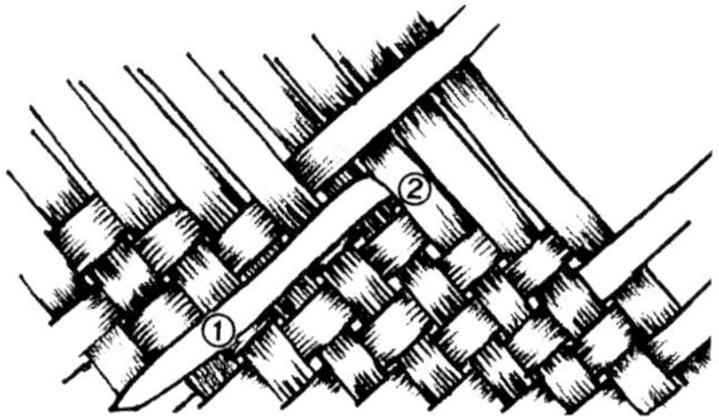

Fig. 113

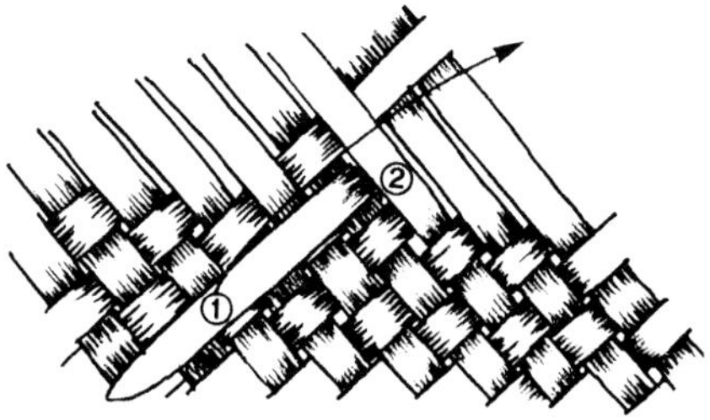

Fig. 114

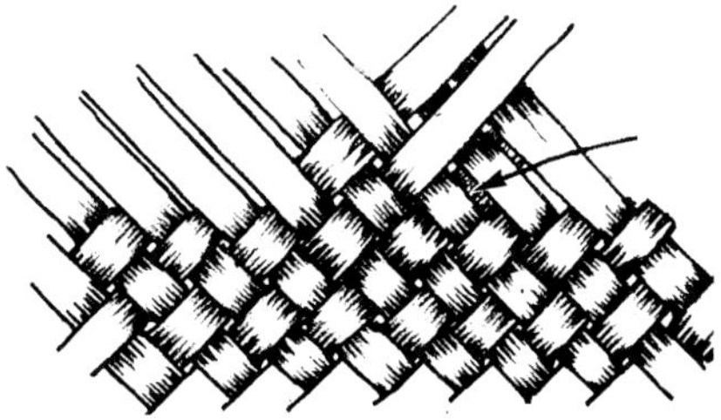

Fig. 115

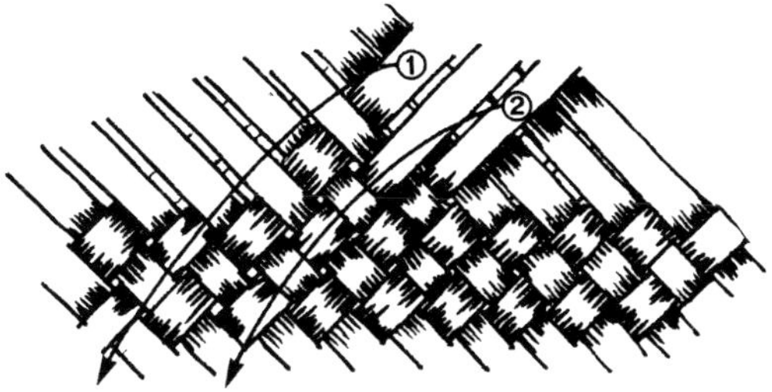

Fig. 116

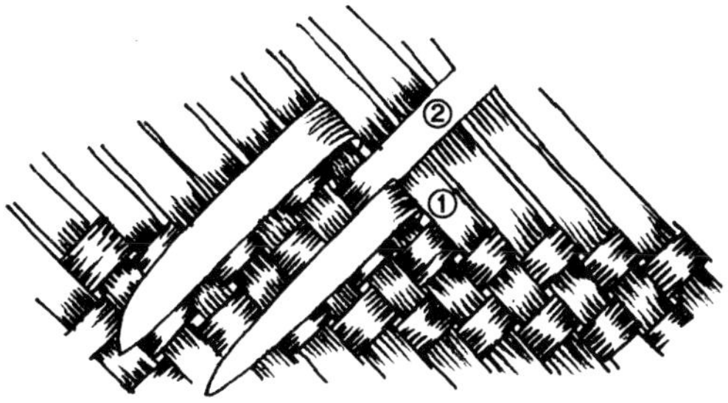

Fig. 117

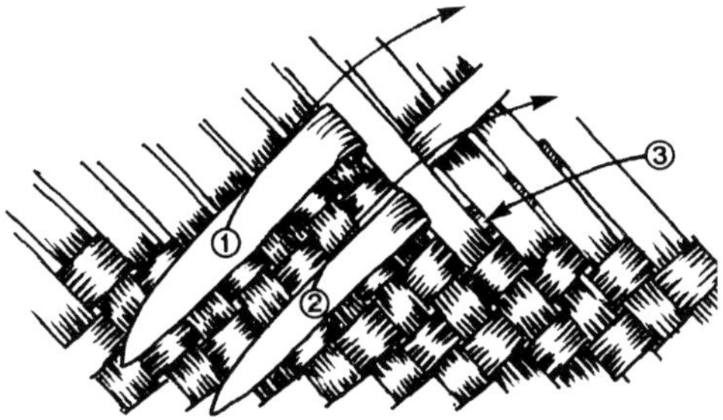

Fig. 118

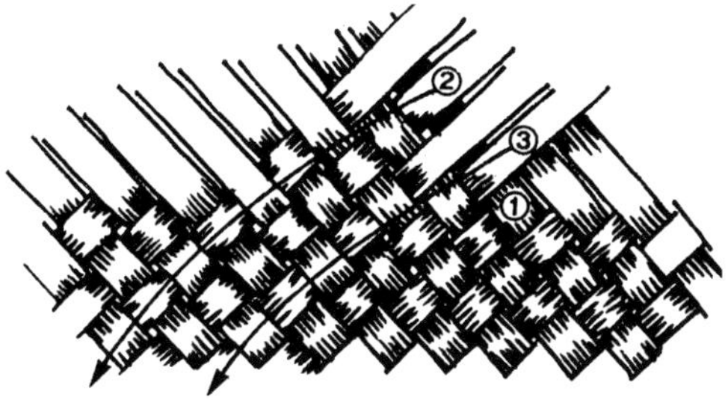

Fig. 119

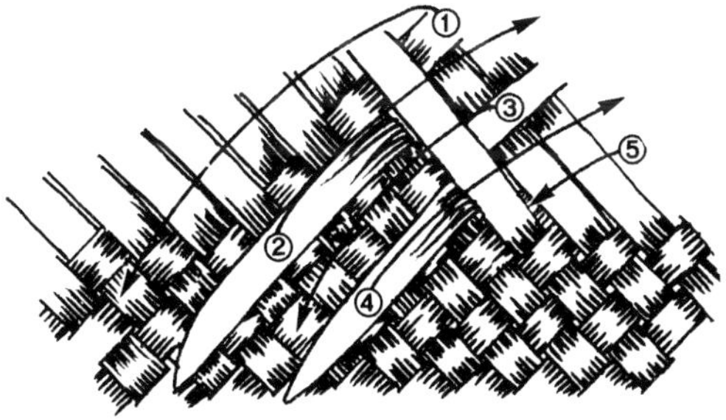

Fig. 120

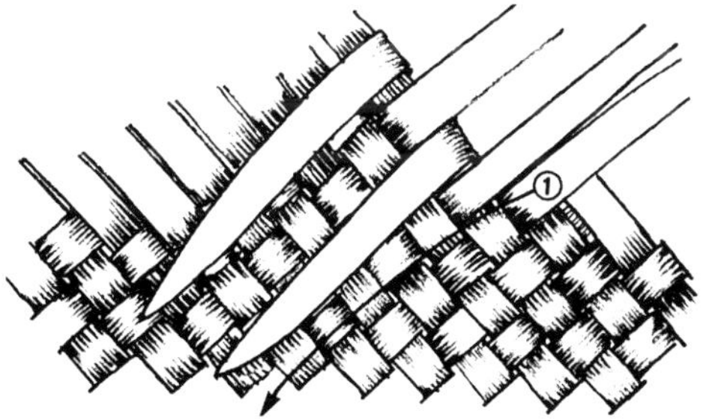

Fig. 121

Lift strip 2 in fig. 113 so that it lies on the top of the work in the position shown in fig. 114.

Return strip 1 to its original position (arrow) as shown in fig. 115.

Lift another strip from beneath at the point marked by the arrow in fig. 115, so that it lies in the position shown in fig. 116.

Fold strips 1 and 2 in fig. 116 back towards you to lie as in fig. 117.

Lift strip 1 so that it lies over strip 2 in fig. 117, to the position shown in fig. 118.

Return strips 1 and 2 to their original positions as indicated in fig. 118. Lift strip 3 from beneath at the point indicated by the arrow so that it lies on top of the work as in fig. 119.

Fold strips 2 and 3 in fig. 119 back towards you. Lift strip 1 so that it lies on the top of the work in the position shown in fig. 120.

Following the arrows in fig. 120:
Fold strip 1 back towards you.
Return strip 2 to its original position.
Fold strip 3 towards you.
Return strip 4 to its original position.

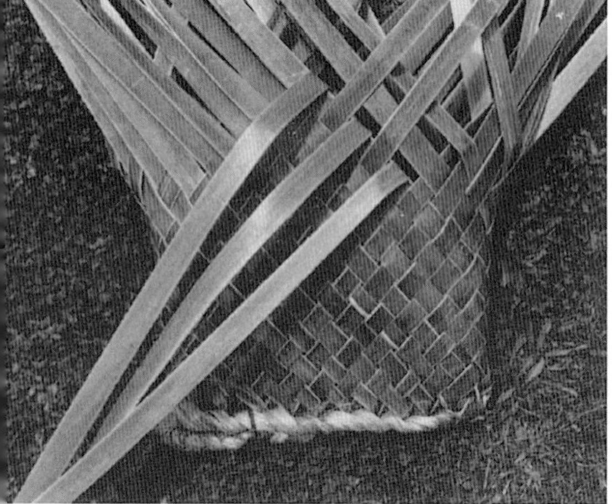
Fig. 122

Lift strip 5 (arrow) from beneath to lie in the position shown in fig. 121.

Fold strip 1 in fig. 121 back towards you.

Lift strip 1 in fig. 123 so that it lies on top of the work in the position shown in fig. 124.

Following the arrows in fig. 125:
Return strip 1 to its original position. Anchor it there by folding strip (a) back into the plait (Appendix 2, page 90).
Fold strip 2 back towards you.
Return strip 3 to its original position.
Fold strip 4 back towards you.
Return strip 5 to its original position.
Lift strip 6 so that it lies on top of the work, then fold it back towards you.
Repeat fig. 123 and 125 until you have worked right around the kete.

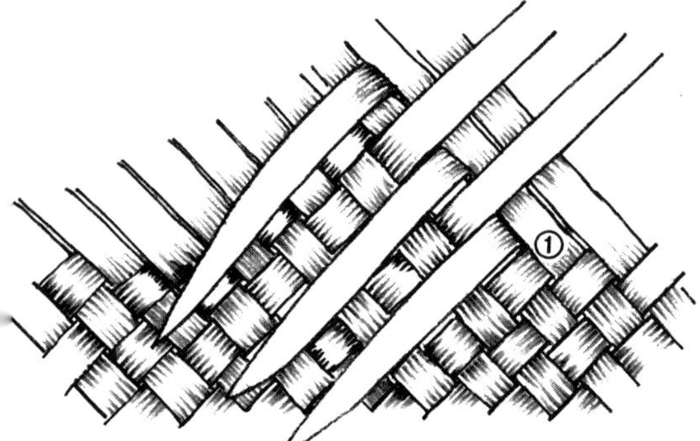

Fig. 123

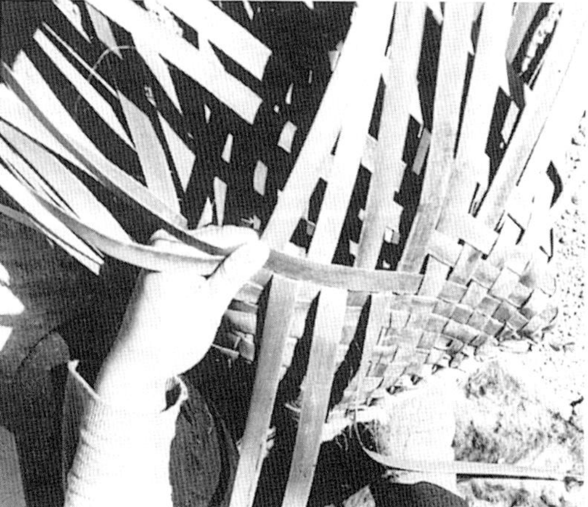
Fig. 124

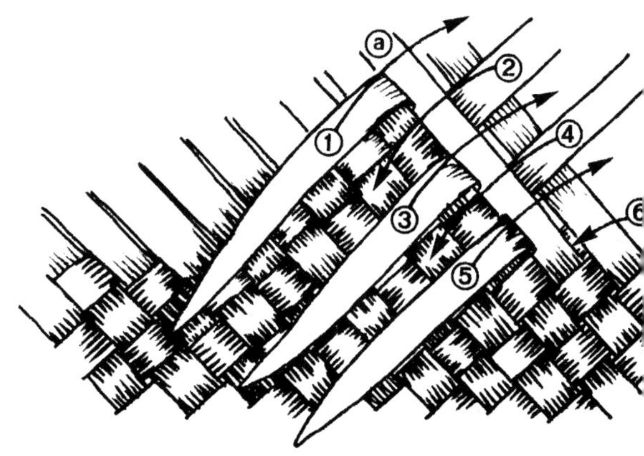

Fig. 125

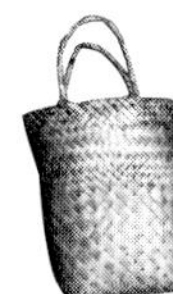

Another band is now plaited, beginning at the movement shown in fig. 111.

If it is found that there is a step in the top and that the plaiting continues to go round and round without making an even finish it means that an incorrect number of strips was put on at the beginning or that one or more strips from one side of the three-ply braid in the base of the kete has come across to the wrong side and increased the number of strands on that side.

It is possible to complete the kete if the step is not too big by just plaiting over it in the final braid at the top of the kete, or to correct by the method shown in Appendix 4. But it may be easier for the beginner to start again — painful as it may seem.

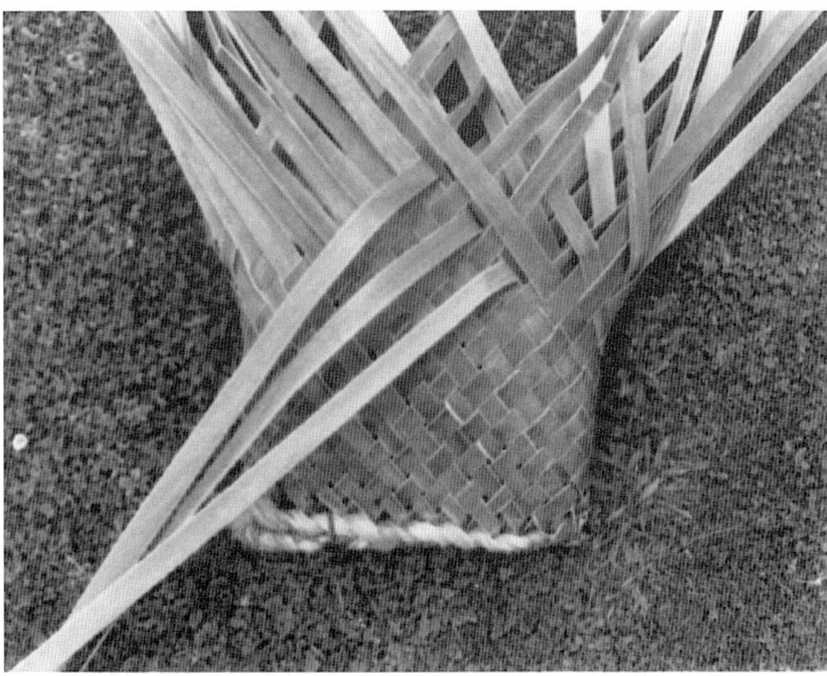

Fig. 126

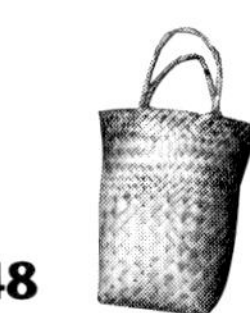

Folding down the top edge of the kete

The ends of the strips of flax that project from the top of the kete and to the right are now to be folded back on themselves and held in place by the strips next to them. All these protruding strips will then be plaited into a three-ply braid that will form the top edge.

Make sure that all the strips that are pointing to the left are over those pointing to the right as can be seen in fig. 127.

Lift any one of the strips from beneath the work, at the point indicated by the arrow, and bring it to the top of the work to lie in the position shown in fig. 128.

Lift the next strip to the right of the last one lifted, to the top of the work in the same way. Then fold it back on itself to lie in the position shown in fig. 129.

Lift the strip indicated by the arrow to the top of the work to lie in the position shown in fig. 130.

Fold strip 1 along the dotted line and bring it down on to the strip indicated by the arrow to lie in the position shown in fig. 131.

Return strip 1 to its original position (arrow) as shown in fig. 132.

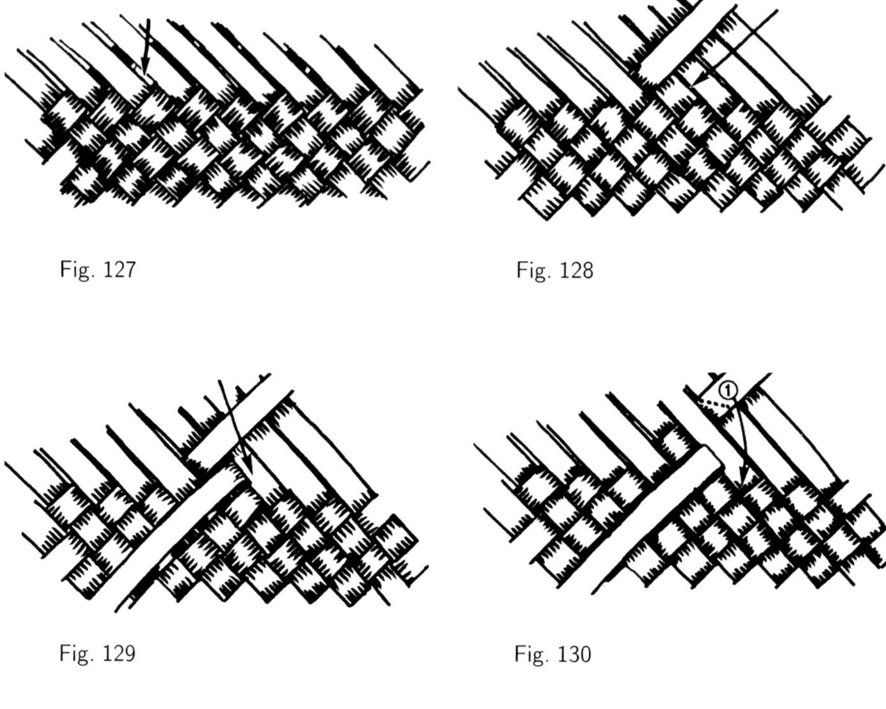

Fig. 127

Fig. 128

Fig. 129

Fig. 130

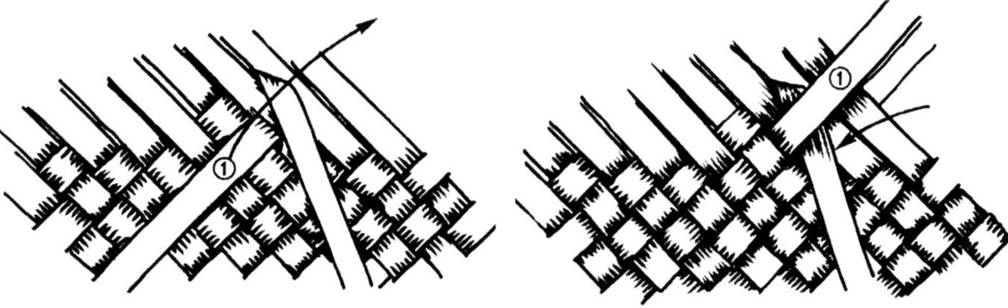

Fig. 131

Fig. 132

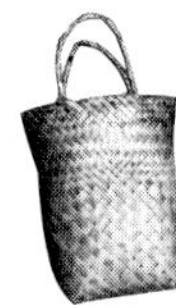

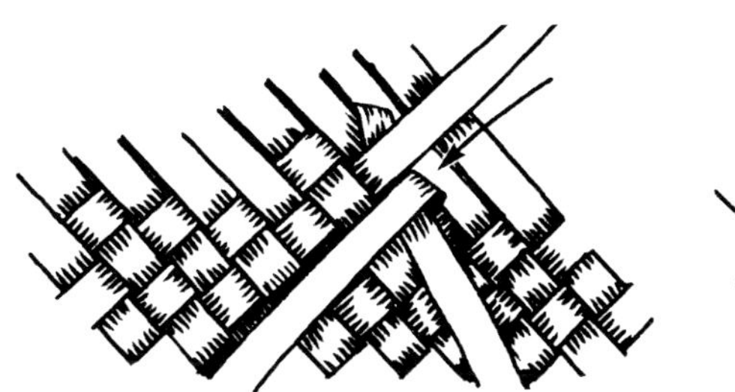

Fig. 133

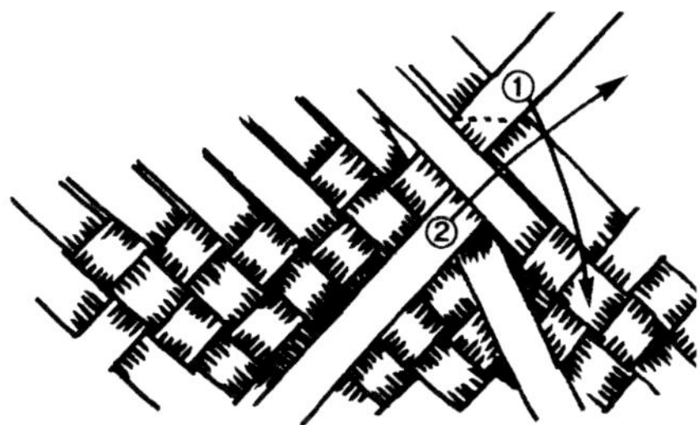

Fig. 134

Lift another strip from beneath the work at the point indicated by the arrow, and parallel to strip 1, so that it lies on top of the work. Then fold it back on itself to the position shown in fig. 133.

Lift the strip from beneath, at the point indicated by the arrow, so that it lies on the top of the work as shown in fig. 134.

Fold strip 1 along the dotted line and bring it down on to the strip indicated by the arrow. Return strip 2 to its original position over strip 1.

Continue to work figs. 132–134 until the top of the kete has been worked right around. It will be necessary to tuck the last strips into the first ones to complete the round.

The strips protruding at the top of the kete should now be interlocked with each other, holding the work in place while the three-ply braid along the top edge is plaited.

All the strips that were pointing to the right of the work are now folded down and pointing to the base of the basket, as in fig. 135.

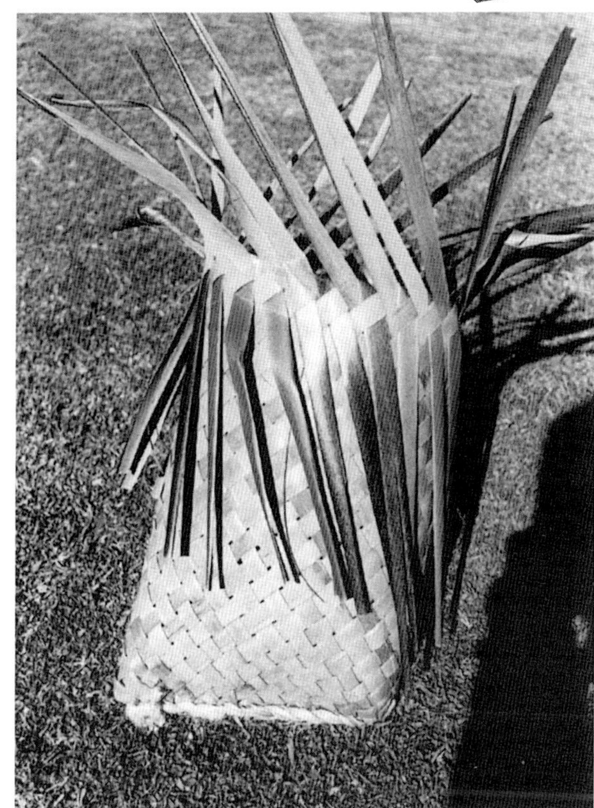

Fig. 135

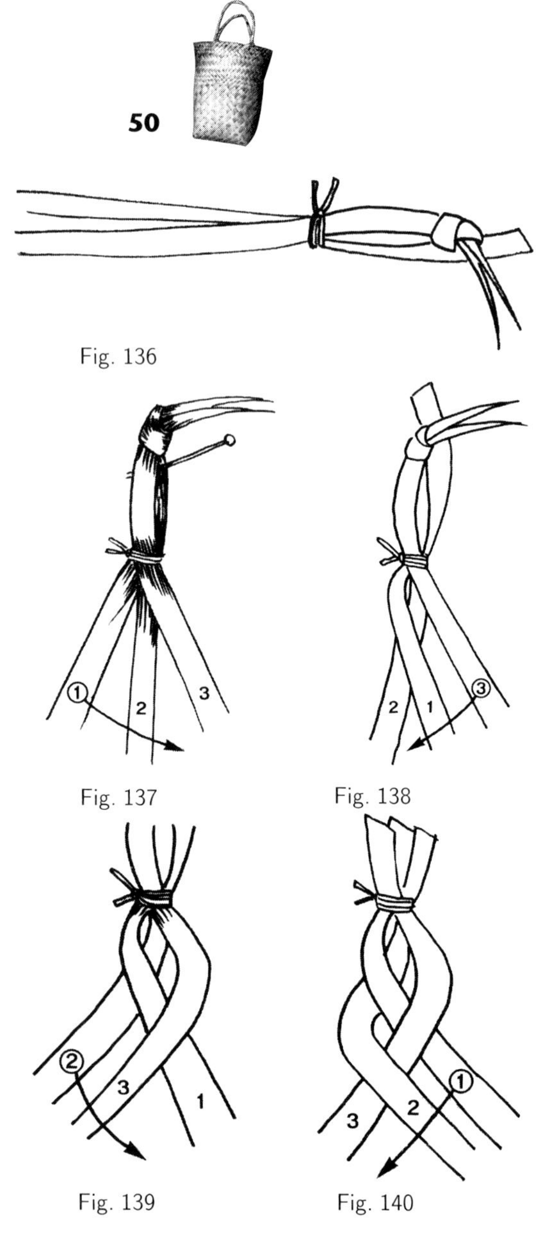

Fig. 136

Fig. 137

Fig. 138

Fig. 139

Fig. 140

Braiding the handle for the satchel kit

Before the three-ply braid for the top edge is worked the handle must be prepared. Any kind of braid can be used for the handle. The three-ply braid is given here as the simplest but the four-ply braid may be preferred for its attractive appearance. The method of doing it is given in the section on making handles for the bucket kete on pages 74–75.

Split and scrape three strips of flax 2 cm wide and as long as possible. Tie them together with a thin strip of flax about 20 cm or more from the end. To keep the final braid of even thickness do not pull all the thick butt ends together. Instead reverse one strip so that there are two butt ends and one thin pointed end from the top of the leaf to tie together. With an overhand knot, tie two of the projecting ends together (see fig. 136) so that these may be hooked over a nail in the wall to hold the work firm while braiding. Spread the three strips into a fan as in fig. 137.

Fold the left-hand strip 1 over the middle strip 2 (arrow). Strip 1 has now become the middle strip (see fig. 138).

Fold the right-hand strip 3 over the middle strip 1 (arrow) to become the new middle strip shown in fig. 139.

Fold the left-hand strip 2 over the middle strip 3 (arrow) to become the new middle strip as shown in fig. 140.

Fold the right-hand strip 1 over the middle strip 2 (arrow) to become the middle strip.

Continue to fold first the left strip and then the right strip over the new middle strip alternately until about 80 cm has been worked. Tie the end with a thin strip.

The positions where the handle is to be inserted are now chosen. Select a strip at each end of the kete and tie a knot in them. These mark the positions where the ends of the handle will be inserted, and will act as a reminder, when they are reached during the braiding of the top edge, that the handle must be inserted. The knots can be seen in fig. 135.

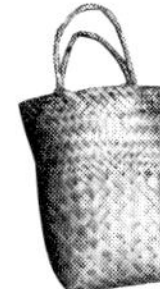

Braiding the top edge

Start braiding about one third of the way along the top. The handles will be added at each end of the kete during the process of the braiding.

Fold a strip protruding from the top of the kete back on itself as indicated by the arrow in fig. 141 to lie in the position shown in fig. 142.

The strip pointing to the base of the kete, and to the left of the last strip worked (strip 1 in fig. 142) is folded along the dotted line and moved in the direction shown by the arrow to lie in the position shown in fig. 143.

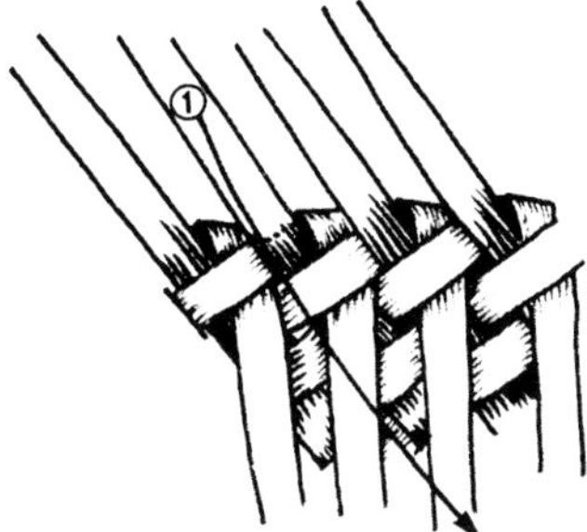

Fig. 141

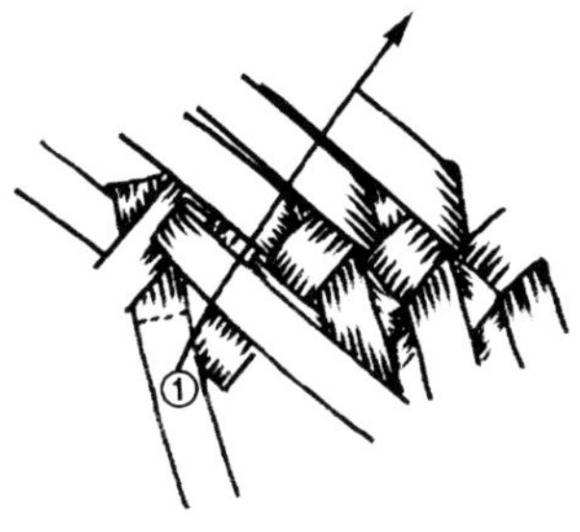

Fig. 142

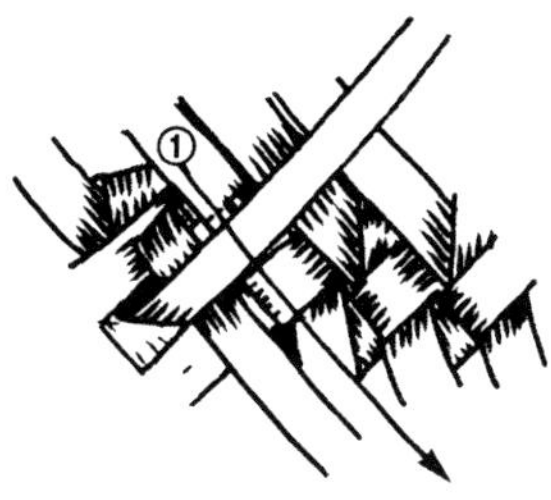

Fig. 143

Strip 1 is folded down on itself (arrow) to lie in the position shown in fig. 144.

Strip 1 is folded along the dotted line and moved as indicated by the arrow to lie in the position shown in fig. 145.

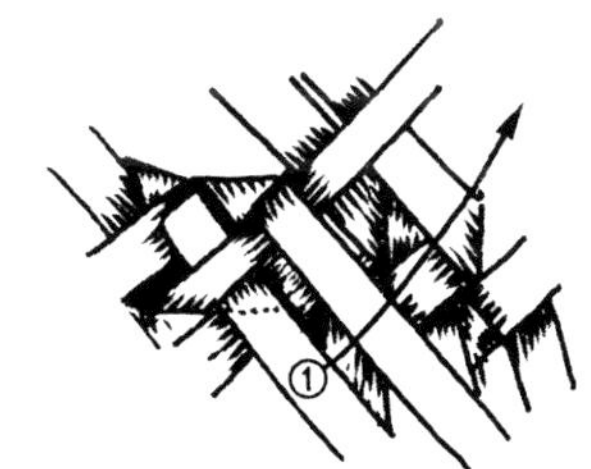

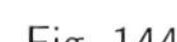

Fig. 144

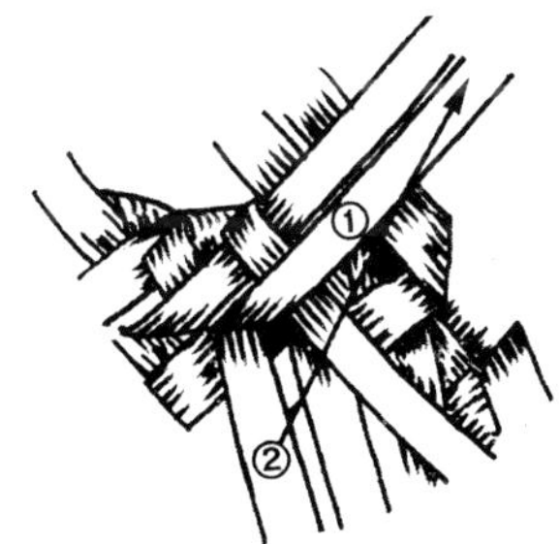

Fig. 145

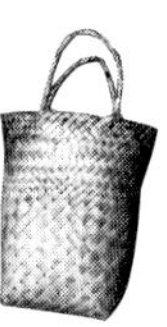

Lift strip 2 (which was beneath the last strip worked) and carry it to the same position as shown by the arrow to lie on top of the last strip in the position shown in fig. 146.

Strip 1 is folded down and over the last two strips worked (arrow), to lie in the position shown in fig. 147.

The next strip (2) protruding from the top of the kete is folded down on to the last strip worked (arrow) to lie in the position shown in fig. 148.

Fold strip 1 up at the dotted line in the direction indicated by the arrow. Then fold strip 2 in the same diagram on top of it. The work should now resemble fig. 149.

Fold double strip 1 in fig. 149 down along the dotted line (arrow). Fold strip 2 in the same diagram down on top of it as in fig. 150.

Continue to work a three-ply braid taking strips alternately from the bottom and then the top. Two strips are taken each time from the top but at the bottom the strips continue to increase.

Keep braiding the top three from the bottom side of the braid and drop the rest. These will be cut off when the kete has been completed.

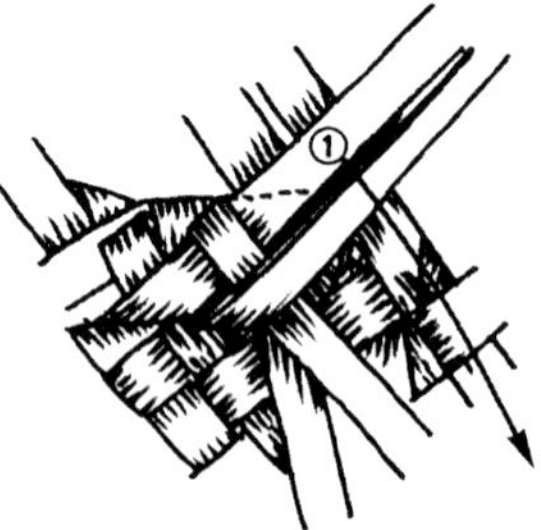

Fig. 146

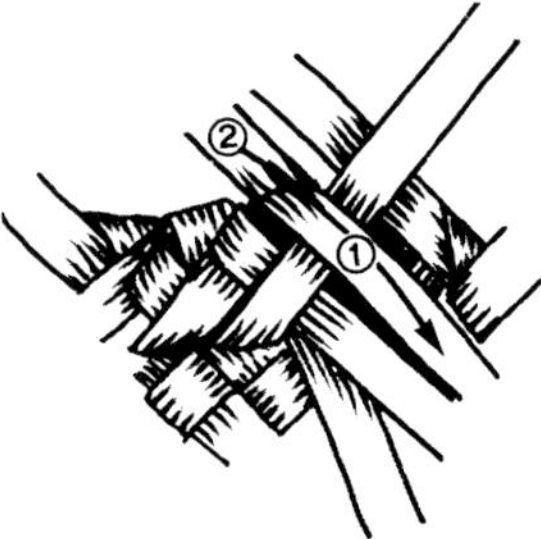

Fig. 147

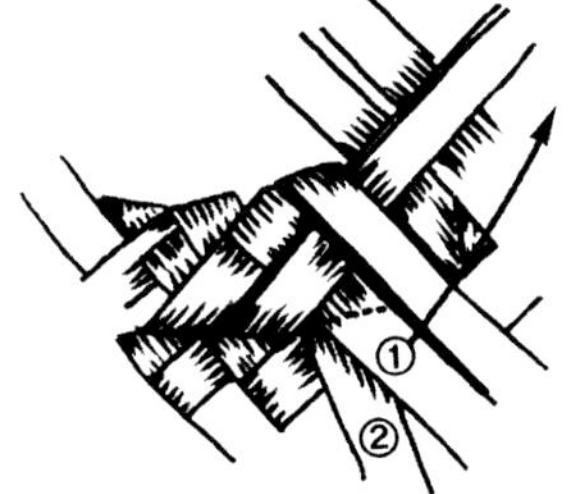

Fig. 148

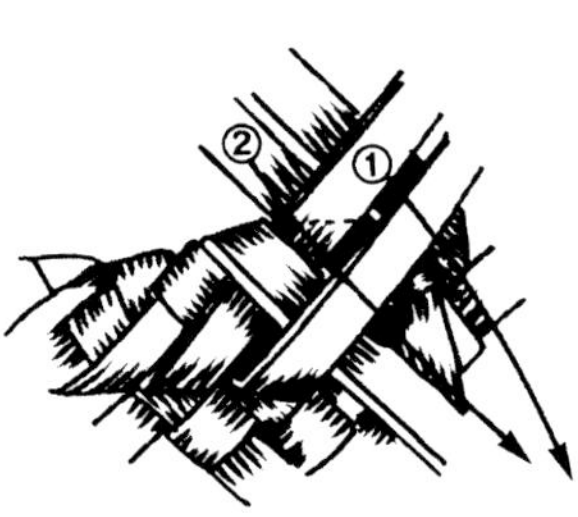

Fig. 149

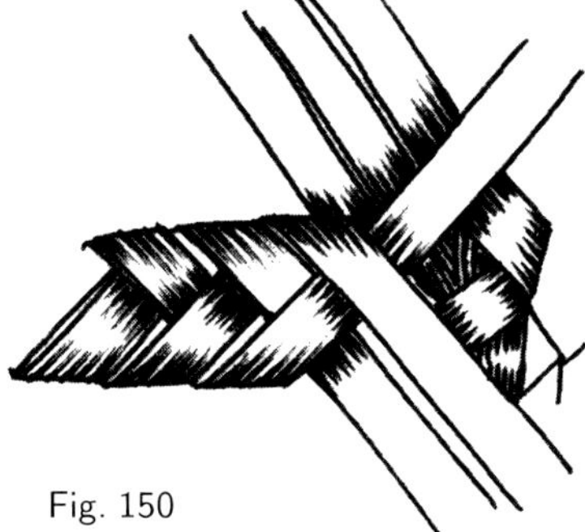

Fig. 150

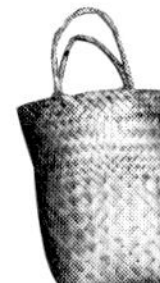

Adding the handle

The first end of the handle is added to the side of the basket at the point where one of the strips was knotted to mark the position. After two top strips have been brought down into the braid, insert one end of the handle between the braid and the side of the kete, as shown in fig. 151.

Strip 1 is brought from behind the handle, around the front of it and down on to strip 2 (arrow) to lie as shown in fig. 152.

Fold two strips up along the dotted line and into the braid.

There will be some more strips left on the lower side of the braid, in the position from which the last two were taken. These are pushed out of the way as indicated by the arrow (fig. 153) and will later be cut off.

The ends of the handle labelled 1 in fig. 154 are brought up on top of the strips labelled 2, and become part of the braid. Continue the braid in the same way. The next step is to bring strip 3 down into the braid.

Braid until the next knotted strip is reached and insert the other end of the handle there. Take care to carry the ends far enough into the braid to ensure that the handle won't pull out when the basket is in use.

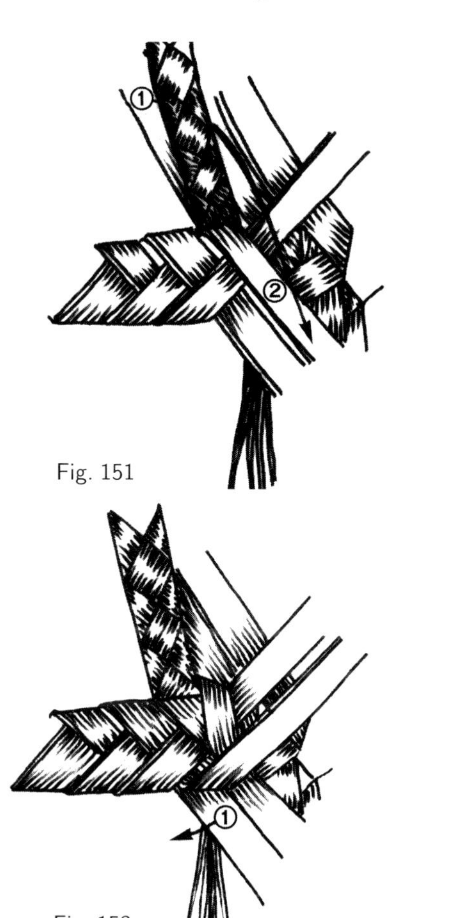

Fig. 151

Fig. 153

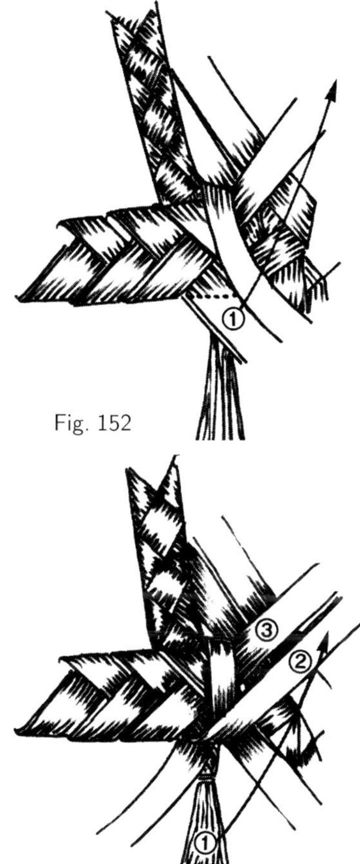

Fig. 152

Fig. 154

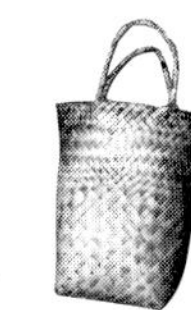

Completing the kete

When the top of the kete has been fully circled continue to braid the ends of the strips, making a 'tail' of about 5 cm. The end of this may be made thinner and neater by dropping strips to the left (or lower side on the kete). At the end tie an overhand knot or use a thin strip of flax to tie the end.

All the ends of the strips are now cut off with a large pair of scissors or a sharp knife. The braided 'tail' is neatly positioned against the side of the plait.

Turn the kete right side out. Start with the corners at the bottom.

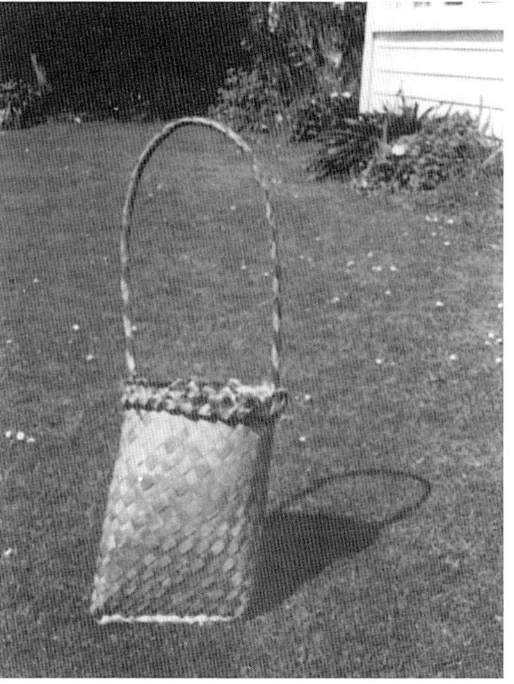

Fig. 155

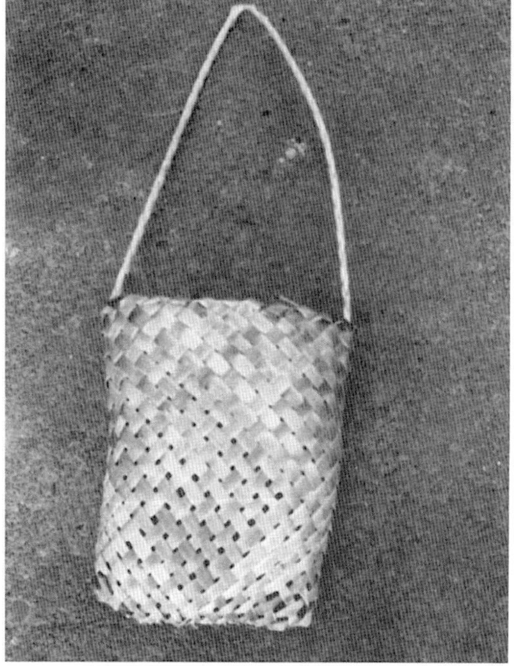

Fig. 156

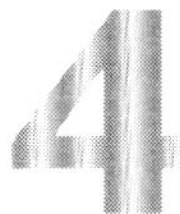

The Bucket Kit

Note: The photographs in this section have been turned top to bottom so that the flax strips follow those in the line diagrams.

This kete is more open at the top than the first one explained. It has four corners in the base instead of two and this makes the bottom flatter. A number of variations can be made in the plaiting of the sides depending upon the skill of the worker or the time available. The same number of strips of flax are required as were used for the satchel kete, that is, 48 strips of scraped flax about 1.5 cm wide and a couple of spare leaves for the handles and tying. The 48 strips are prepared in the way that has been covered beginning at fig. 7 and working to fig. 11. The base braid is made in exactly the same way as for the satchel kete (see figs. 12–21). Plait the base triangles using the same methods outlined in figs. 22–69. The first new step to be learned is forming the four corners.

Plaiting the corners

This kete has four corners instead of two and the bottom should be almost 'box shaped'. In plaiting the corners the base triangles are not held so closely together, as the kete is more open from the bottom up. The three-ply braid at the end where you are to make the first corners is bent up into what will be the side of the kete.

Untie the four strips on the left-hand side of the three-ply braid, taking special care to keep them from crossing to the other side of the braid.

Fold strips 1 and 2 back (arrows) to the positions shown in fig. 159.

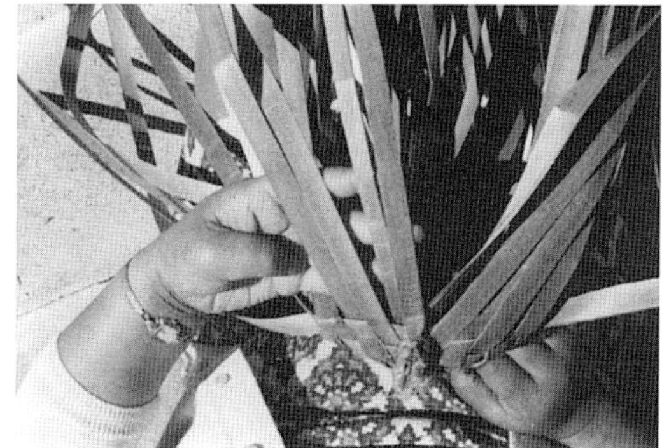

Fig. 157

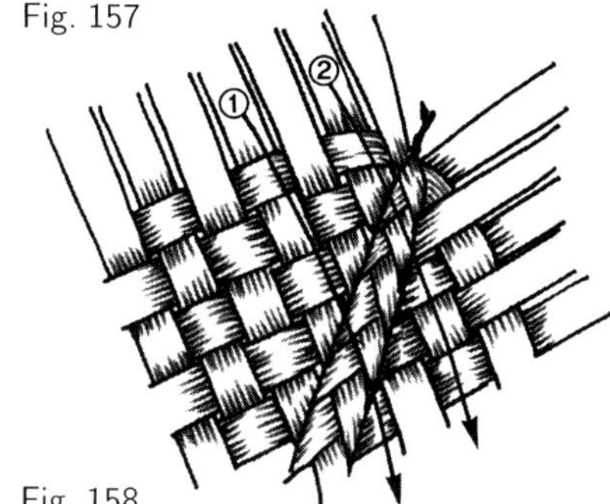

Fig. 158

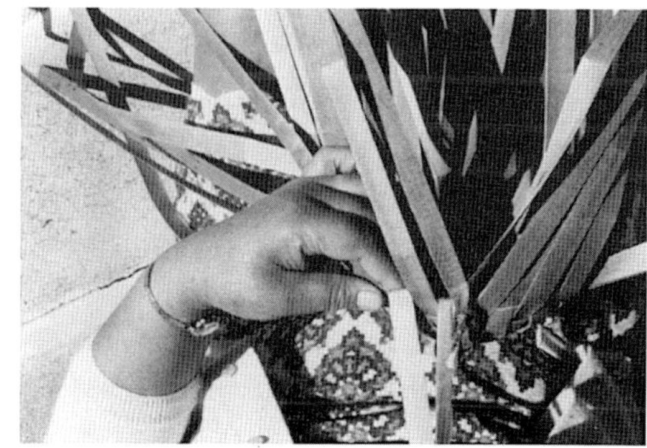

Fig. 159

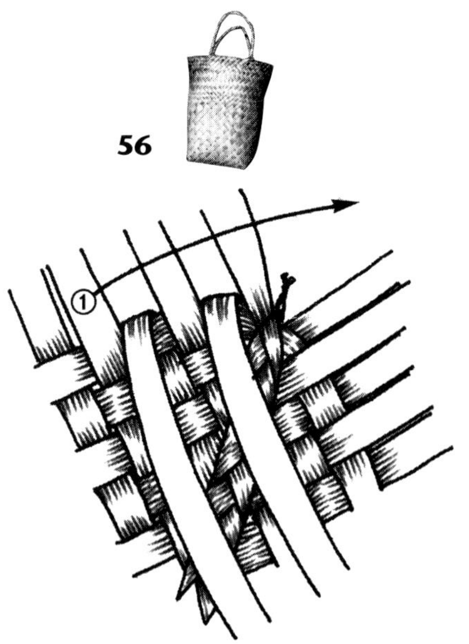

Fig. 160

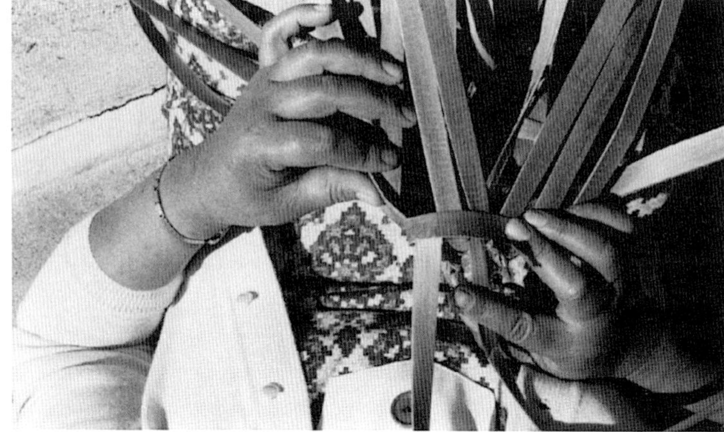

Fig. 161

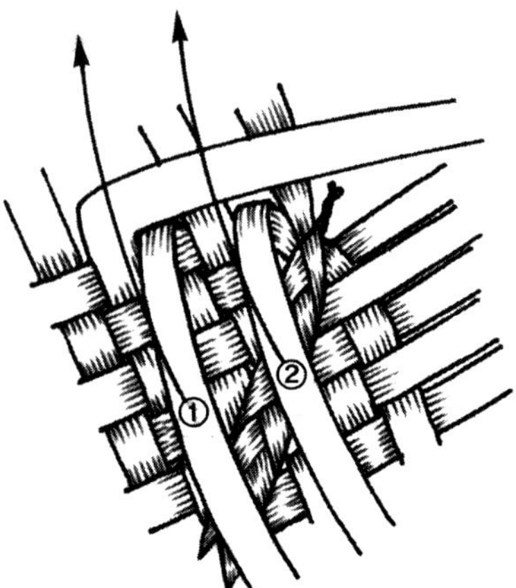

Fig. 162

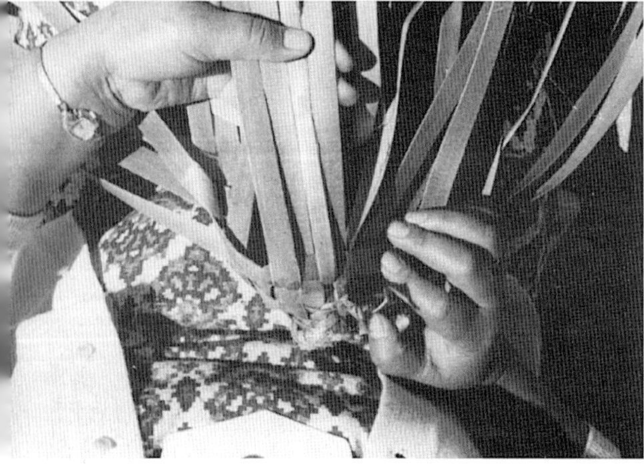

Fig. 163

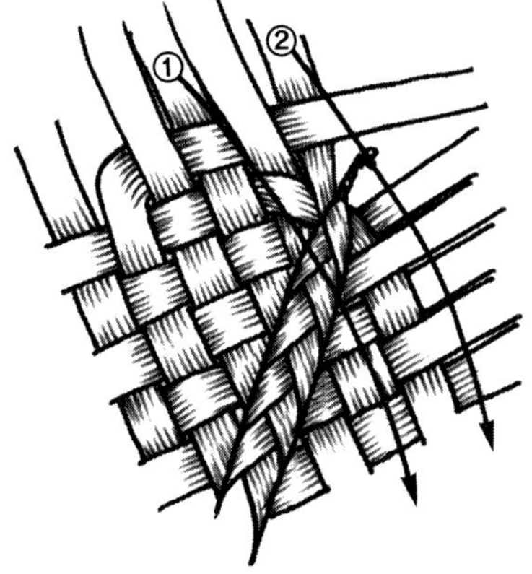

Fig. 164

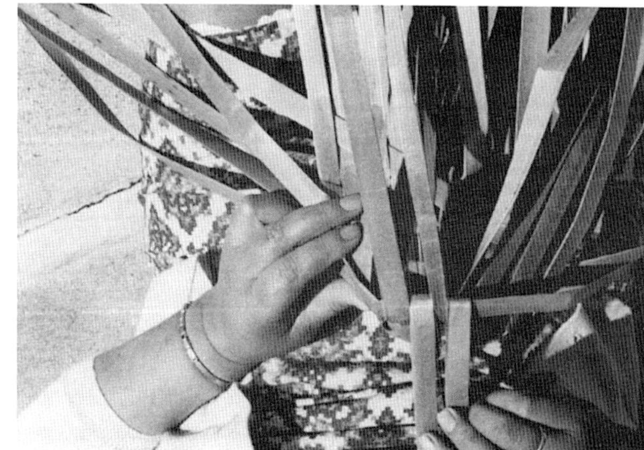

Fig. 165

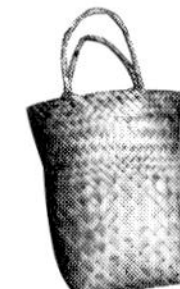

Move strip 1 (arrow) to lie in the position shown in fig. 161. The dull side remains uppermost and the strip is not folded in any way; the strips to the left of it are bent to allow it to form the corner.

Strips 1 and 2 are returned to their original positions as shown in fig. 163.

Strips 1 and 2 are folded back (arrows) to the positions shown in fig. 165.

Strip 1 is moved to the right (arrow) to lie in the position shown in fig. 167. Return the two strips that were folded back to their original positions as shown in fig. 168.

Fold the next two strips that come from beneath the work back to the positions shown in fig. 169.

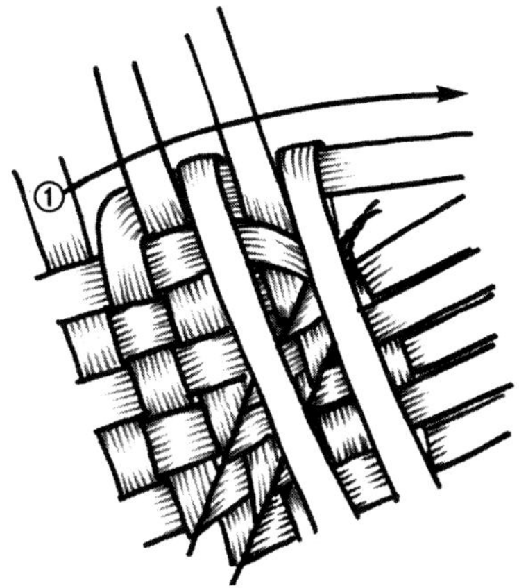

Fig. 166

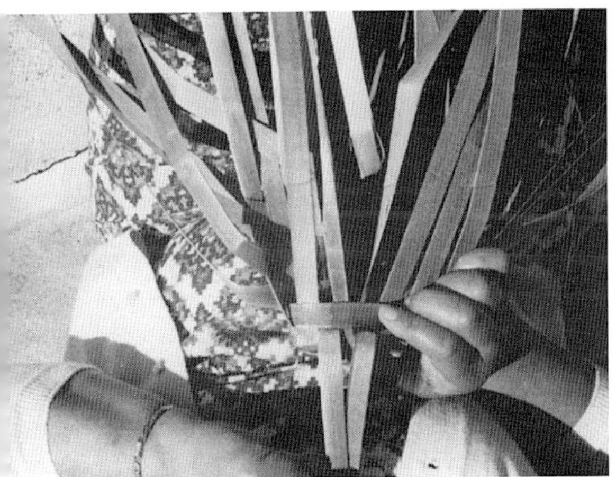

Fig. 167

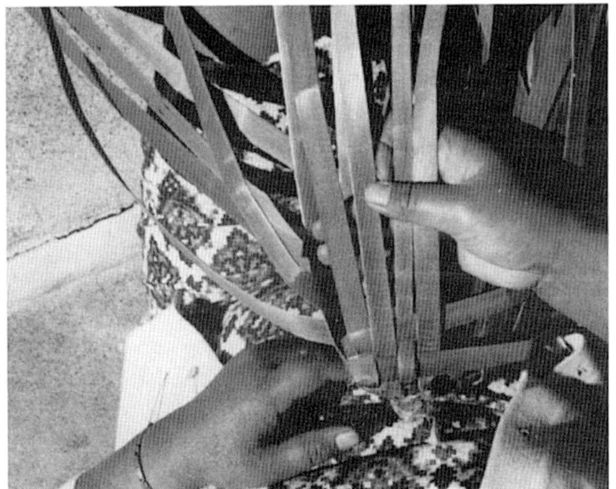

Fig. 168

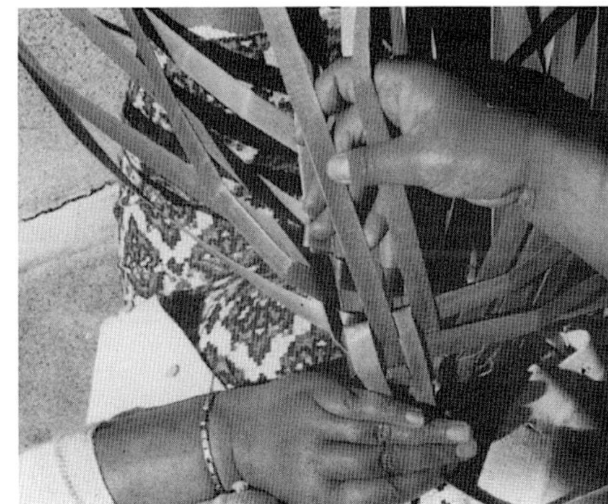

Fig. 169

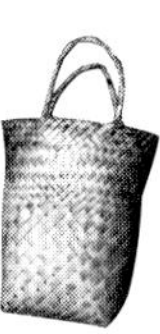

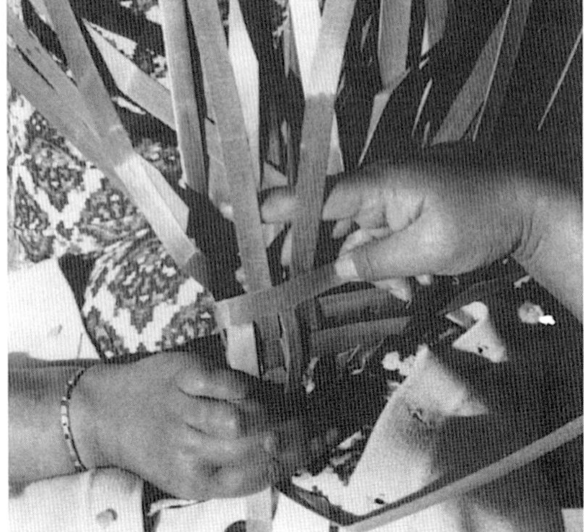

Fig. 170

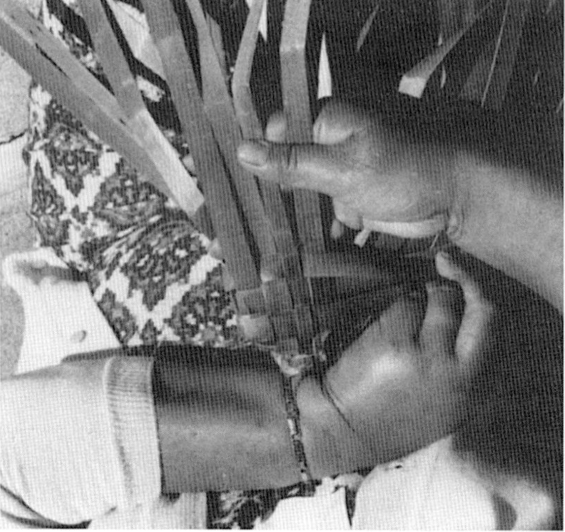

Fig. 171

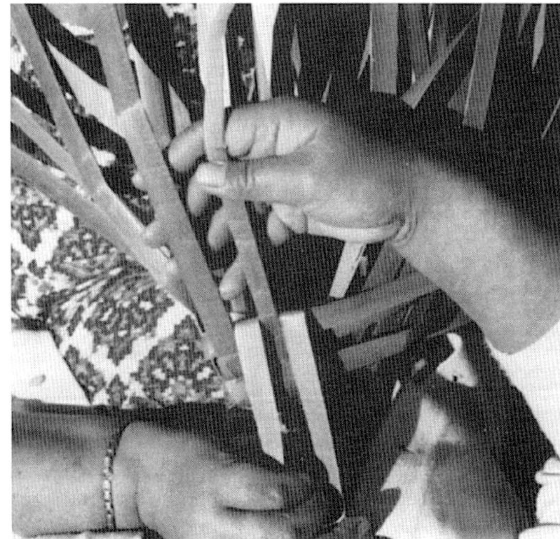

Fig. 172

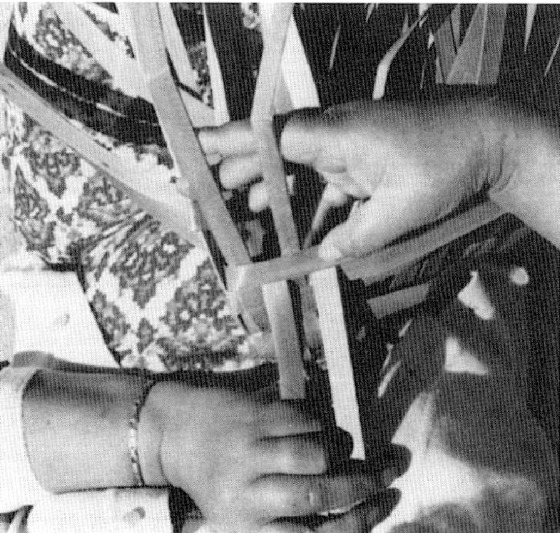

Fig. 173

Bring another strip from the left across into the position shown in fig. 170.

Return the two strips that were folded back to their original positions as in fig. 171.

Fold the next two strips that come from beneath the work back to the positions shown in fig. 172.

Bring another strip from the left across into the work as shown in fig. 173.

Return the two strips that were folded back to their original positions. Continue to follow the same movements shown in figs. 171–173 until you have plaited to a height equal to the base triangle.

The corner on the right-hand side of the three-ply braid is now formed in exactly the same way except that new strips will be brought into the work from the right instead of the left.

Untie the four strips tied together at the right of the three-ply braid. Fold the two strips that come from beneath the work back to the positions shown in fig. 175.

Bring the first strip to the right of the four working strips across and into the position shown in fig. 176.

Return the two strips that were folded back to their original positions, as in fig. 177.

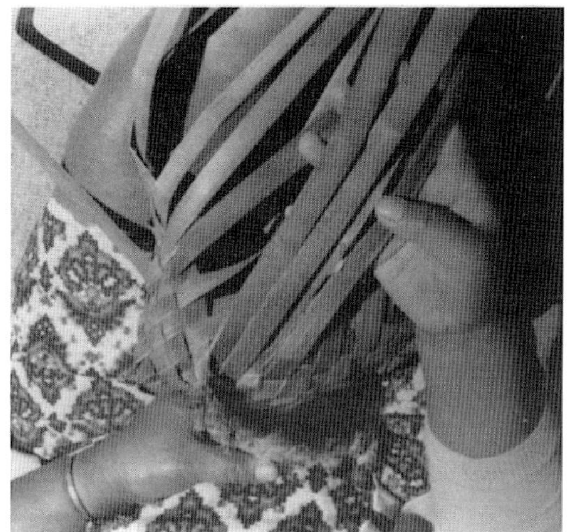

Fig. 174

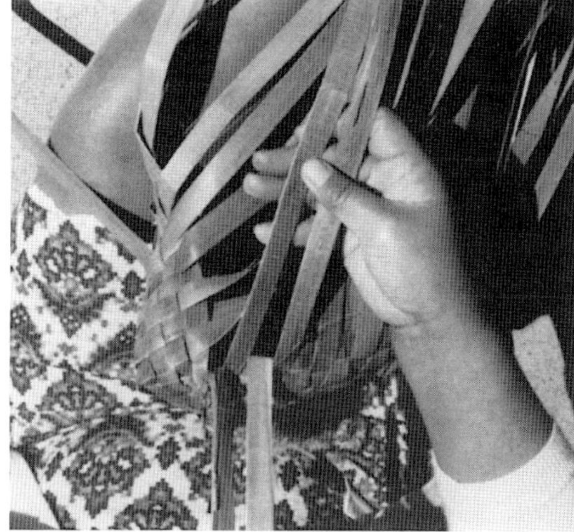

Fig. 175

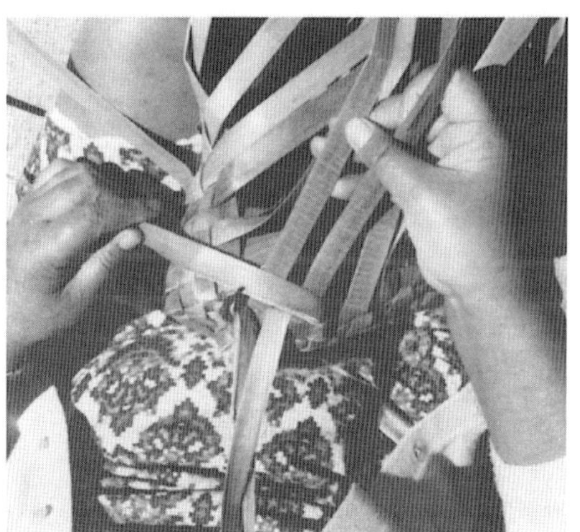

Fig. 176

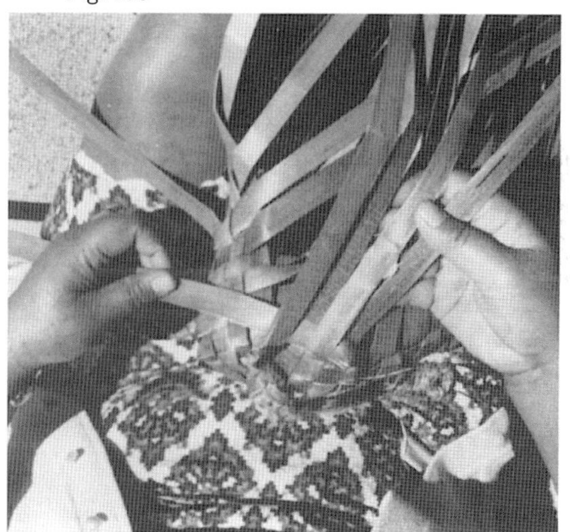

Fig. 177

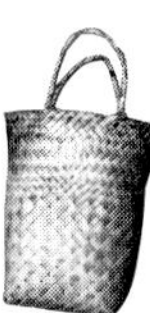

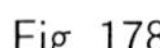

Fig. 178

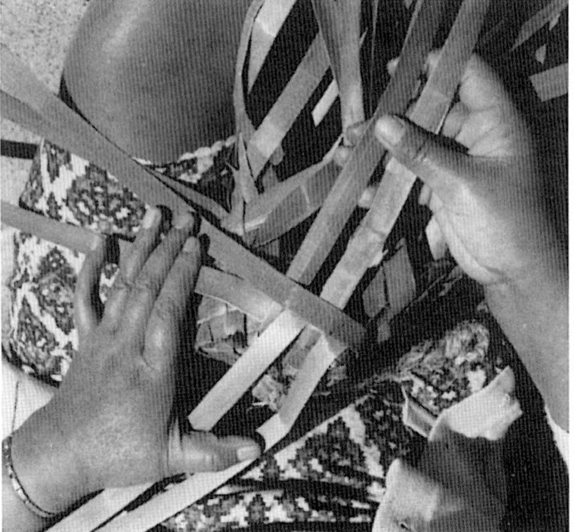

Fig. 179

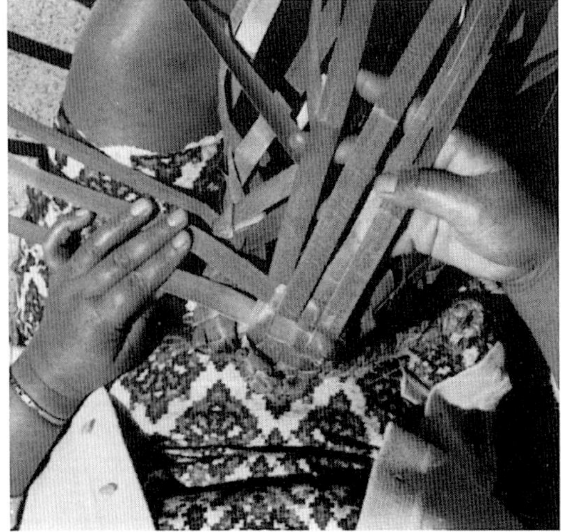

Fig. 180

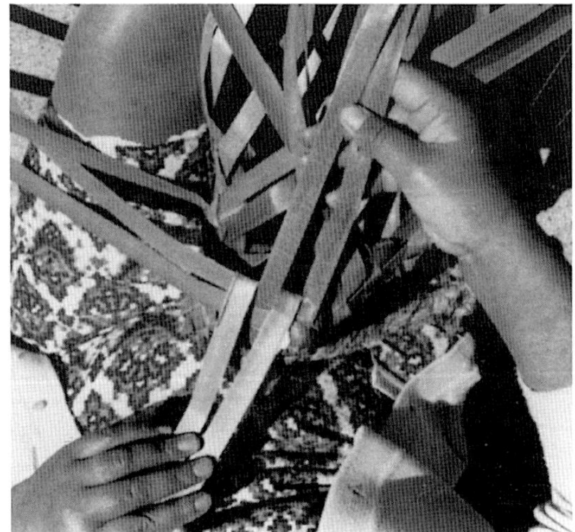

Fig. 181

The two strips that come from beneath the work are folded back to the positions shown in fig. 178.

Bring the next strip to the right of the four working strips across into the work as shown in fig. 179.

Return the two strips that were folded back to their original positions as shown in fig. 180.

Fold the two strips that come from beneath the work back to the positions shown in fig. 181.

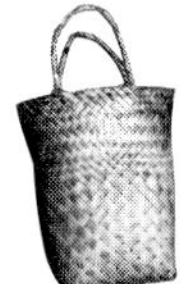

Bring the next strip to the right of the four working strips across into the work as shown in fig. 182.

Return the two strips that were folded back to their original positions. Continue to make the same moves shown in figs. 180–182 until the work reaches the height of the base triangle.

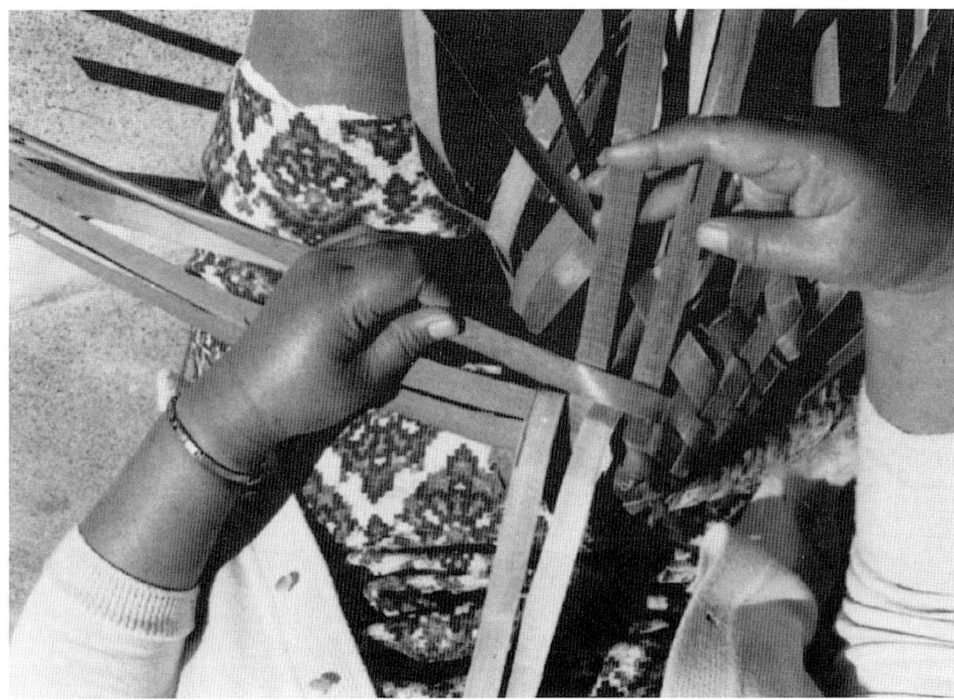

Fig. 182

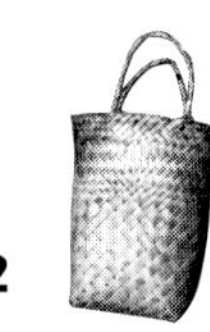

Filling the gap between the corners

The gap between the two corners should now be plaited in. Lift the three strips that come from beneath the work and fold them back to the positions shown in fig. 184.

Bring the first strip from the right-hand corner across into the work as shown in fig. 185.

Return the three strips that were folded back to their original positions as shown in fig. 186.

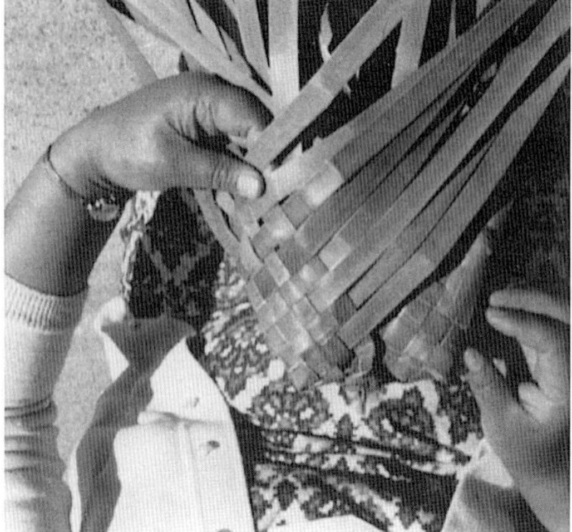

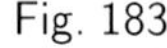

Fig. 183

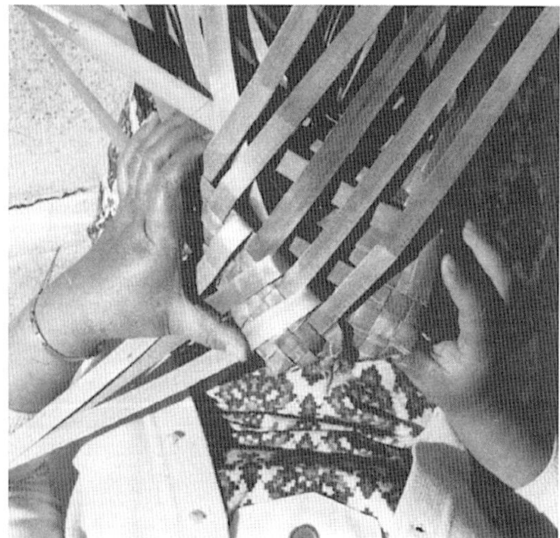

Fig. 184

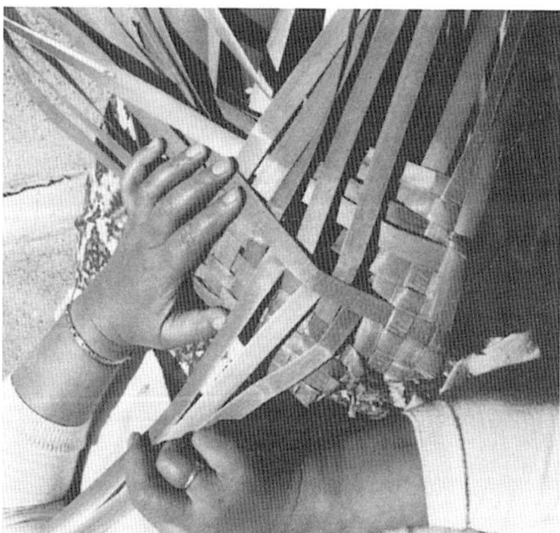

Fig. 185

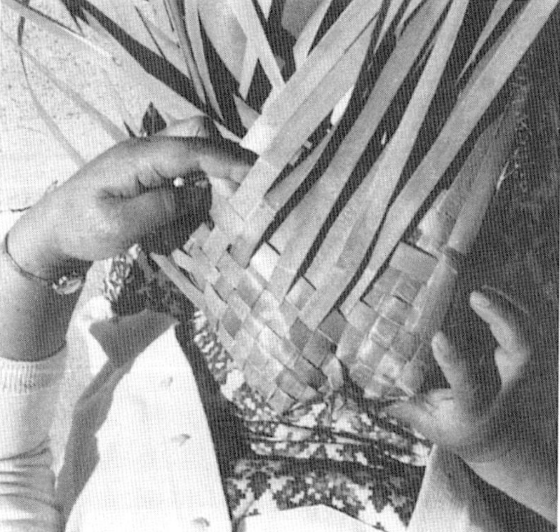

Fig. 186

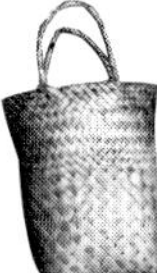

Lift the three strips that come from beneath and fold them back to the positions shown in fig. 187.

Bring the next strip from the right-hand corner across and into the work as shown in fig. 188.

Return the three strips that were folded back to their original positions as shown in fig. 189.

Lift the two strips that come from beneath and fold them back to the positions shown in fig. 190.

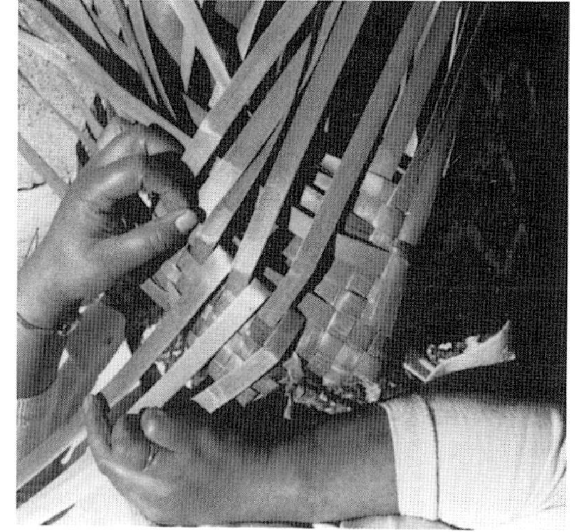

Fig. 187

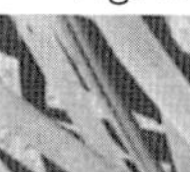

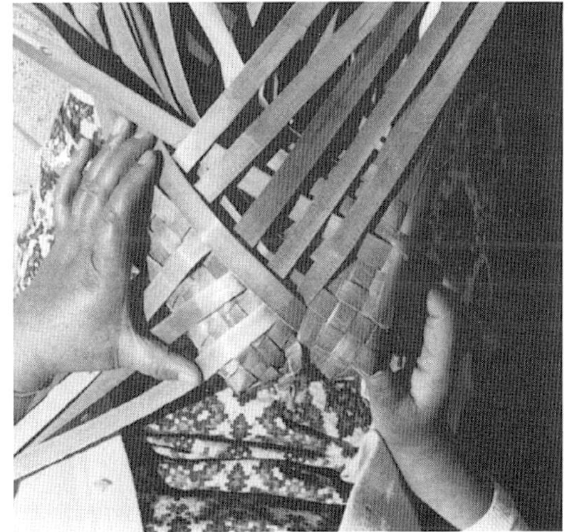

Fig. 188

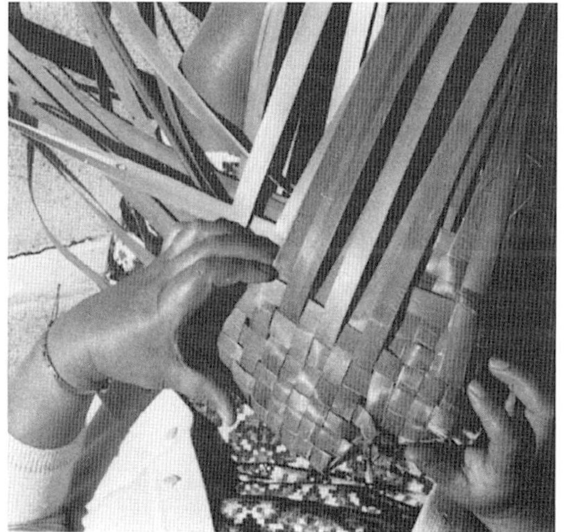

Fig. 189

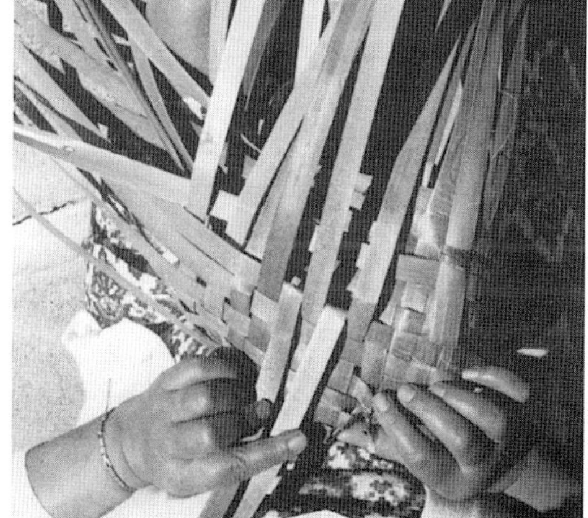

Fig. 190

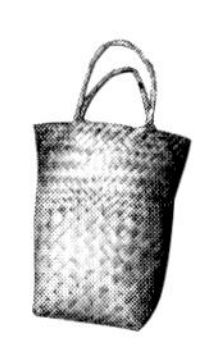

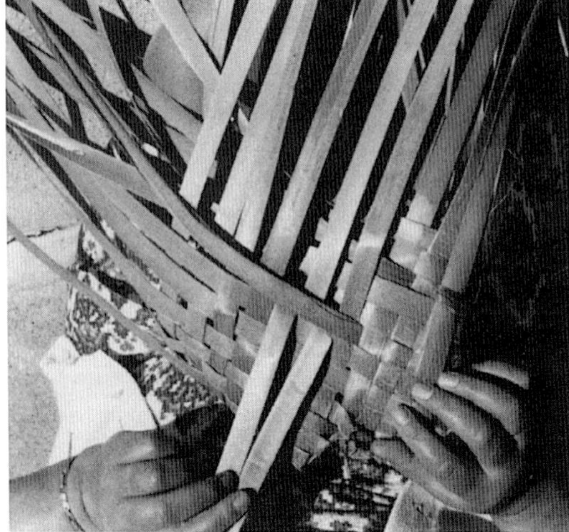

Fig. 191

Bring the next strip from the right-hand corner across and into the work as shown in fig. 191.

Return the two strips that were folded back to their original positions, as shown in fig. 192.

Lift the two strips that come from beneath and fold them back to the positions shown in fig. 193.

Bring the next strip from the right-hand corner across and into the work as shown in fig. 194.

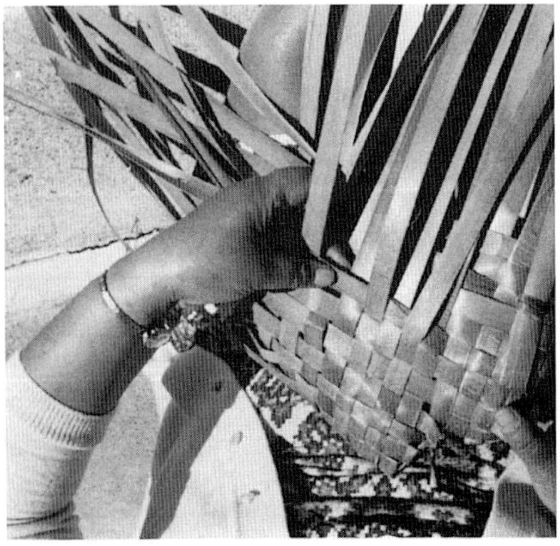

Fig. 192

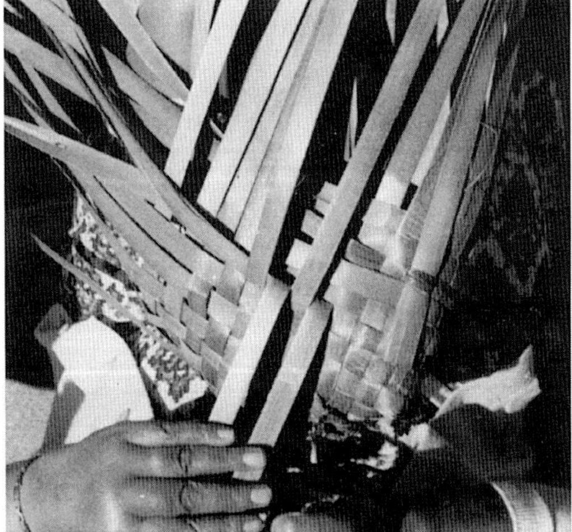

Fig. 193

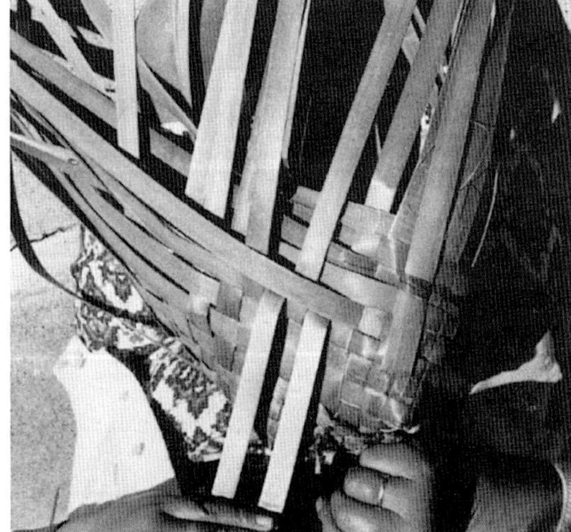

Fig. 194

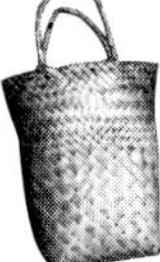

Return the two strips that were folded back to their original positions as shown in fig. 195.

Lift the strip that comes from beneath the work and fold it back to the position shown in fig. 196.

Bring the next strip from the right-hand corner across and into the work.

Continue in the same way until the gap is fully filled.

Now turn the kete around and plait the corner at the other end of the three-ply braid in the same way.

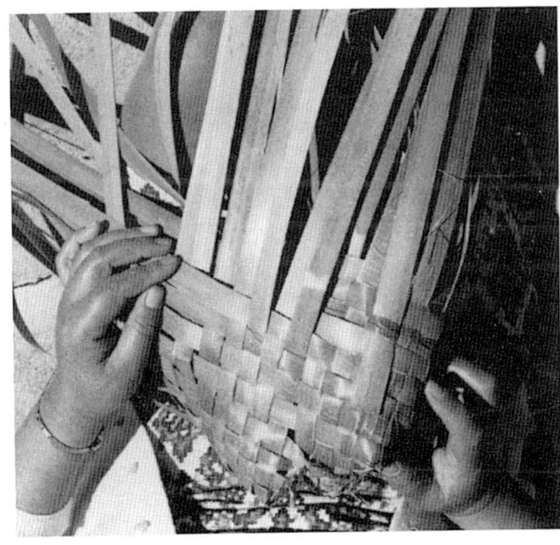

Fig. 195

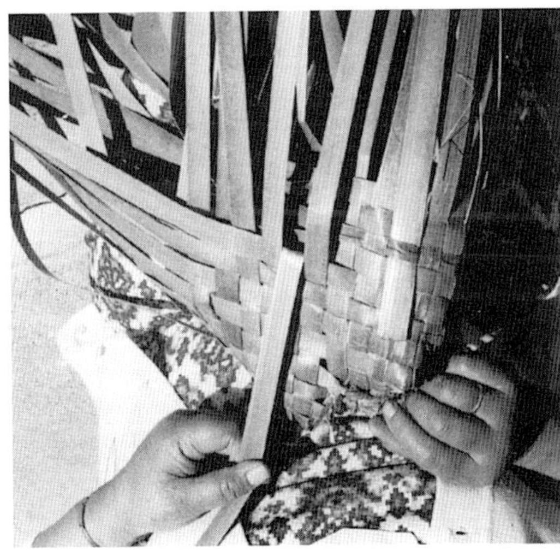

Fig. 196

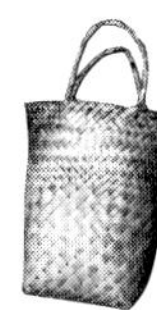

Plaiting the sides

When the sides have been plaited up to the height of about 15 cm, each strip is split down the centre from the pointed end of the strip to the plaited part. From this point on the strips will now be half the width and the rest of the plaiting will be of a finer plait.

Split the strips on the inside of the work first. That is, those that are pointing to the right of the work. Push your thumbnail through the strip near the place where it enters the plaited area and split to the end of the strip. Split all the strips on the inside of the work working from left to right and then split those on the outside in the same way. The work will now resemble fig. 198.

Lift a strip from beneath at the point indicated by the arrow in fig. 198, to lie on top of the work as in fig. 199.

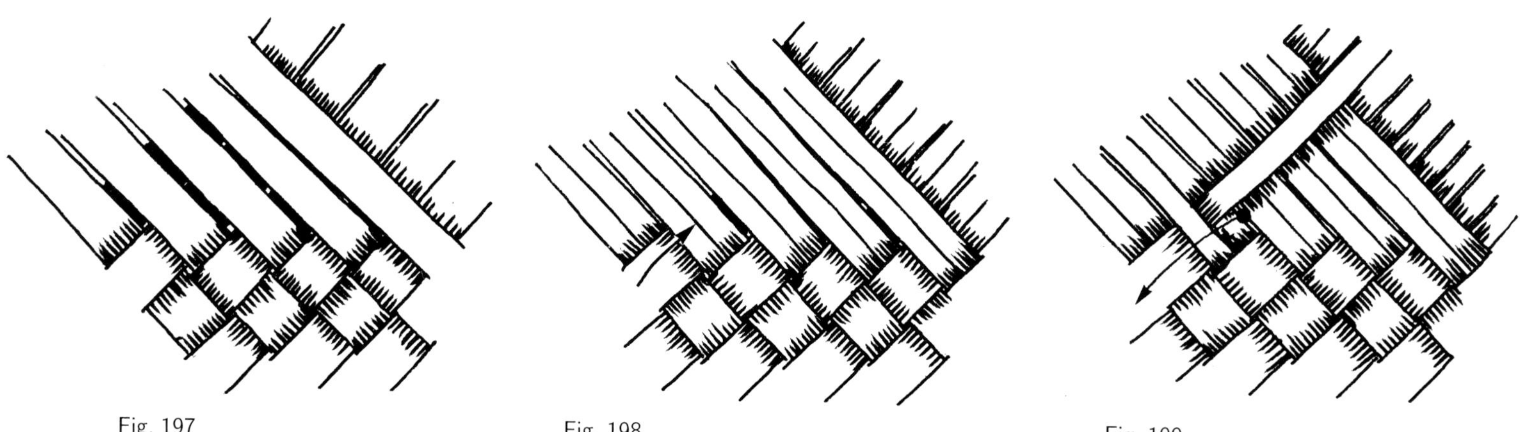

Fig. 197 Fig. 198 Fig. 199

Lift the next strip to right, from beneath at the point indicated and fold it back (arrow) to lie in the position shown in fig. 200.

Lift strip 1 so that it lies over strip 2 and on top of the work in the position shown in fig. 201.

Fold strip 1 back as indicated by the arrow (fig. 201). Return strip 2 to its original position.

Lift another strip from beneath and fold it back (arrow). Lift strip 1 so that it lies on top of the work as shown in fig. 203.

Return strip 1 to its original position. Fold strip 2 back (arrow). Return strip 3 to its original position. Lift another strip from beneath and fold back as indicated.

Lift strip 1 so that it lies over strips 2 and 3 (fig. 204).

Return strip 1 (fig. 205) to its original position. Fold strip 2 back (arrow). Return strip 3 to its original position. Lift a new strip from beneath and fold back as indicated by the arrow (fig. 205).

Repeat figs. 204 and 205 until you have worked right around the kete.

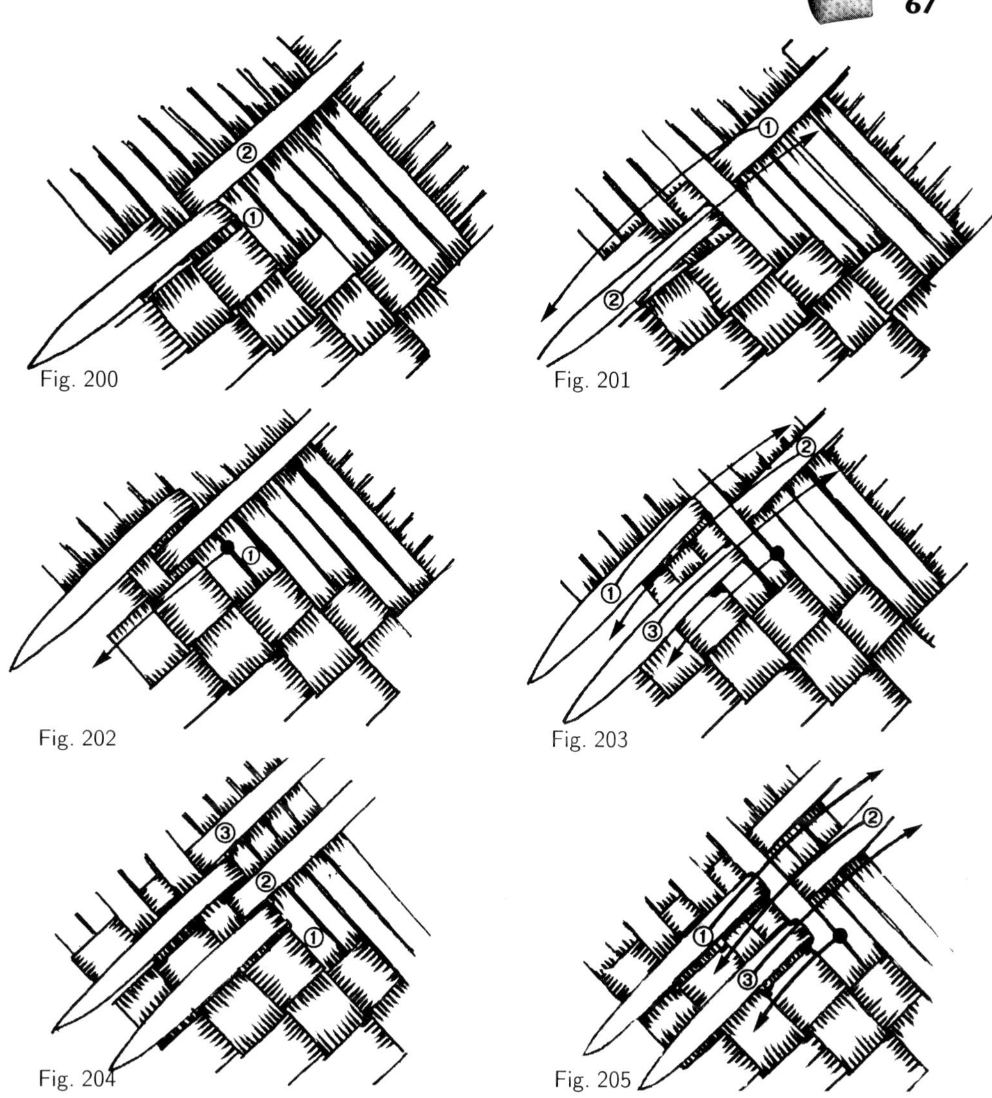

Fig. 200

Fig. 201

Fig. 202

Fig. 203

Fig. 204

Fig. 205

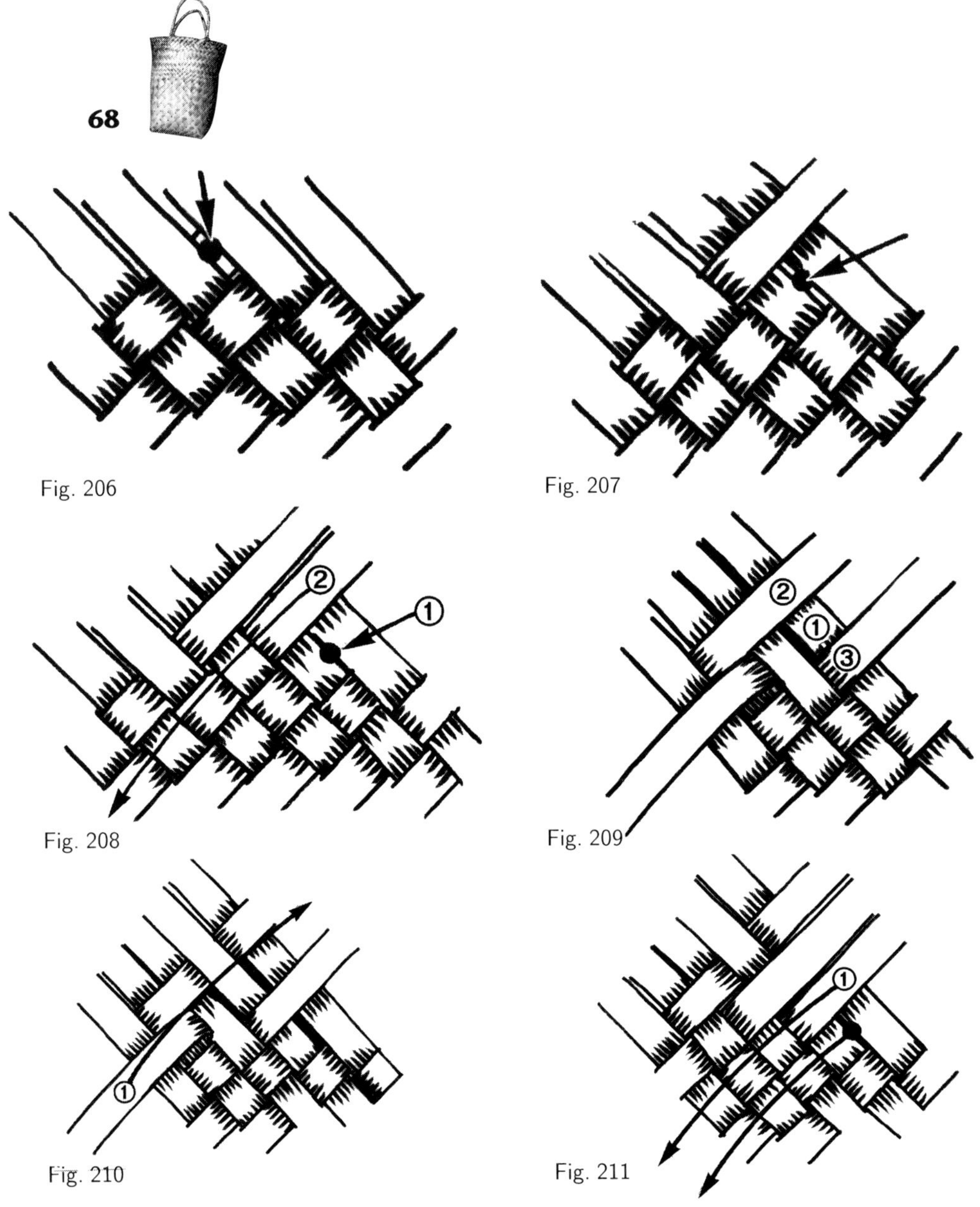

Fig. 206

Fig. 207

Fig. 208

Fig. 209

Fig. 210

Fig. 211

Plaiting in tōrua

When a full round of the finer plait has been completed, you can begin plaiting the rest of the sides of the kete. Simplest for the beginner is the takitahi — the simple over-under plait that has been used so far. You can continue to plait the whole body of the kete in the same way, following figs. 109 to 125, or if you feel competent at this you may like to try the plait known as tōrua in central and eastern districts and pae in Taranaki and Wanganui. It is the commonly used plait where each strip passes under two strips and over two strips. Another pattern that can add interest to this area of the kete is illustrated in Appendix 5.

Lift a strip from beneath the work at the point indicated by the arrow, so that it lies on top as shown in fig. 207. Lift another strip from beneath at the point indicated.

Lift another strip (1) from beneath at the point indicated (fig. 208). Fold strip 2 back (arrow). The work should now resemble fig. 209.

Lift strip 1 so that it lies on top of the work over strip 2 but under strip 3 (fig. 209).

Return strip 1 to its original position (fig. 210).

Fold strip 1 back (arrow). Lift another strip from beneath and fold it back as indicated by the arrow (fig. 211).

Lift strip 1 so that it lies over strips 2 and 3 (fig. 212).

Return strips 1 and 2 to their original positions (fig. 213).

Fold strips 1 and 2 back (arrows). Lift another strip from beneath and fold back as indicated by the arrow (fig. 214).

Lift strip 1 so that it lies on top of strips 2 and 3 (fig. 215).

Return strips 1, 2 and 3 to their original positions (fig. 216).

Fold strips 1, 2 and 3 back (arrows). Lift another strip from beneath and fold back as indicated by the arrow (fig. 217).

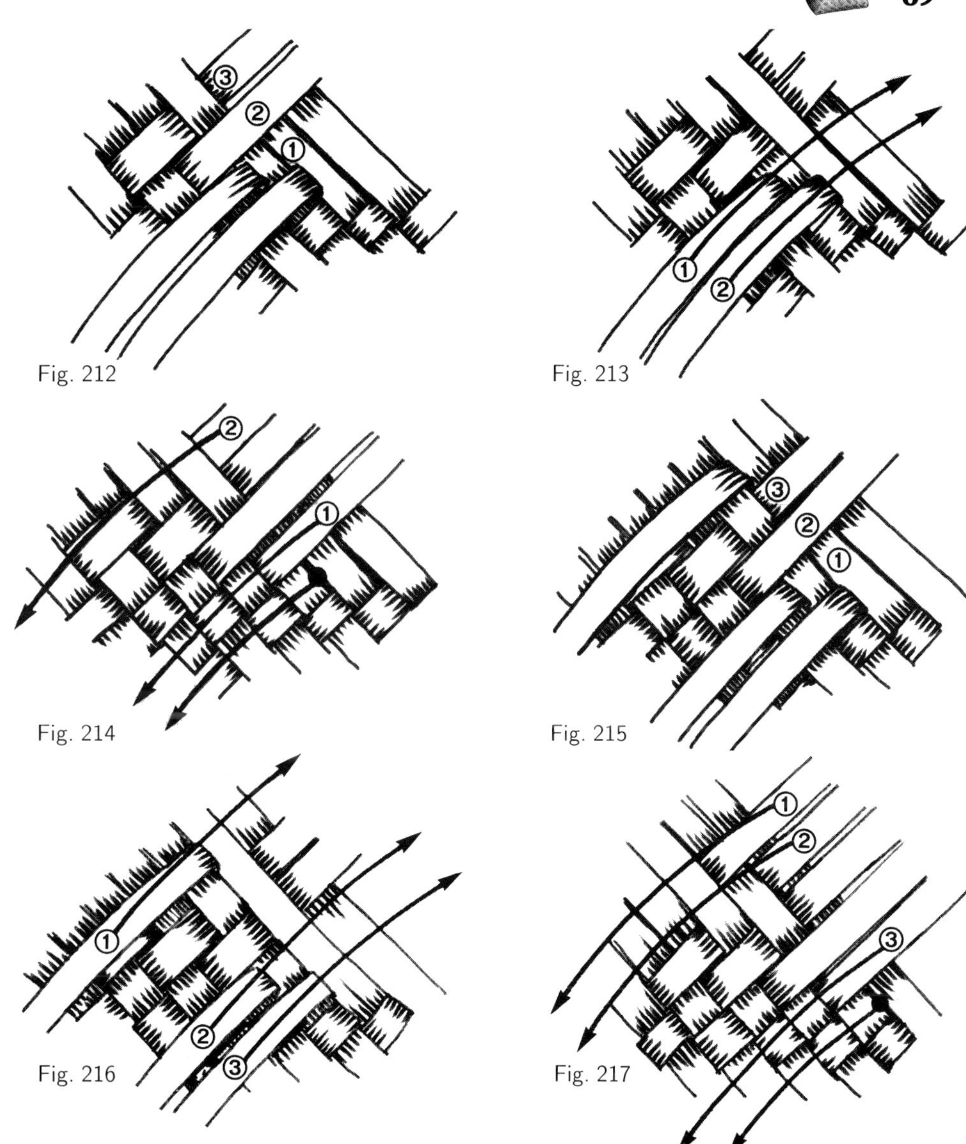

Fig. 212

Fig. 213

Fig. 214

Fig. 215

Fig. 216

Fig. 217

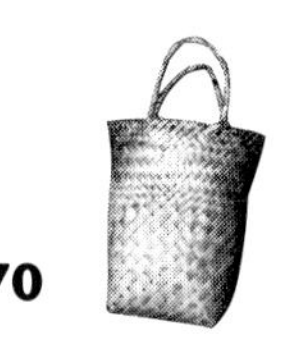

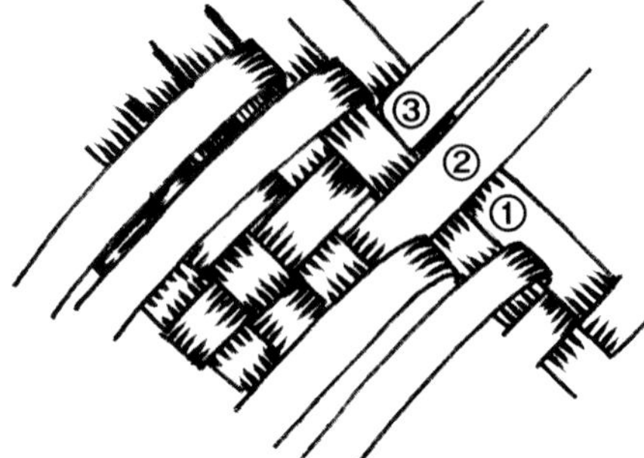

Fig. 218

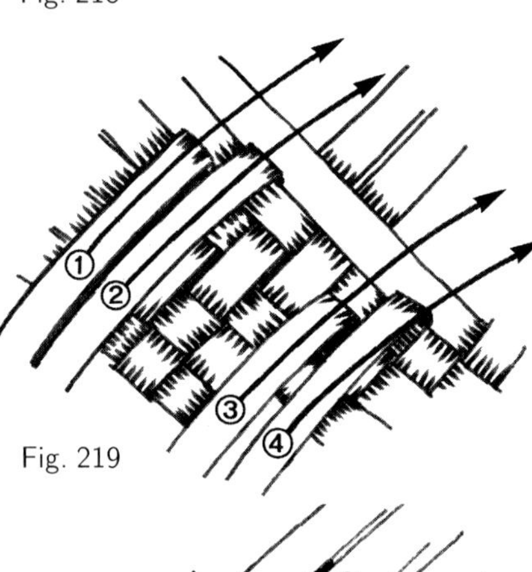

Fig. 219

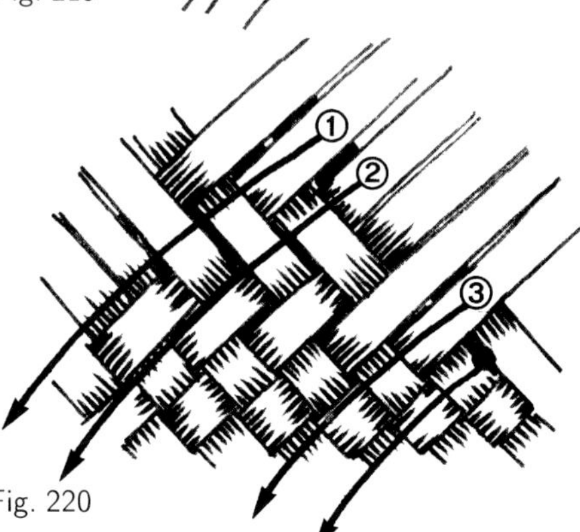

Fig. 220

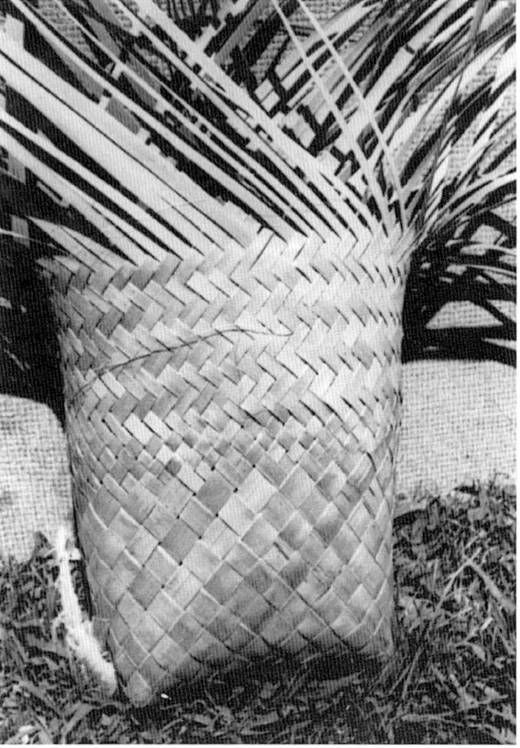

Fig. 221

Lift strip 1 so that it lies over strips 2 and 3 (fig. 218).

Return strips 1, 2, 3 and 4 to their original positions (fig. 219).

Strips 1, 2 and 3 are folded back. Another strip is lifted from beneath and folded back (arrow) as in fig. 220.

Repeat the movements shown in figs. 218–220 until you have worked right around the kete.

Plait another band around the kete in the same way, to add to the height of the sides (figs. 206–220). The kete should now resemble fig. 221.

Before attempting to finish off at the top edge, plait another band of two rows of the simple over-and-under plait called takitahi. This holds the working edge firmly while the finish is being completed.

Folding down the top edge of the kete

Lift any strip from beneath at the point indicated by the arrow, so that it lies on top of the work as shown in fig. 223.

The next strip to the right is lifted from beneath (arrow) and folded back to the position shown in fig. 224.

Lift strip 1 so that it lies over strip 2 in the position shown in fig. 225.

Return strip 1 to its original position. Lift another strip from beneath (arrow).

Fold strips 1 and 2 back (arrows) as shown in fig. 226.

Lift strip 1 so that it lies over strip 2 in fig. 227, to the position shown in fig. 228.

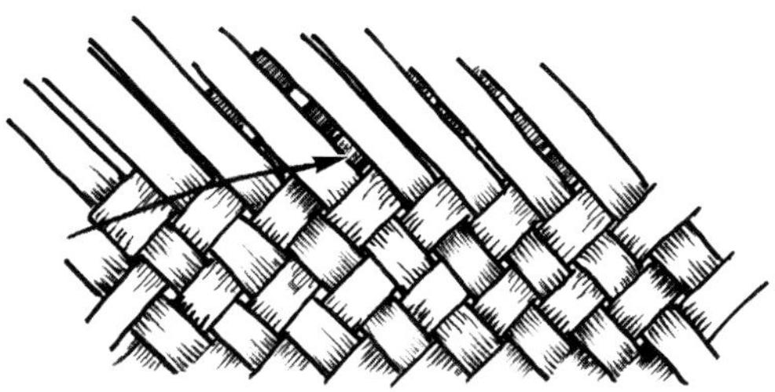

Fig. 222

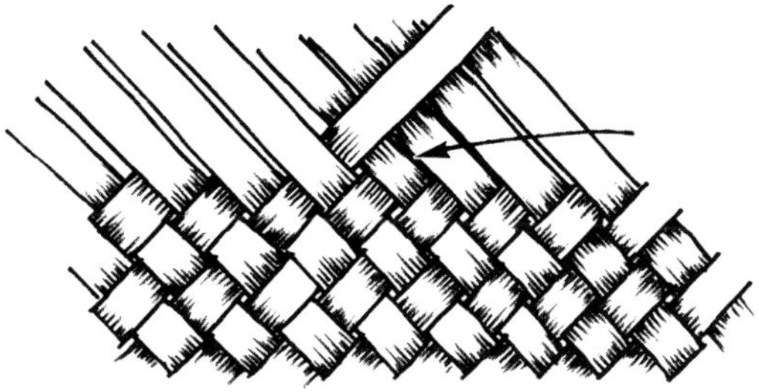

Fig. 223

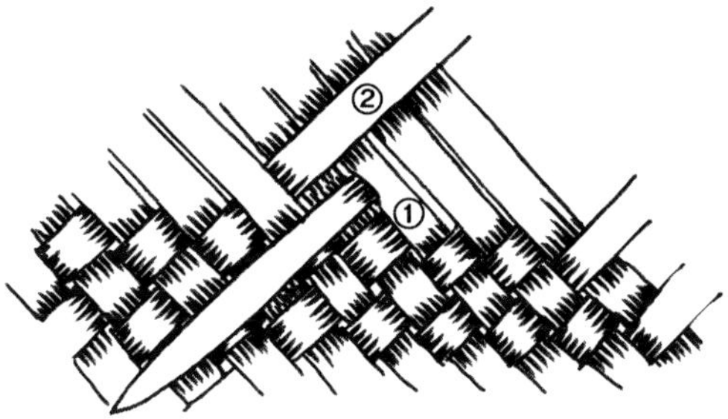

Fig. 224

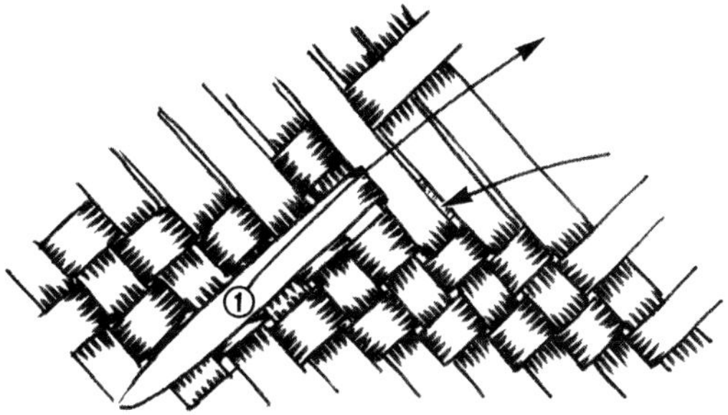

Fig. 225

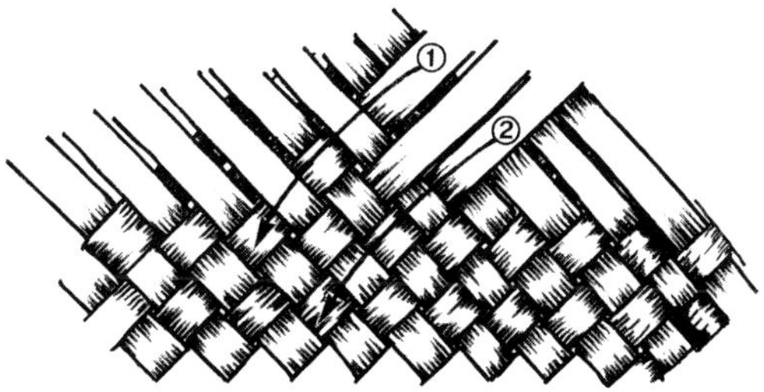

Fig. 226

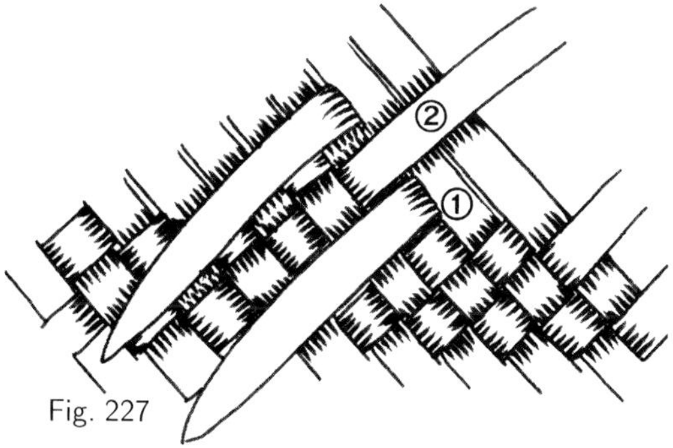

Fig. 227

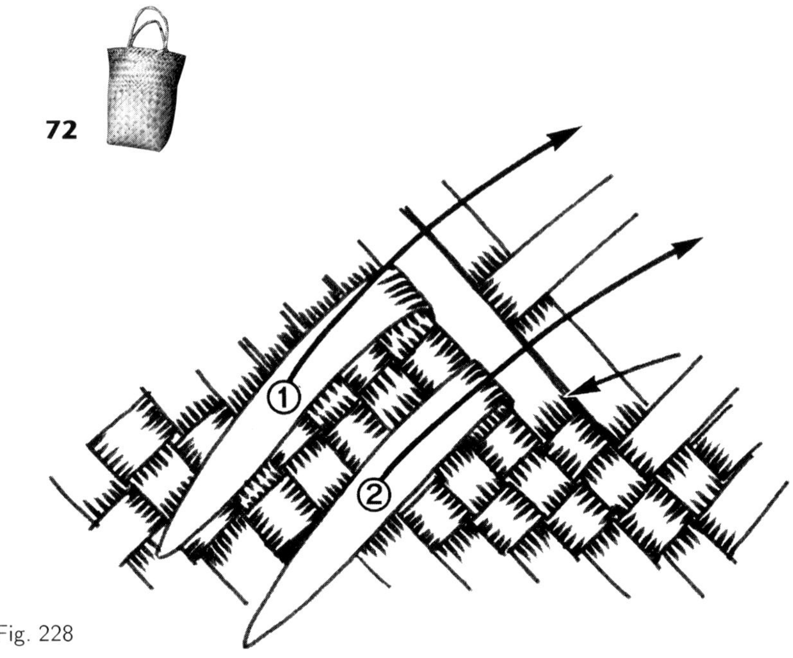

Fig. 228

Return strips 1 and 2 to their original positions. Lift another strip from beneath at the point indicated by the arrow in fig. 228.

Fold strips 1 and 2 back (arrows, fig. 229).

Lift strip 1 so that it lies over strips 2 and 3 (fig. 230).

Following the arrows in fig. 231:
Fold strip 1 along the dotted line and bring it down in the direction indicated.
Return strip 2 to its original position.
Fold strip 3 back.
Return strip 4 to its original position.
Lift another strip from beneath and fold back.

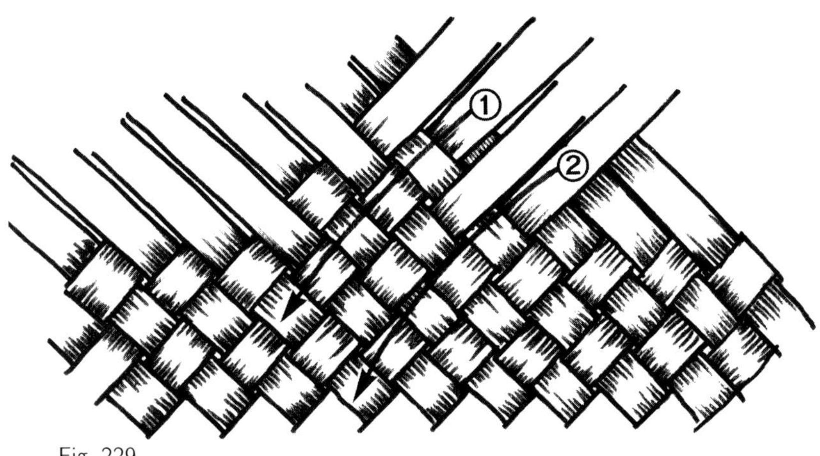

Fig. 229

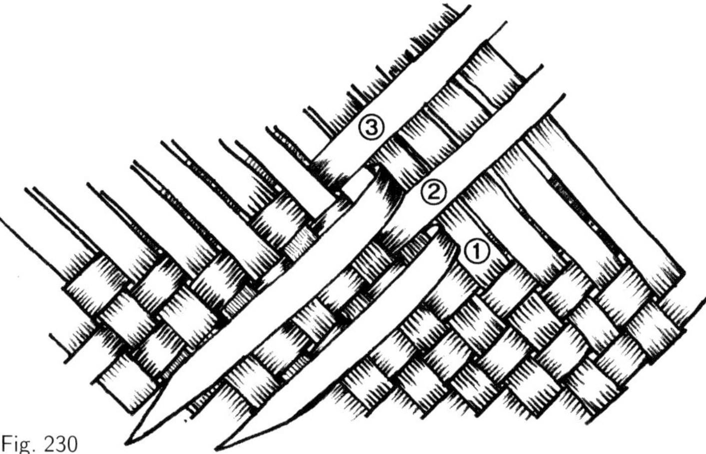

Fig. 230

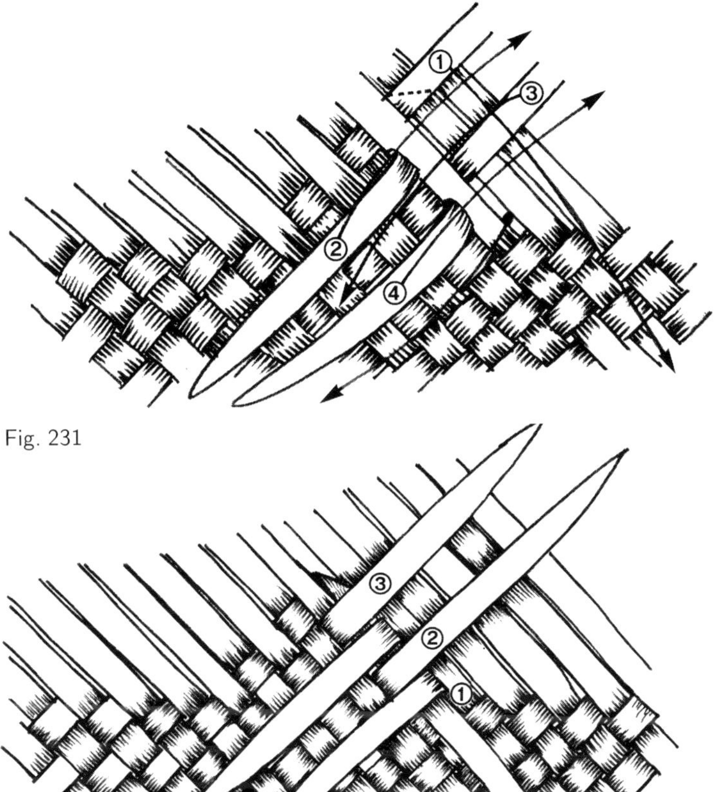

Fig. 231

Fig. 232

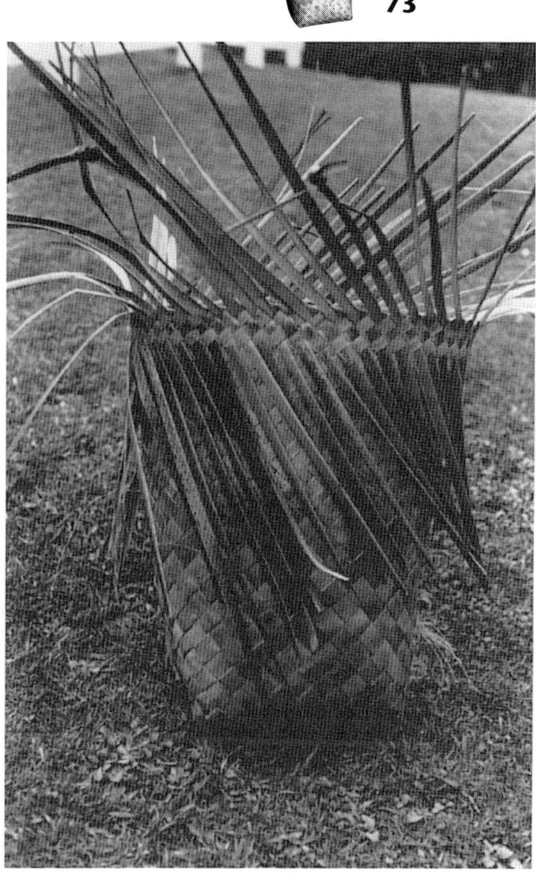

Fig. 233

The work should now resemble fig. 232.

Lift strip 1 so that it lies over strips 2 and 3.

Work figs. 231 and 232 until the whole of the kete has been circled. The last strips will have to be tucked into the plait to complete the full round.

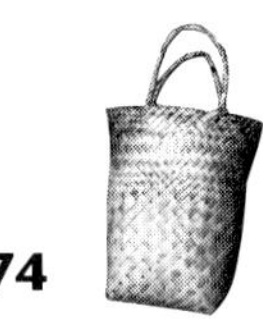

Braiding the handles for the bucket kit

The handles are made in the same way as for the satchel kit. This time two will be needed and they will be about 75 cm long. They can be made in three ply, but the four-ply plait is perhaps more attractive and directions for making it are given here.

Split and scrape four strips of flax 1 cm wide and about 75–100 cm long. The braid is started in the same way as the three-ply braid already explained except that four strips are used. Tie the four strips of scraped flax together with a thin strip of flax, leaving ends about 20 cm long protruding. Reverse two of the strips so that there are two thick butt ends and two of the thinner ends from the pointed end of the leaf together at the tied end. This will keep the braid an even thickness throughout. Tie together two of the strips protruding at the end with an overhand knot (see Appendix 1), and hook these over a nail on the wall to hold the plait while you work.

Spread the strips into a fan. Lift strip 2 and take it over strip 3 (arrow) to the position shown in fig. 235.

Put the right hand between the strips 2 and 4 and reach behind for strip 1. Bring it to the front between strips 2 and 4 and take it over strip 2 (arrow) to the position shown in fig. 236.

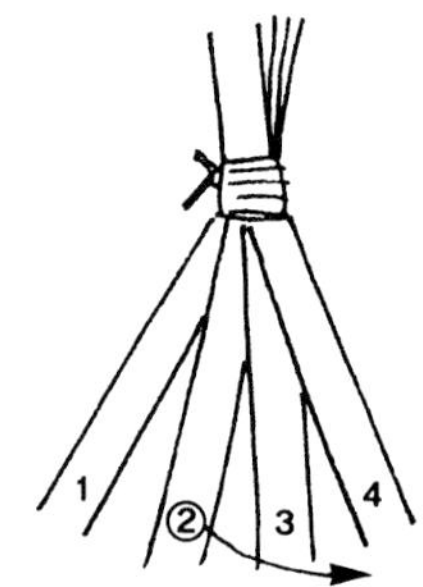

Fig. 234

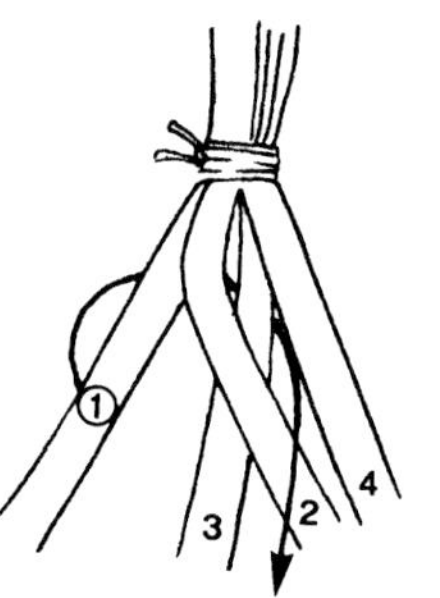

Fig. 235

Fig. 236

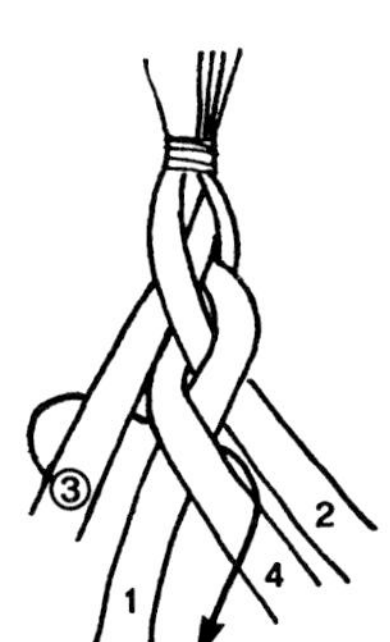

Fig. 237

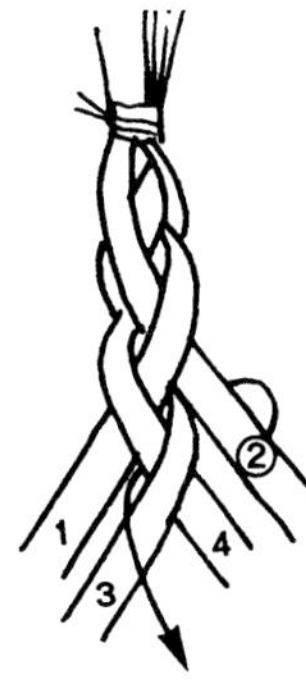

Fig. 238

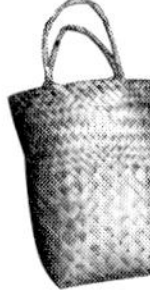

Put the left hand in between strips 3 and 1 and reach behind for strip 4. Bring it to the front between strips 1 and 3 and take it over strip 1 (arrow) to the position shown in fig. 237.

Put the right hand between strips 2 and 4 and reach behind for strip 3. Bring it to the front between strips 2 and 4 and take it over strip 4 (arrow) to the position shown in fig. 238.

Put the left hand between strips 1 and 3 and reach behind for strip 2. Bring it to the front between strips 1 and 3 and take it over strip 3.

Repeat the movements shown in figs. 237 and 238 until the braid is 35 cm long.

To end the braid, split a thin strip of flax off the side of one of the braid strips (fig. 239).

Pass the thin strip around the braid and loop it through itself as shown in fig. 240. Tighten it. This will hold the end of the braid until it is braided into the kete.

The completed handles are shown in fig. 241. Add the handles in the same way as was done in the satchel kit (figs. 151–154).

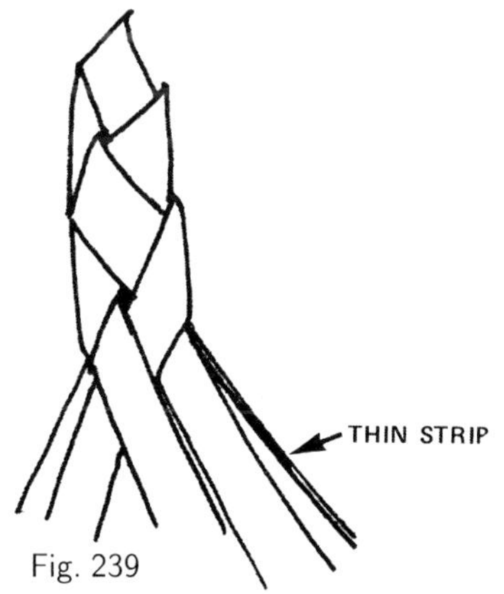

Fig. 239

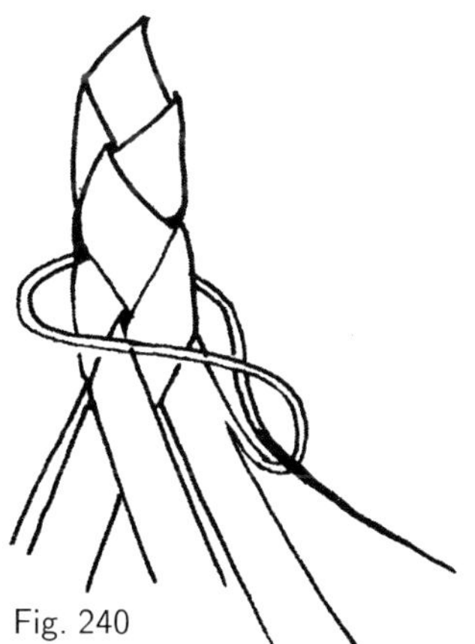

Fig. 240

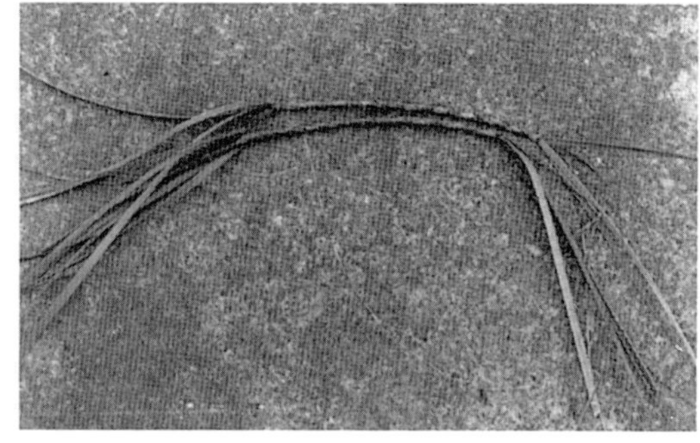

Fig. 241

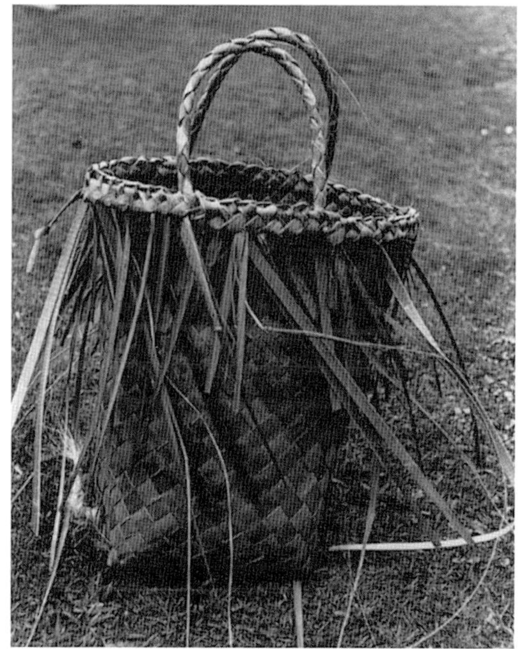

Fig. 242. The kete with handles attached.

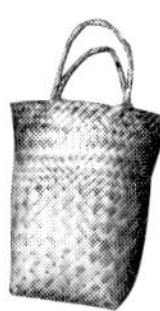

Completing the kete

Cut off the waste ends as near to the braid as possible, as shown in fig. 243.

Turn the kete the right way out. Begin by pushing the corners in with the thumbs.

The completed bucket kit, fig. 244.

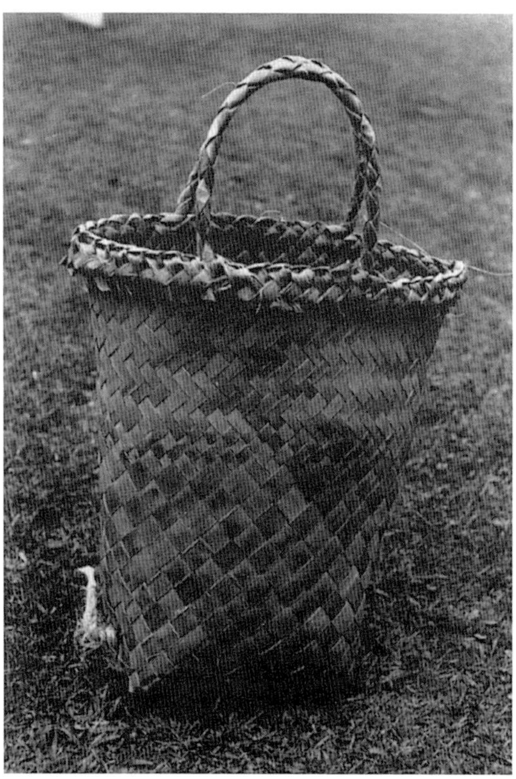

Fig. 243

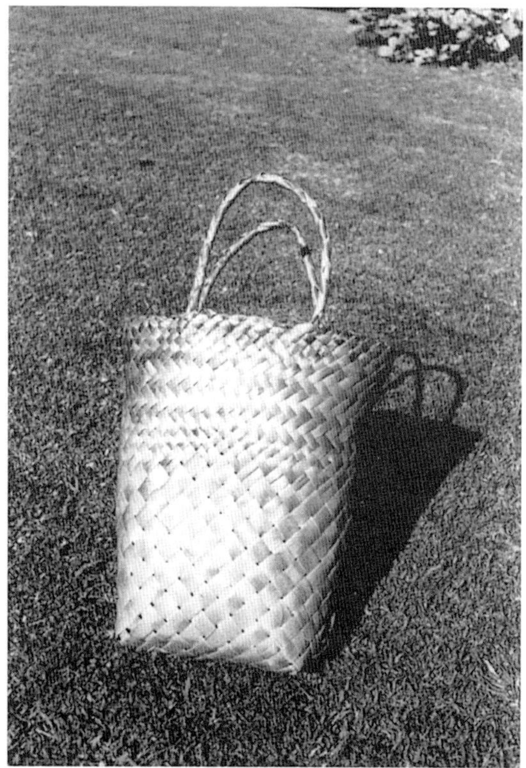

Fig. 244

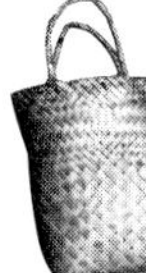

An alternative (and more common) commencement method

The commencement method already shown for the two beginners' kete is not often used by experienced kete makers. It has been shown in the book because setting up the strips in pairs avoids some confusion and it is easy to remember the sequence: the top strip is folded back towards the worker, and the bottom one moved to the left. In the method shown below the strips are laid out on to the commencement braid one at a time as shown in fig. 245. Because the strips are more spaced out and not so congested, the commencement braid is longer, resulting in a straight-sided basket.

It is best to use an even number of strips on each side of the commencement braid. Add them one at a time, first to one side and then to the other, until the braid is as long as desired for the length of the kete.

Strip 1 in fig. 246 is folded back towards the worker as indicated by the arrow to lie in the position shown in fig. 247. The dull side will be uppermost.

Strip 1 in fig. 247 is moved to the left as indicated by the arrow to lie in the position shown in fig. 248.

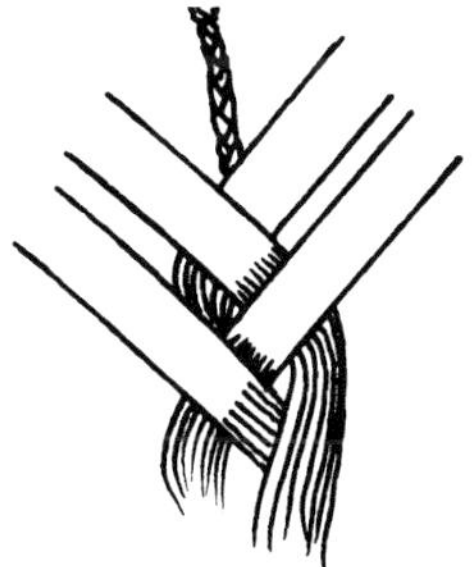

Fig. 245

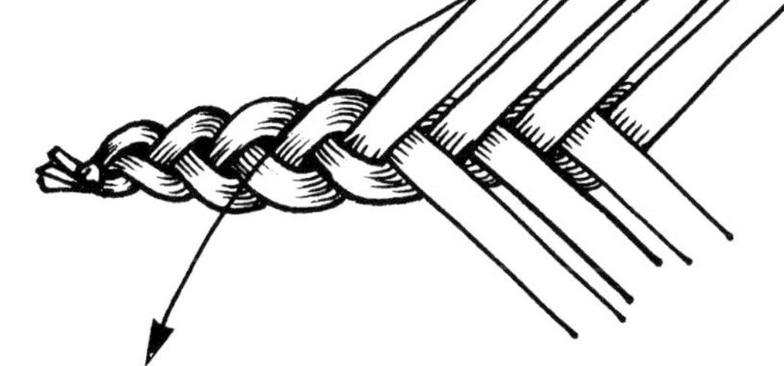

Fig. 246

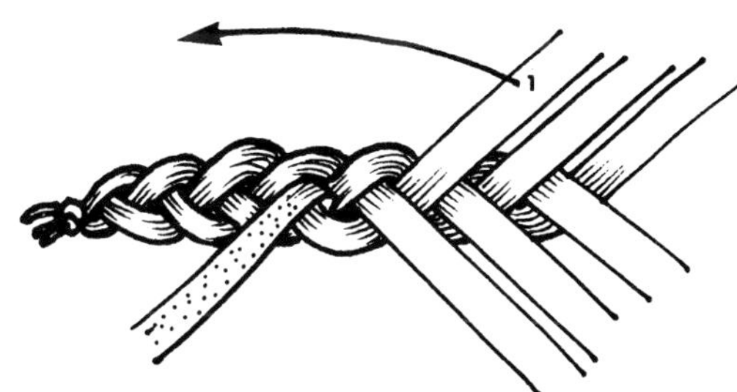

Fig. 247

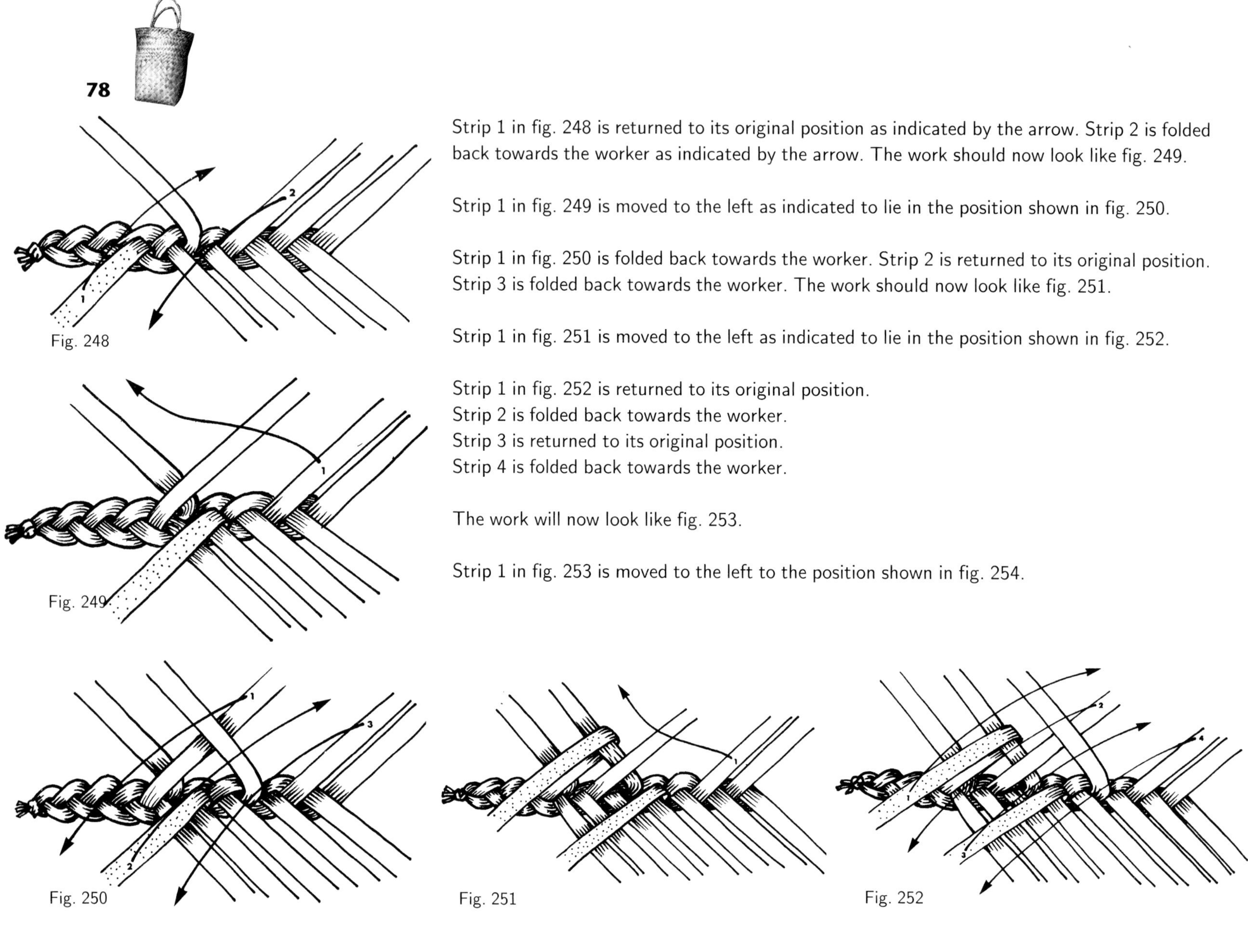

Fig. 248

Fig. 249

Fig. 250

Fig. 251

Fig. 252

Strip 1 in fig. 248 is returned to its original position as indicated by the arrow. Strip 2 is folded back towards the worker as indicated by the arrow. The work should now look like fig. 249.

Strip 1 in fig. 249 is moved to the left as indicated to lie in the position shown in fig. 250.

Strip 1 in fig. 250 is folded back towards the worker. Strip 2 is returned to its original position. Strip 3 is folded back towards the worker. The work should now look like fig. 251.

Strip 1 in fig. 251 is moved to the left as indicated to lie in the position shown in fig. 252.

Strip 1 in fig. 252 is returned to its original position.
Strip 2 is folded back towards the worker.
Strip 3 is returned to its original position.
Strip 4 is folded back towards the worker.

The work will now look like fig. 253.

Strip 1 in fig. 253 is moved to the left to the position shown in fig. 254.

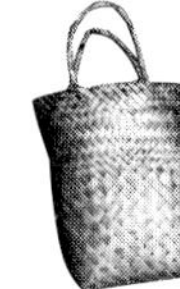

This sequence is repeated until all the strips are used and the commencement braid is complete. The sequence is:

(1) Plait: that is, return all strips that have been previously folded towards you back to their original positions. Fold all strips that come from beneath the work back towards you.
(2) Fold the next strip on the right back towards you.
(3) Plait again, that is, return the folded strips to their positions. Fold all strips that come from beneath the work back towards you.
(4) The next strip on the right is moved to the left.

Repeat these four movements in the sequence until all the strips have been used and a triangle formed (see fig. 48).

Now turn the work over so that the three-ply braid is uppermost. The plaited area is towards the worker and the end of the three-ply braid projecting to the left (see fig. 51).

The strips of the other side of the braid are now plaited by the same method. The bottom is now complete and the rest of the kete is completed in the same way as has already been shown for the other kete.

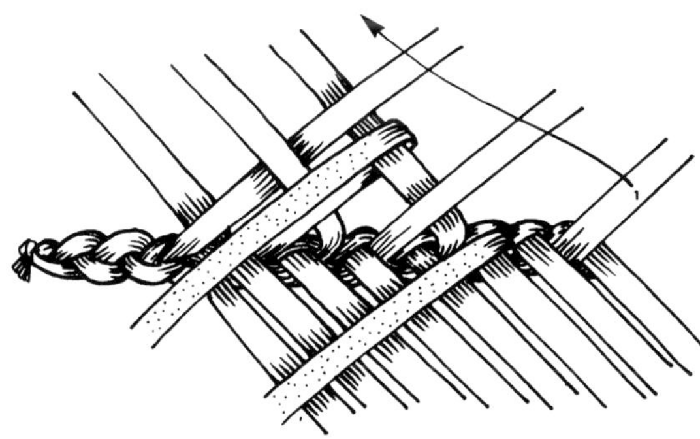

Fig. 253

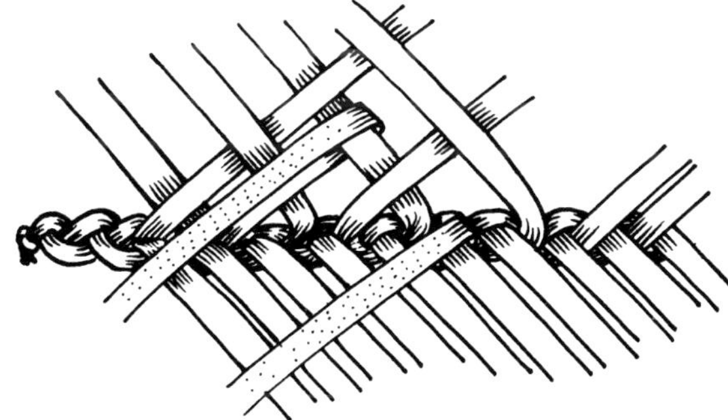

Fig. 254

5 MAKING A HAT

With the skills you already have and the addition of a couple of new ones you can make a flax hat.

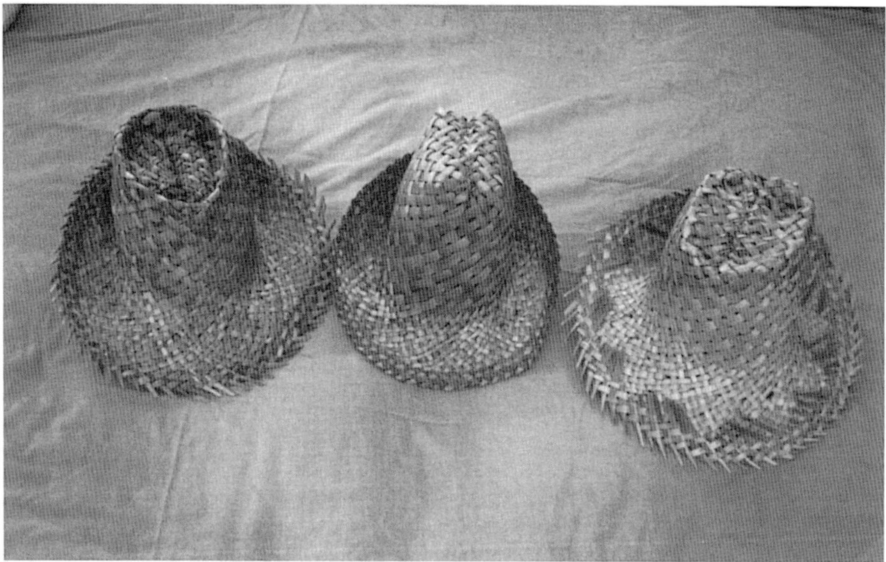

Fig. 255

Referring to the earlier directions in this book, tear 44 strips off the flax leaves following figures 7–10. The tuft of fibre at the end of each strip should be quite small so that the commencement braid that will be inside the crown of the hat will be narrow. Scrape the strips to soften them (fig 11). Make an extra 11 strips about 40 cm in length but these do not need the fibre tufts. They need to be about 50 cm long, with both ends cut off. Scrape all the strips to soften them (fig. 11).

For this hat the preferred commencement braid is the one where the strips are added in pairs. This has already been practised for the satchel kit (figs. 12–21). It makes a neater shape for the crown of the hat. Take the fibre tufts of the 44 strips into a three-ply braid, adding them in pairs as practised for the satchel kit. There should be 22 strips on each side of the braid.

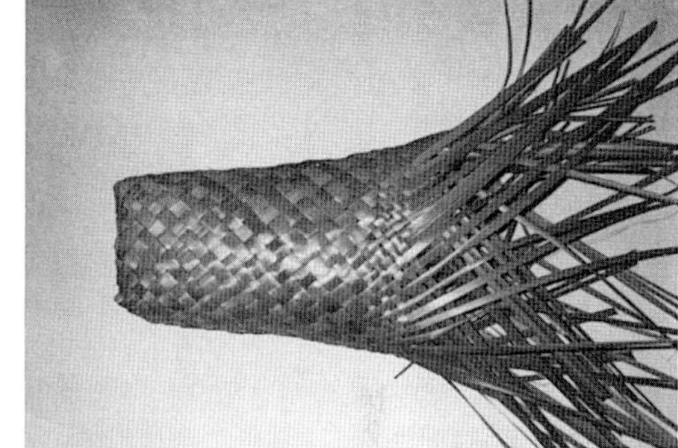
Fig. 256

Plait a triangle on each side of the braid following figs. 22–69.

Plait four corners as practised for the bucket kit following figs. 157–182.

Now plait the sides, following the directions for Filling the gap (figs. 183–196) and Plaiting the sides (figs. 109-126). The weaver must decide the height of the sides of the crown. It should be remembered that the crown must be high, perhaps taller than you would wish, to allow room for the braid that will be on the inside of the crown. The extra height also allows you more freedom to shape and flatten the top of the crown by pushing the four corners in. But this is not done until the plaiting has been completed.

The working strips are now split in half following figs. 197–205 and the plaiting continues for about three rows using the narrower strips. The work should look like fig. 256.

Plaiting the brim

The next process is one not already covered in this book. It entails adding extra strips that force the work to widen to form the brim. First take the extra 11 strips you prepared for the brim. Split each strip in half, making a total of 22. Put them aside until needed.

You can work from the inside or outside of the hat, whichever suits you best. Here we will work from the outside, perhaps the easiest method.

Plait a triangle on the working edge as shown in fig. 257.

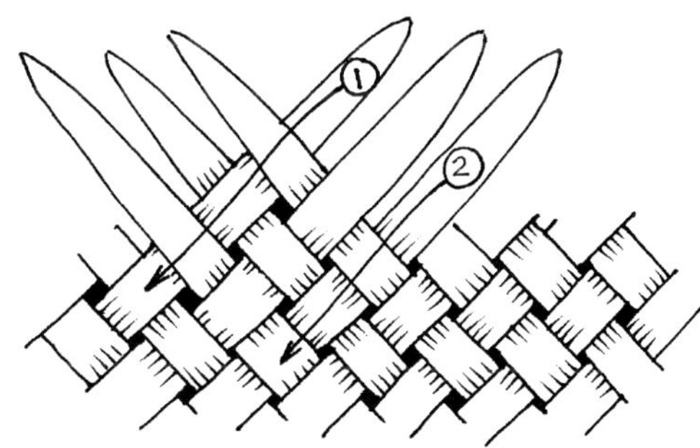

Fig. 257

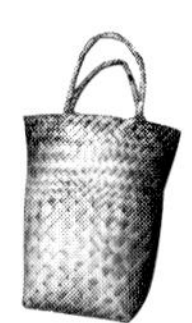

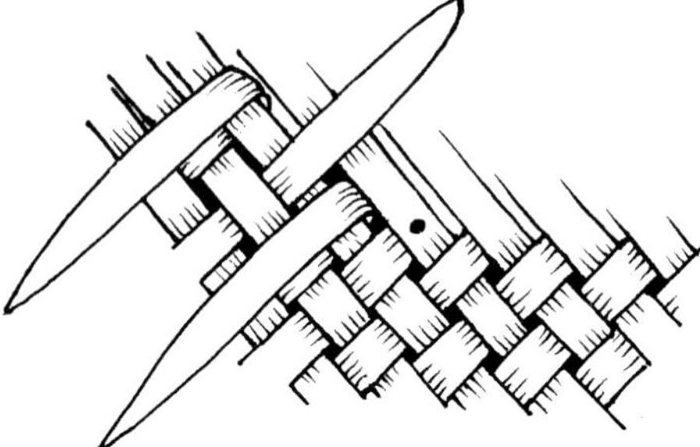

Fig. 258

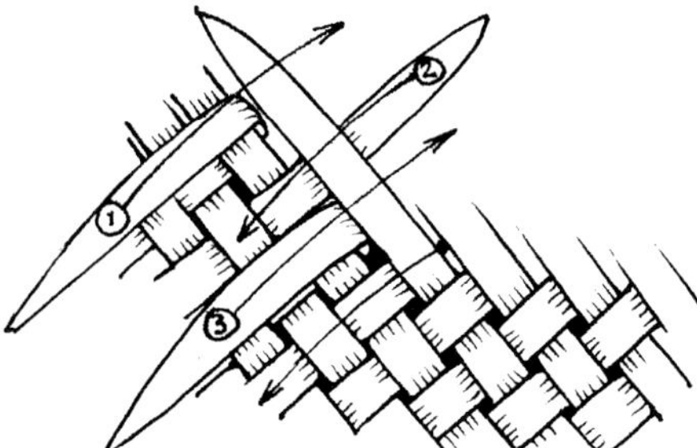

Fig. 259

Fold strips 1 and 2 in fig. 257 back in the direction indicated to lie in the positions shown in fig. 258.

Lift the strip indicated with a black dot in fig. 258 from beneath to lie in the position shown in fig. 259.

Return strip 1 in fig. 259 to its original position as indicated.
Fold strip 2 back as indicated by the arrow.
Return strip 3 to its original position.
Lift a strip from beneath at the position marked with a black dot and fold it back in the direction indicated by the arrow to lie in the position shown in fig. 260.

Lift the strip indicated with a black dot in fig. 260 from beneath so that it lies in the position shown in fig. 261.

Fold strip 1 in fig. 261 back in the direction indicated.
Return strip 2 to its original position.
Fold strip 3 back as indicated.
Return strip 4 to its original position.
Fold strip 5 back in the direction indicated.
The work should look like fig. 262.

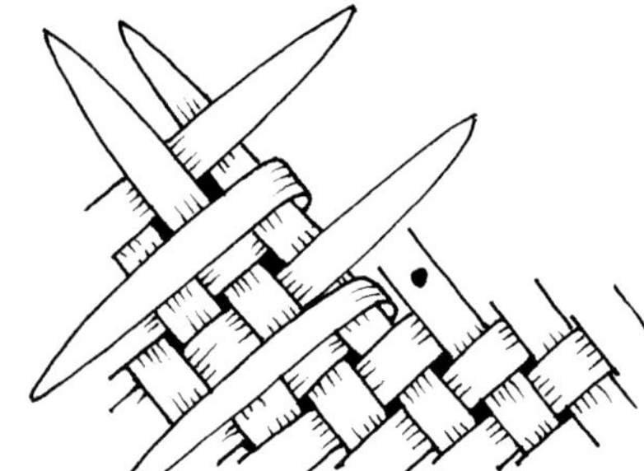

Fig. 260

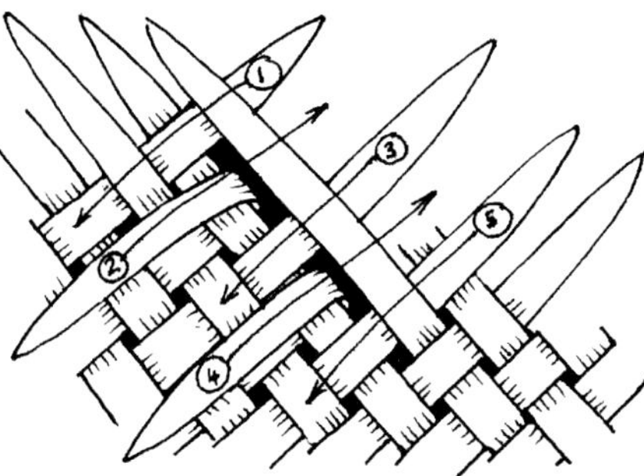

Fig. 261

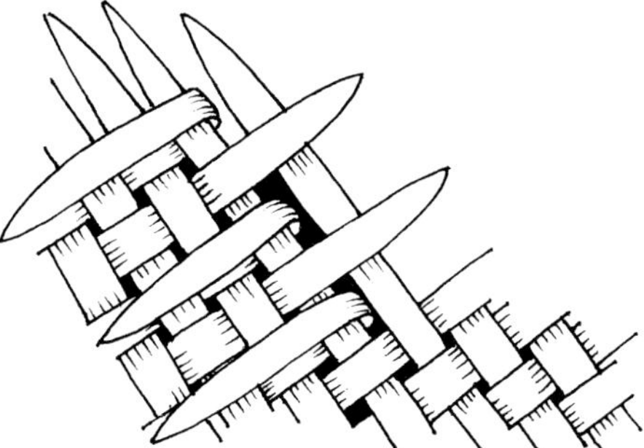

Fig. 262

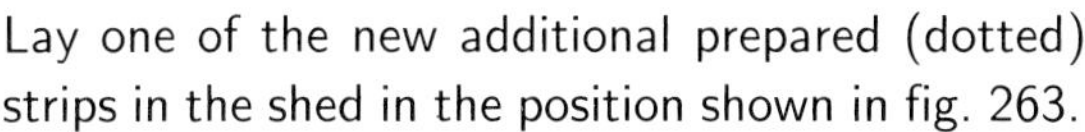

Lay one of the new additional prepared (dotted) strips in the shed in the position shown in fig. 263.

Return strip 1 in fig. 263 to its original position as indicated.
Fold strip 2 back in the direction indicated by the arrow.
Return strip 3 to its original position.
Fold strip 4 back as indicated.
Return strip 5 to its original position.
The new (dotted) strip has been locked in position.
Now lift the strip indicated by a black dot in fig. 263 from beneath so that it lies in the position shown in fig. 264.

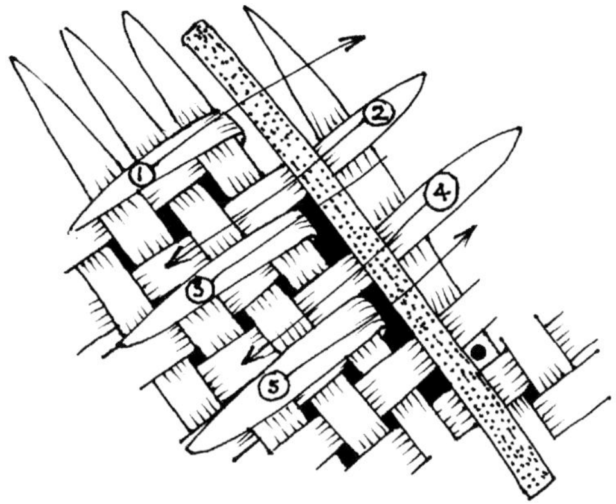

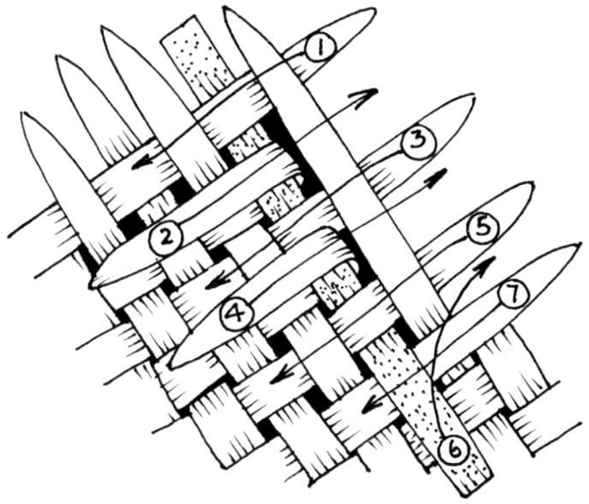

Fold strip 1 in fig. 264 back in the direction indicated.
Return strip 2 to its original position.
Fold strip 3 back in the direction indicated.
Return strip 4 to its original position.
Fold strip 5 back in the direction indicated.
Bend strip 6 in the direction indicated to lie in the position shown in fig. 265a. (Alternatively it can be **folded** as shown in fig. 265b).
Now fold strip 7 in fig. 264 back in the direction indicated to lie in the position shown in fig 265a and 265b.

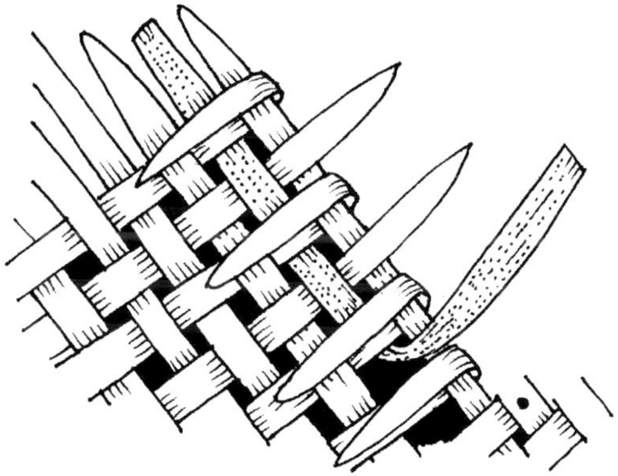

Lift the strip indicated by a black dot in fig. 265a/265b from beneath so that it lies in the position shown in fig. 266.

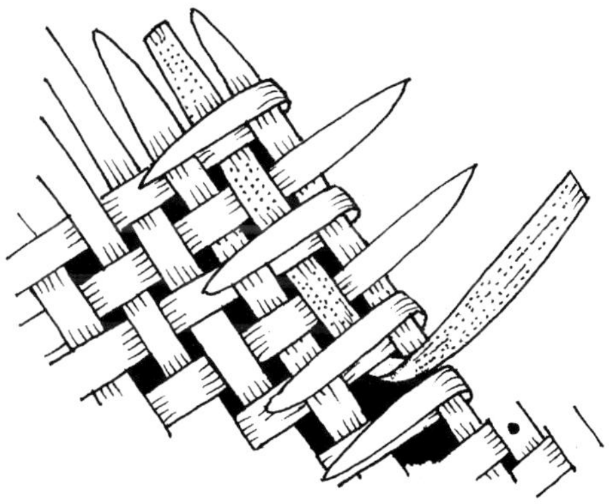

Fig. 263

Fig. 264

Fig. 265a

Fig. 265b

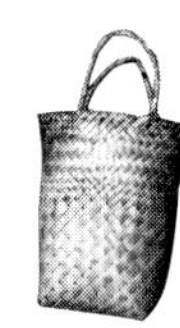

Return strip 1 in fig. 266 to its original position as indicated by the arrow.
Fold strip 2 back as indicated.
Return strip 3 to its original position.
Fold strip 4 back as indicated.
Return strip 5 to its original position.
The new (dotted) strip 6 is folded back as indicated by the arrow to lie in the position shown in fig. 267.
Now return strip 7 to its original position.
Now lift another strip from beneath at the point indicated by a back dot in fig. 266 and fold it back in the direction indicated.
The work should now look like fig. 267.

Lay a new short strip in the shed. This is the same movement as shown in fig. 263.
Continue the movements shown in figs. 263–267 until you have worked right around the brim. The work should look like fig. 268.

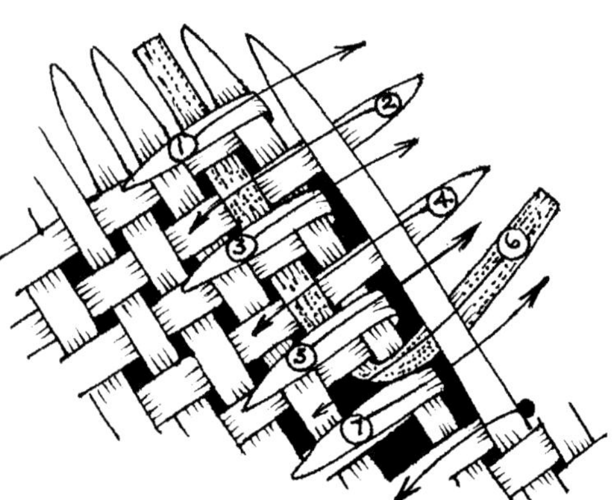

Fig. 266

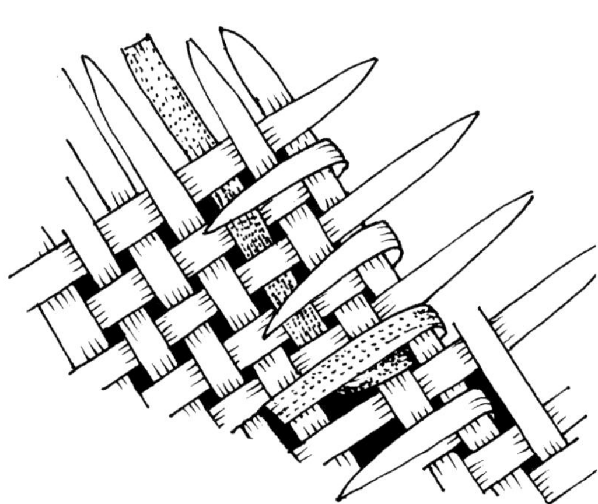

Fig. 267

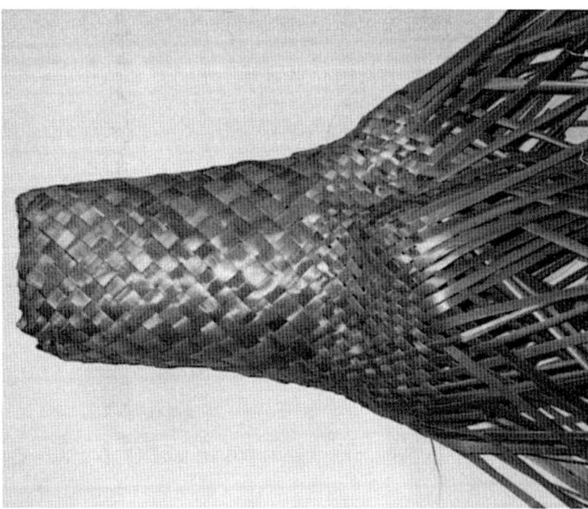

Fig. 268

The added strips should have pushed the work out to form the brim of the hat. If you wish to make a wider brim, repeat the same movements for Plaiting the brim (figs. 257-268), adding another row of new strips. If fewer strips are added by spacing the additional strips further apart, the brim will turn up or down sharply and may need to be stretched after completion. If more are added by placing them closer together, the brim becomes flat. If even more are added the brim takes on a wavy form. You should experiment to find the number of additional strips that suits the tension of your work as well as your aesthetic preferences.

As a decorative element the additional strips can be placed with the dull side of the leaf strips uppermost to create a contrast. Alternatively other materials such as kiekie, pingao or cabbage tree can be introduced, or even long narrow strips of leaf or bundles of leaf from introduced plants such as bulbs, palms or raffia can be used. Dyeing the strips is another possibility. This is a useful way of experimenting with dye since a comparatively small number of strips are required and so small tests can be made and then used in the hat.

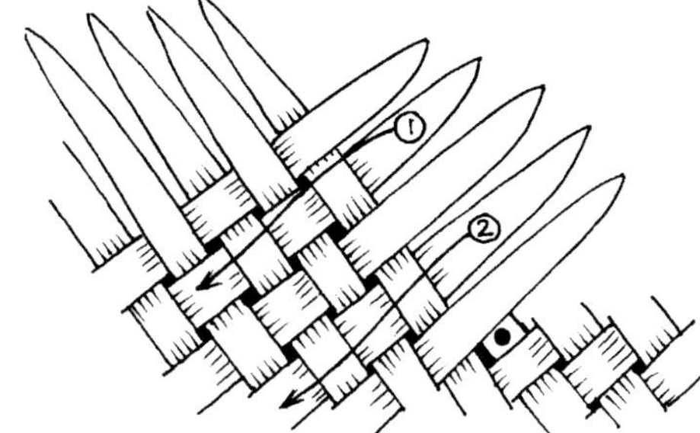

Fig. 269

Finishing the edge of the brim

To plait the edge of the brim continue to work on the outside of the hat.
First plait a raised triangle on the working edges as shown in fig. 269.

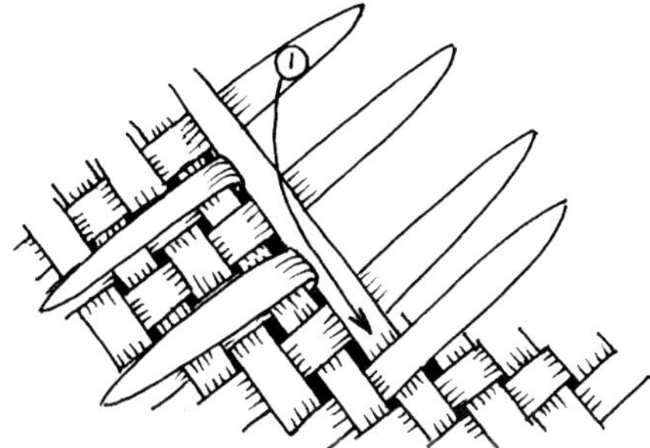

Fig. 270

Fold strips 1 and 2 in fig. 269 back in the direction indicated by the arrows.
Lift the strip indicated by a black spot in fig. 269 from beneath so that it lies in the position shown in fig. 270.

Fold strip 1 in fig. 270 in the direction indicated by the arrow to lie in the position shown in fig. 271.

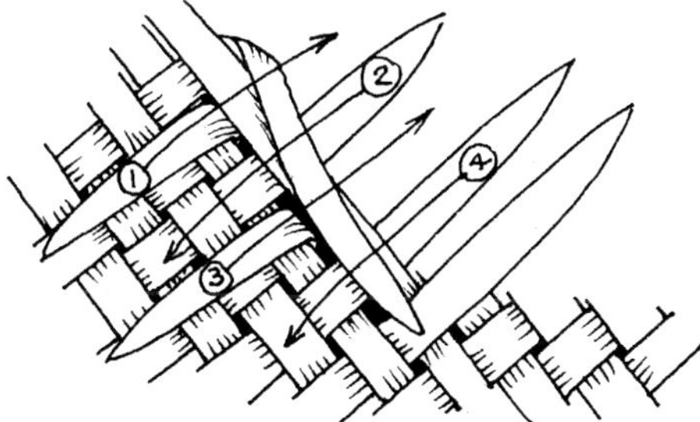

Fig. 271

Return strip 1 in fig. 271 to its original position.
Fold strip 2 back in the direction indicated.
Return strip 3 to its original position.

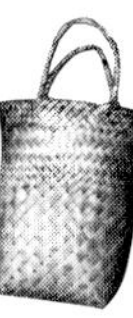

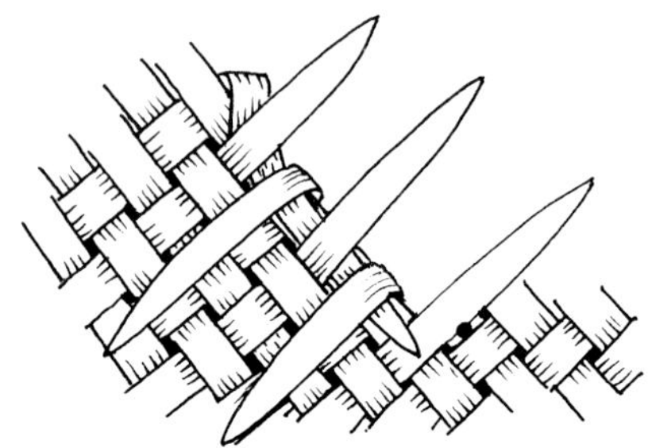

Fig. 272

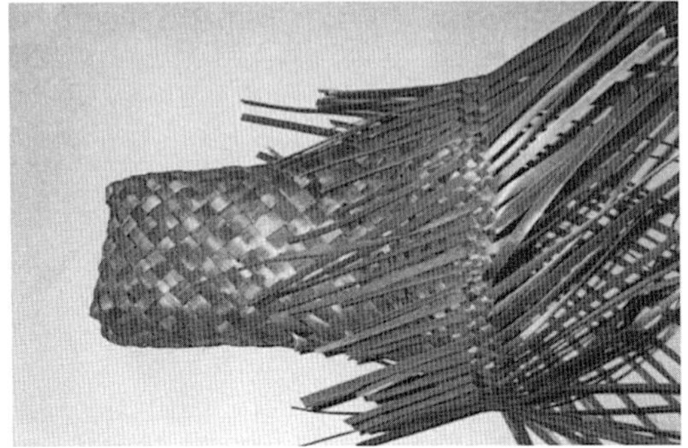

Fig. 273

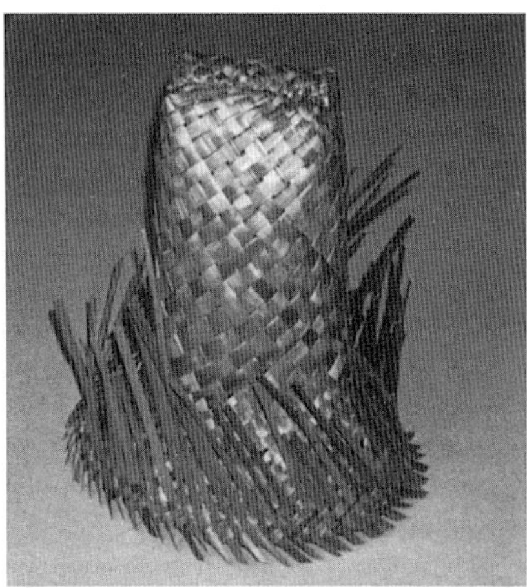

Fig. 274

Fold strip 4 back in the direction indicated.
The work should look like fig. 272.
The first folded strip has been locked in position.

Lift a strip from beneath at the position indicated by the black dot.
The work should look the same as fig. 270.

Repeat the movements shown in figs. 270–272 until you have worked right around the edge of the brim. You will need to thread the last few strips back into the work. The plaiting is now complete.

To tidy the shape, work around the brim two or three times pulling to left and right. This tightens the edges and straightens out any untidy plaiting. See fig. 273.

Next cut off the protruding strips around the edge of the brim. Leave a centimetre or more protruding as a decorative trim and to guard against unravelling. A large pair of scissors makes this a simple job. The work will look like fig. 274.

Now trim off the remaining ends on top of the brim. These can be cut close to the work. The hat should now look like fig. 275.

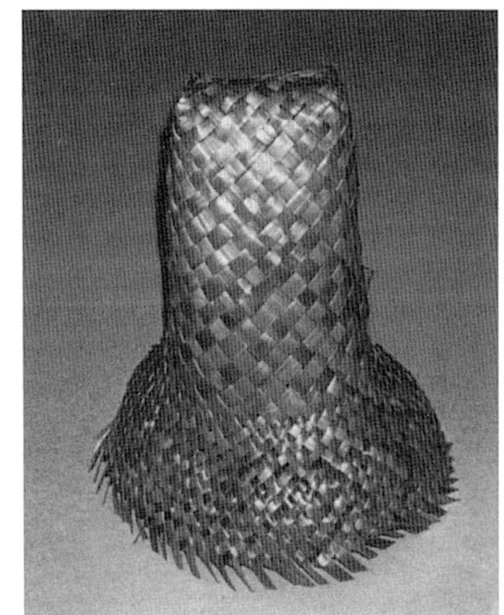

Fig. 275

If preferred, one or both fringes may be cut to a serrated trim as shown in fig. 276.

To finish, manipulate the crown until it is tidy. Lightly handle and rub the sides to ease out uneven areas. Shape the corners by lightly pushing on them from the inside. Then using the thumbs, push the corners in quite firmly from the outside. Push the crown down leaving a ridge around the outside of it. Now push up the centre of the crown from the inside (fig. 277).

Now fold up the brim and shape it as you please. No doubt you will soon develop your own preferred method of handling this manipulation and reshaping.

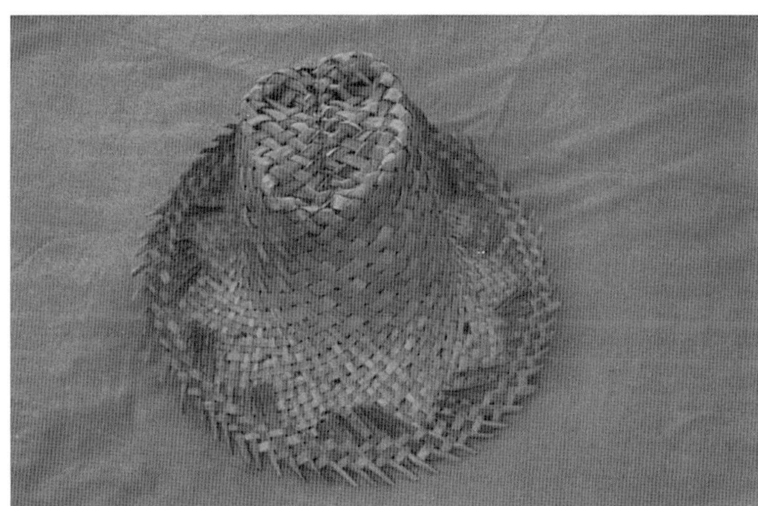

Fig. 276

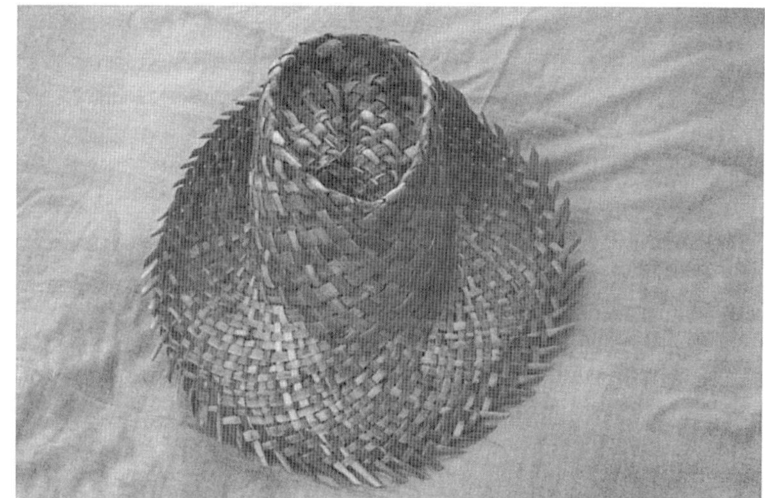

Fig. 277

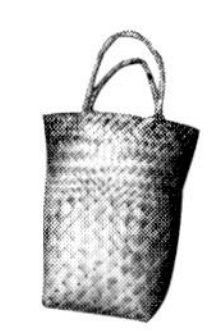

An alternative finish

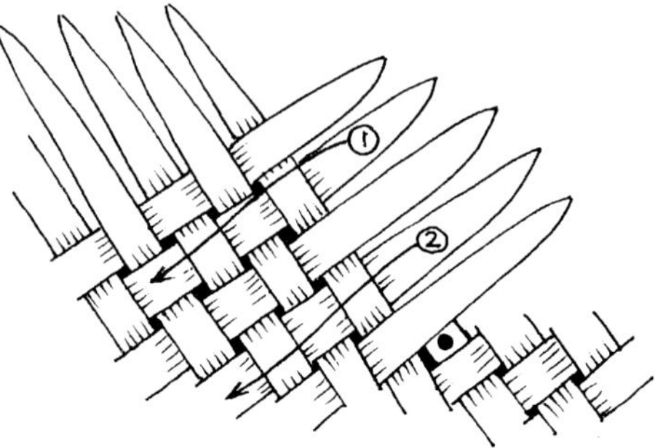

Fig. 278

This finish for the edge of the rim requires a single additional movement. It makes a smooth edge to the brim with no protruding strips.
Form a triangle on the edge of the brim as shown in fig. 278.

Fold strips 1 and 2 in fig. 278 back in the direction indicated by the arrows.
Lift the strip indicated by a black dot from beneath so that it lies in the position shown in fig. 279.

Fold strip 1 in fig. 279 in the direction indicated so that it lies in the position shown in fig. 280.

Return strip 1 in fig. 280 to its original position.
The work should look like fig. 281.

This is the new movement.
Fold strip 1 in fig. 281 in the direction indicated so that it lies in the position shown in fig. 282.

Fold strip 1 in fig. 282 back in the direction indicated.
Return strip 2 to its original position.
Fold strip 3 back as indicated.

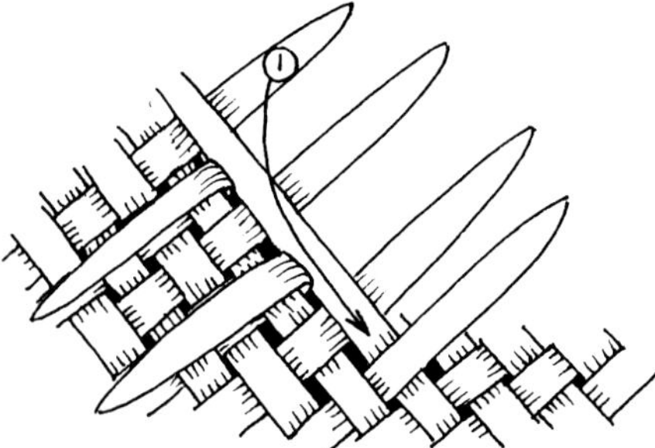

Fig. 279

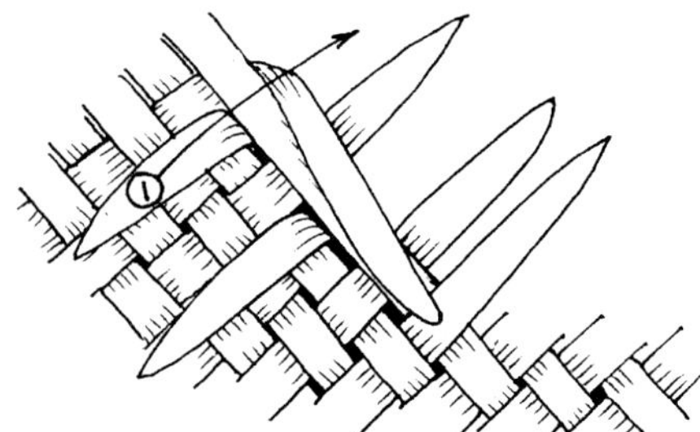

Fig. 280

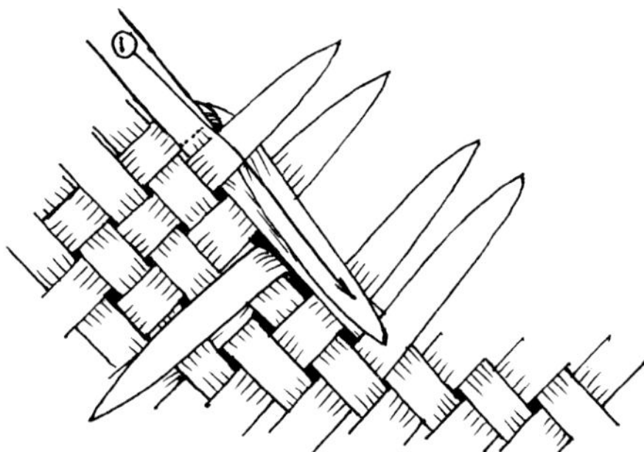

Fig. 281

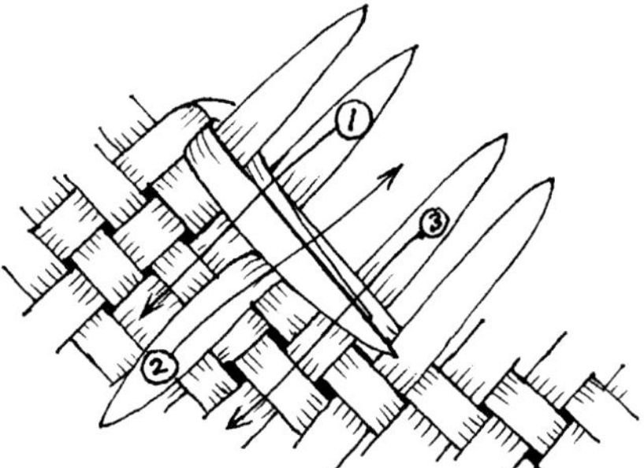

Fig. 282

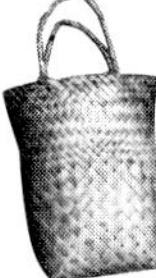

The work should look like fig. 283

Lift the strip indicated by a black dot in fig. 283 from beneath so that it lies in the position shown in fig. 284.

Fold strip 1 in fig. 284 in the direction indicated.
This is the same movement as that shown in fig. 280.
Repeat the movements shown in figs. 281–284 until you have worked right around the brim.
To finish you will need to thread the final strips into the weave. Trim off the protruding strips. The completed brim has a smooth edge (fig 285).

If you wish to conceal the finish beneath the brim fold the brim up before beginning to finish the edge. Then work around the brim in the same way (figs. 278–284) but on the underside.

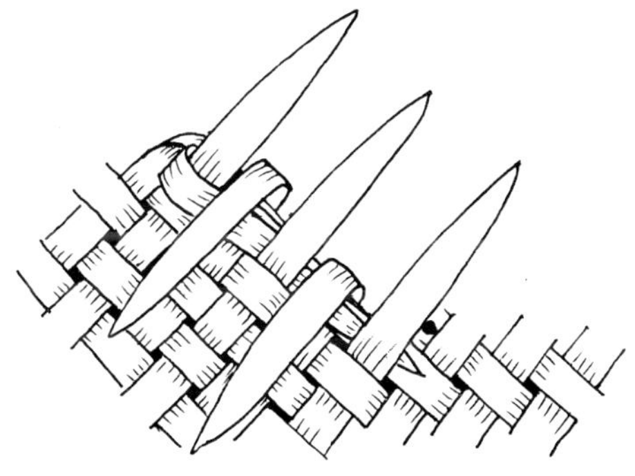

Fig. 283

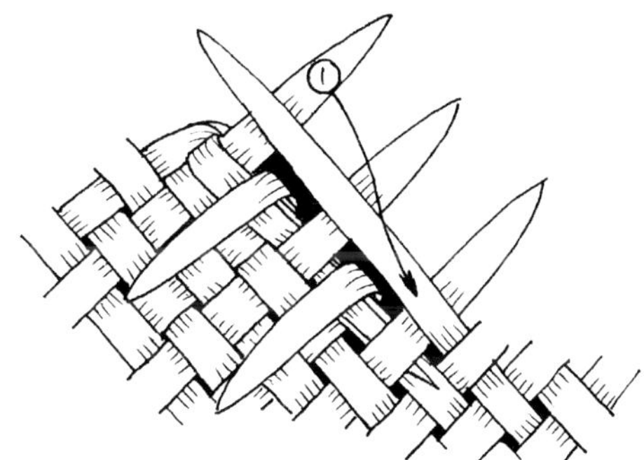

Fig. 284

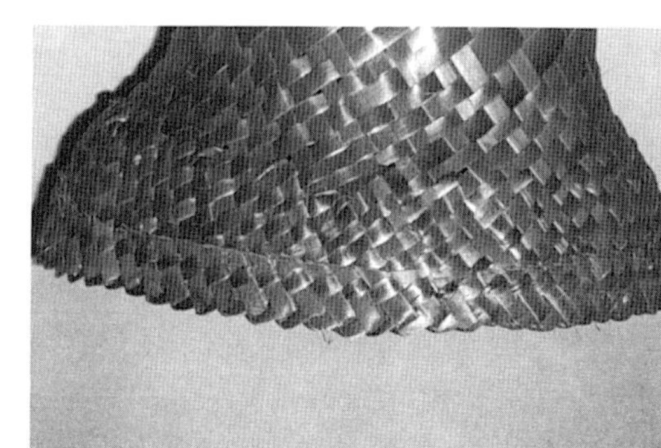

Fig. 285

Appendixes

1. How to make an overhand knot

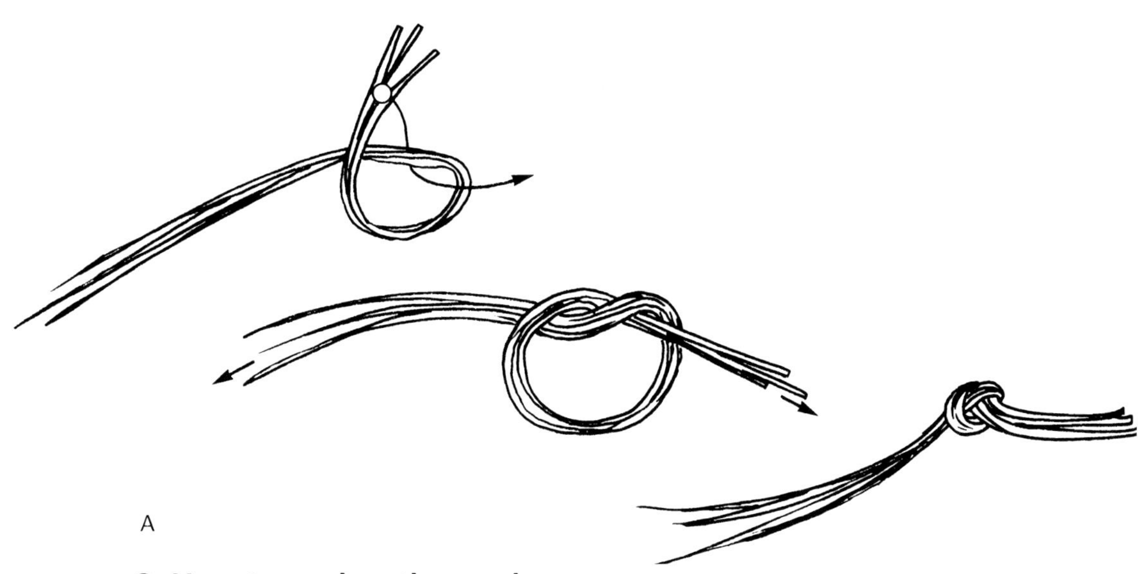

A

2. How to anchor the work

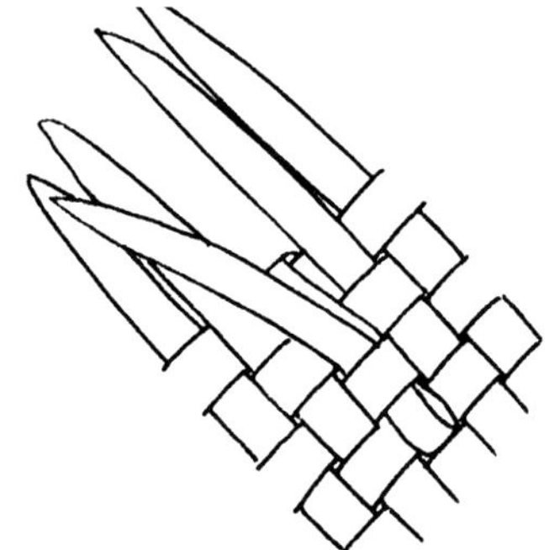

B

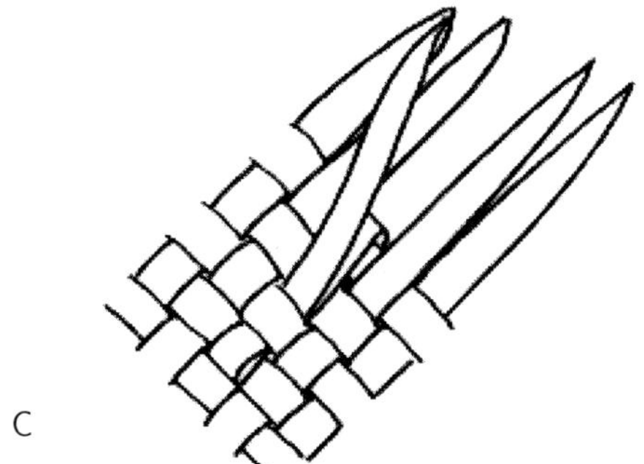

C

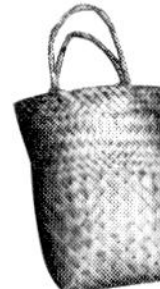

3. Keeping the working edge even

Lift strip 1 so that it lies over strips 2 and 3 (D).

Return strips 1, 2 and 3 to their original positions (E).

The strip marked with the large black dot in F has just been returned to its original position. No strips are worked to the left of it. All future work is to the right of the strip with the black dot. To keep the work firm and close pull strips 1 and 2 in the direction indicated by the short arrows before working them. As you work, pull all strips that come from beneath before you work them. Fold strips 1 and 2 back as indicated by the arrows. Lift another strip from beneath and fold back as indicated by the arrow.

Continue to plait using these three figures. and holding the two strips that cross beneath the black dot between the thumb and first finger of the left hand.

If some of the earlier work has come undone, there may be more than three strips to the right of the black dot. The rule is that all the strips to the right of the dot must be worked.

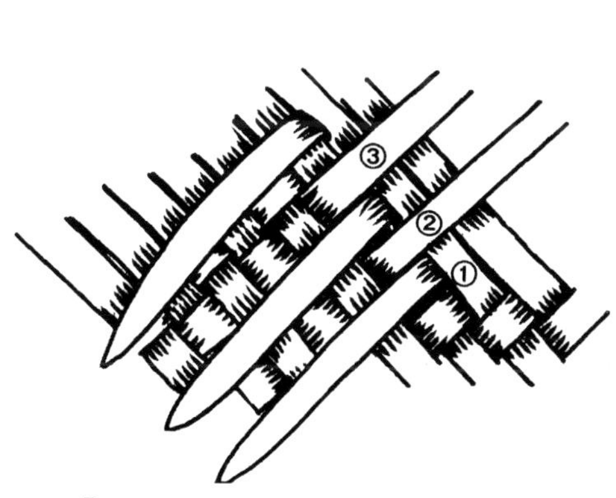

D

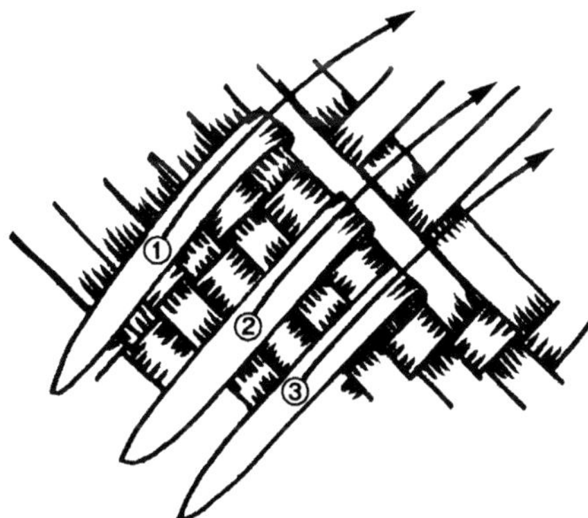

E

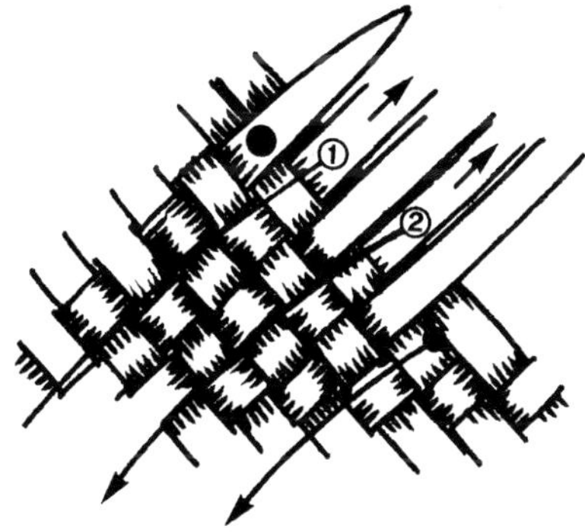

F

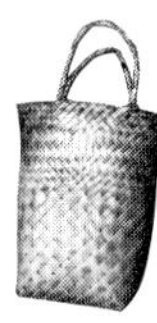

4. How to make a correction in the number of strips on the working edge

G

Sometimes you will find, when plaiting the sides of the kete, that there are more strips pointing to the left than to the right. When this occurs, the plaiting will go round and round the basket, and each round of plaiting will refuse to end off evenly at the top. This is due to one of two reasons: either to using an incorrect number of strips when the three-ply braid for the base is made, or to allowing a strip to cross the three-ply braid and be plaited as one from the other side when making the corners.

A correction can be made by turning one of the working strips so that it points in the opposite direction. The following diagrams show how to make a correction when there are two too many strips pointing to the right.

Strip 1 is bent, so that it changes direction and points to the left (G). The same surface remains uppermost.

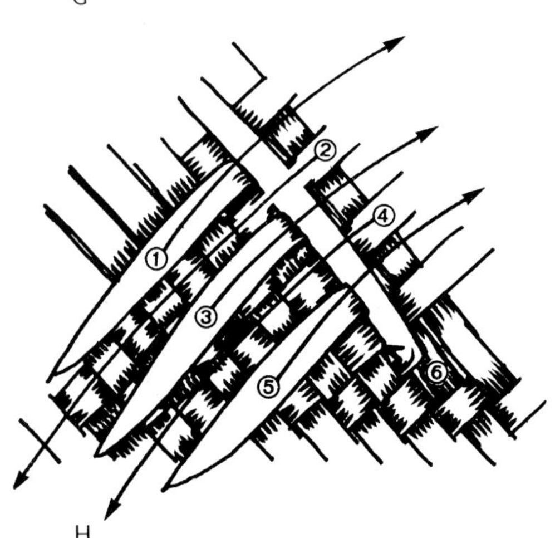

H

Strip 1 is returned to its original position (H).
Strip 2 is folded back as indicated by the arrow.
Strip 3 is returned to its original position.
Strip 4 is folded back as indicated by the arrow.
Strip 5 is returned to its original position.
Strip 6 is lifted so that it lies on top of the work.

Now continue to plait in the usual way.

When there are too many strips pointing to the left a correction can be made in a similar way by altering the direction of one of the strips so that it points to the right.

5. A pattern to try

When you have completed a few kete in takitahi and tōrua you may wish to experiment with other patterns. The one illustrated here is in two colours for clarity only but can as well be worked in natural flax.

Since 48 is the total number of strips used in this kete, any pattern based on a number of strips that will divide into 48 may be used. That is, any pattern or plait using two, three, four, six, or eight strips for each basic unit can be used.

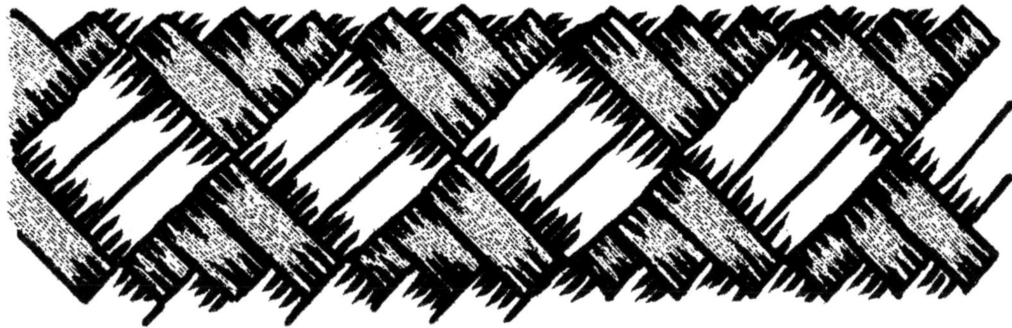

1. A pattern that can be used to add interest to the upper half of the bucket kete.

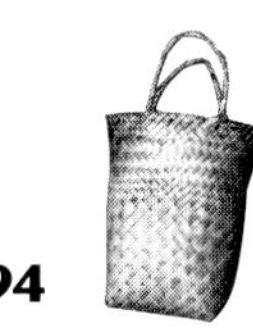

6. How to prepare hard flax

For very hard flax that has a strong fibre the following method can be used for separating the strip from the butt and leaving the tuft of fibre.

Cut the strips away from the butt.

On the dull (underside) of the strip make a cut across with a sharp-pointed knife as shown in J. Do not cut through the fibre, merely the fleshy leaf part, to enable this to be separated off.

Turn the strip over so that the cut is on the upper side.

Place the knife under the strip, beneath where the cut was made, with the strip held between the right thumb and the back of the blade of the knife, as in K.

Pull the knife up and towards the right, so that the dull surface of the strip separates from the strip itself, leaving the tuft of fibre shown in L.

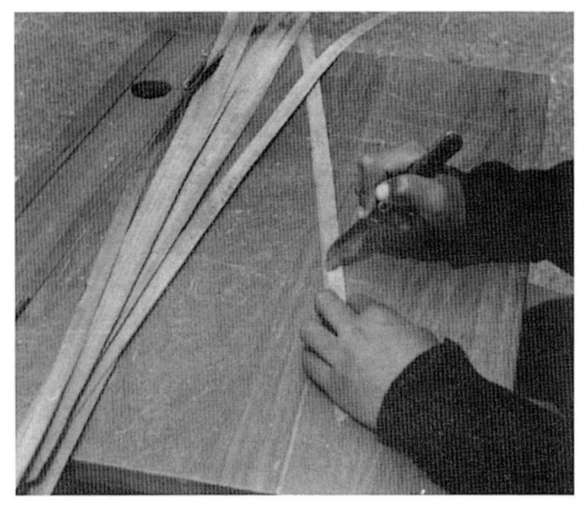

J

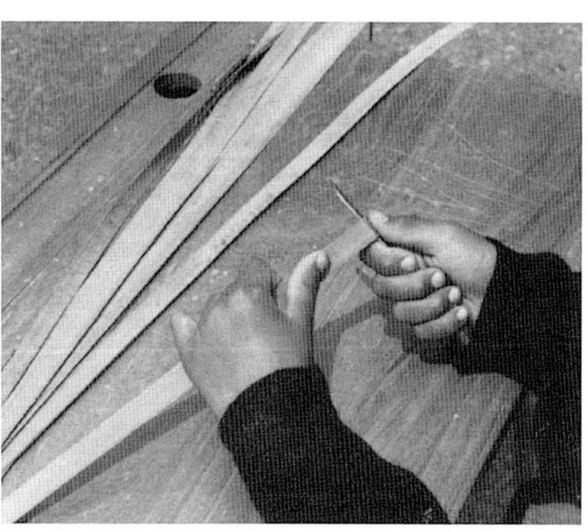

K

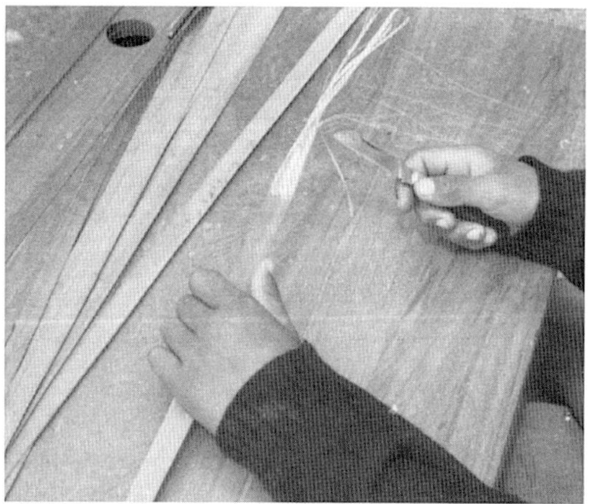

L

Glossary

Here are the meanings of some of the terms used in the book that may cause confusion.

Braid/whiri See plaiting.

Dextrals Te Rangihiroa used the terms dextrals and sinistrals to differentiate between the sets of elements (sets of strips) used in plaiting and braiding. Those that point to the right are dextrals (fig. 1). For most people their right hand is the more dexterous. We see the root of the word appearing in other words referring to the skilful use of one's hands. A person who can use both hands equally well is ambidextrous. See sinistrals.

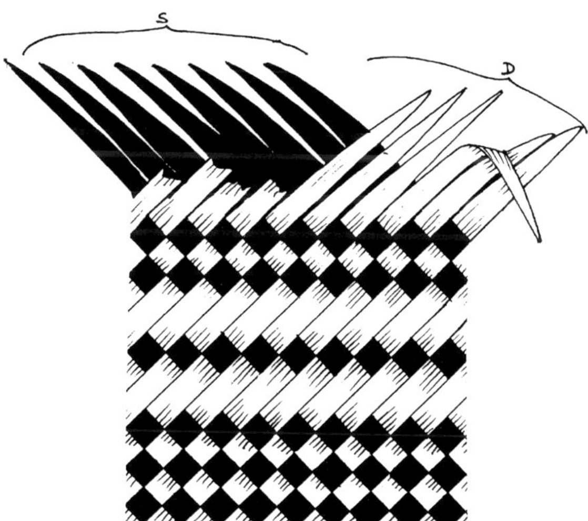

Fig. 1

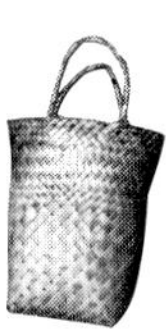

Plaiting The term used by Te Rangihiroa (1923, 705) among others, to describe the method of interlacing strips of flax used to make kete, whariki, tatua and other traditional items. Technically, plaiting and braiding are identical. The working elements in both are laid diagonally. When the work forms a narrow band it is called a braid (whiri) (fig. 2). When it is wide as in a mat or kete it is plaiting (raranga) (fig. 4). There appears to be no definite line of demarcation between the two (fig. 3).

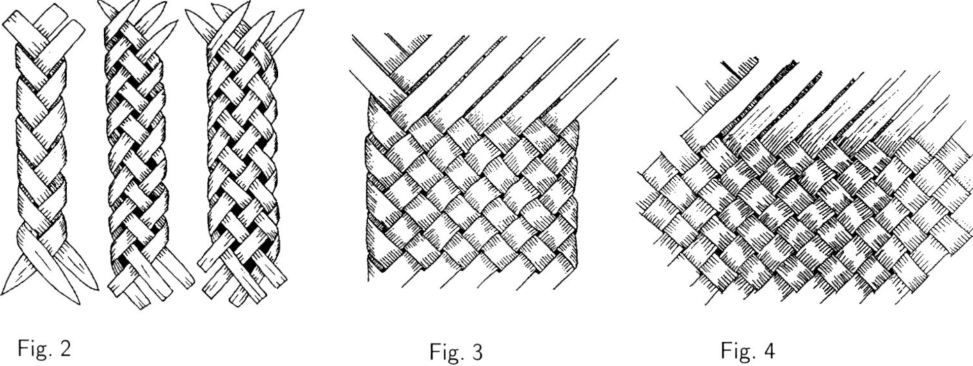

Fig. 2 Fig. 3 Fig. 4

Shed This is a term taken from weaving. It refers to the gap created when alternating wefts are lifted to form a shed. Into this the next weft is laid (fig. 5). In this book the term has been applied to plaiting and used to describe the shed formed when a set of dextrals are lifted to insert a sinistral (fig 6).

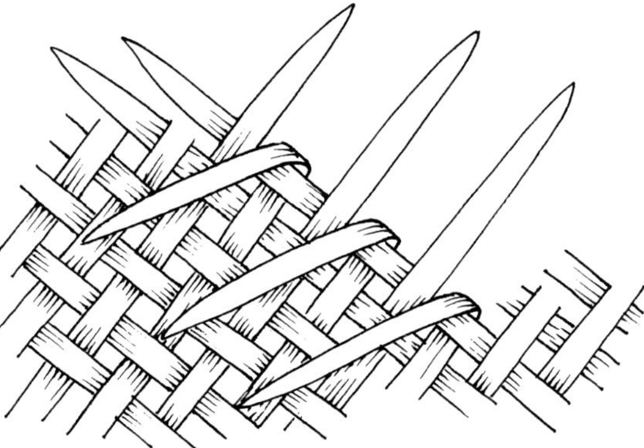

Fig. 5

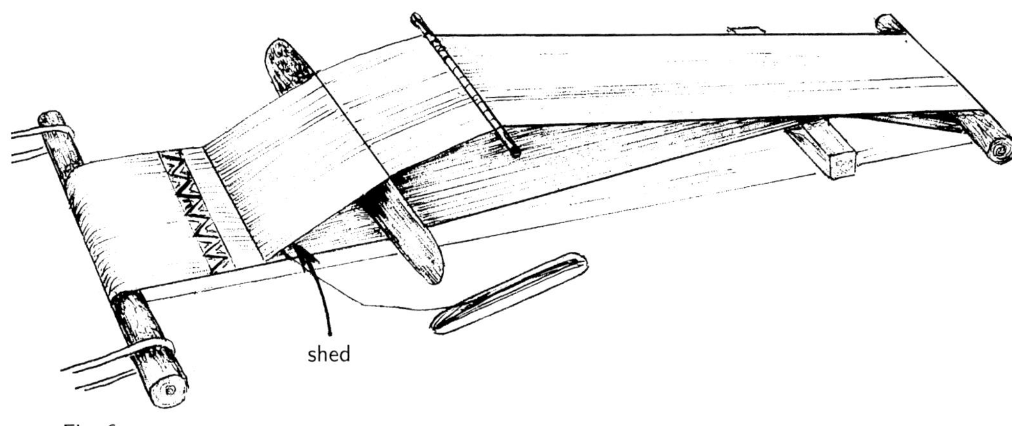

Fig. 6

Sinistrals A term used by Te Rangihiroa to distinguish the strips that point to the left in plaiting (fig. 1). The word sinistral comes from Latin and is related to the word sinister with its suggestion of wickedness and evil. Somewhere in the back of my mind is a story about a Roman who stabbed another man with a knife held in his left hand, while with his right hand he was giving the handshake of friendship. Very sinister behaviour. It helps to remember that sinistrals applied to the strips point to the left. Superstitions and stories about the dangers and evils associated with the left and the left hand appear in many cultures.

Further reading

Anon. 1952. 'Basket Weaving'. *Te Ao Hou*, no. 3. Wellington, Department of Maori Affairs.

— 1953. 'Kawiu Pa Makes up for Lost Time' (an article on mat plaiting). *Te Ao Hou*, no. 5. Wellington, Department of Maori Affairs.

Best, E. 1899. 'The Art of the Whare Pora'. *Transactions of the New Zealand Institute*, vol. 31. Wellington.

— 1925a. 'Fishing Methods and Devices of the Maori'. *Dominion Museum Bulletin*, no. 7. Wellington.

— 1925b. 'Games and Pastimes of the Maori'. *Dominion Museum Bulletin*, no. 8. Wellington.

Blackman, M. 1985. 'Two Early Maori Cloaks'. *New Zealand Craft*, Autumn, 1985. Wellington, The Crafts Council.

Brown, C. 1965a. 'Maori Flax Sandals and How to Make Them'. *Te Ao Hou*, no. 50. Wellington, Department of Maori Affairs.

— 1965b. 'How to Make a Tipare or Headband'. *Te Ao Hou*, no. 52. Wellington, Department of Maori Affairs.

— 1967. 'How to Make a Rourou or Food Basket'. *Te Ao Hou*, no. 59. Wellington, Department of Maori Affairs.

— 1978. *Kete Making*. The Arts of the Maori Instructional Booklet. Wellington, Department of Education.

Buck, P.H. (See Te Rangihiroa)

Connor, J. 1983. 'A Descriptive Classification of Maori Fabrics: Cordage, Plaiting, Windmill Knotting, Twining, Looping and Netting'. *Journal of the Polynesian Society*, vol. 92, no. 2. Wellington.

Duff, R. 1942. 'A Moriori Plaited Textile'. *Dominion Museum Records*, vol. 1. Wellington.

Fischel, W.G. 1951. 'Maori Textile Techniques'. *Ciba Review*, no. 84. Basle.

Gorbey, K. 1979. 'Rangimarie Hetet and Digger Te Kanawa, Korowai Weavers' (poster). Hamilton, Waikato Art Museum.

Goulding, J.H. 1971. 'Identification of Archaeological and Ethnological Specimens of Fibre Plant Material Used by the Maori'. *Records of the Auckland Institute and Museum*, vol. 8. Auckland.

Hamilton, A. 1899–1901. *Maori Art*. 2nd ed. 1977. London, Holland Press.

Hector, J., Haultain, T. and Kebbell, J. 1871. 'Report of the Commissioners Appointed to Enquire into the Preparation of the Phormium Fibre of New Zealand Flax'. *Appendix to the Journals of the House of Representatives of New Zealand*, 1871, E1 G-No. 4. Wellington.

Hindmarsh, Gerard. 'Flax, the Enduring Fibre' in *New Zealand Geographic*, Number 42 April–June 1999.

Hopa, N. 1971. *The Art of Piupiu Making*. Wellington, A.H. & A.W. Reed.

Kururangi, M. 1976. *Weaving*. The Arts of the Maori Instructional Booklet. Wellington, Department of Education.

Ling Roth, H. 1923. *The Maori Mantle*. Halifax, England. Bankfield Museum (republished Bedford, Ruth Beam, Carlton, 1979).

Mead, H.M. 1952a. 'Flax'. *Te Ao Hou*, no. 2. Wellington, Department of Maori Affairs.

— 1952b. 'Te Waka Harakeke (A Toy Canoe)'. *Te Ao Hou*, no. 3. Wellington, Department of Maori Affairs.

— 1953. 'Making a Koronae'. *Te Ao Hou*, no. 4. Wellington, Department of Maori Affairs.

— 1968. *The Art of Taaniko Weaving*. Wellington, A.H. & A.W. Reed.

— 1969. *Traditional Maori Clothing*. Wellington, A.H. & A.W. Reed.

— 1999 (1968). *Te Whatu Taniko, Taniko Weaving, Technique and Tradition*. Reed Publishing (NZ) Ltd.

Moschner, I. 1958. 'Katalog der Neuseeland — Sammlung (A. Reischek), Wien'. *Archive fur Volkerkunde*, Band XIII. Wien.

Pendergrast, M.J. 1984a. *Raranga Whakairo: Maori Plaiting Patterns*. Coromandel, Coromandel Press (reprinted by Reed Books, 1991).

— 1984b. *Feathers and Fibre. A Survey of Traditional and Contemporary Maori Craft*. Auckland, Penguin Books (NZ) Ltd.

— 1987a. *Fun with Flax*. Auckland, Reed Methuen.

— 1987b. *Te Aho Tapu: The Sacred Thread*. Auckland, Reed Methuen, 1987.

Phillipps, W.J. 1950. 'Notes on Maori Plaits'. *Journal of the Polynesian Society*, vol. 69. Wellington.

— 1953. 'Patterns for Baskets'. *Te Ao Hou*, no. 6. Wellington, Department of Maori Affairs.

— 1954. 'A Maori Drinking Cup Used in Otago'. *Journal of the Polynesian Society*, vol. 163. Wellington.

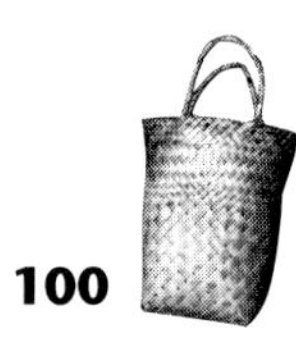

— 1955. 'Notes with Illustrations of Maori Material Culture'. *Dominion Museum Records in Ethnology*, vol. 1, no. 4. Wellington.

— 1957. 'Plaits and Plaiting'. *Te Ao Hou*, no. 18. Wellington, Department of Maori Affairs.

— 1966. *Maori Life and Custom*. Wellington, A.H. & A.W. Reed.

Pownall, G. 1976. *New Zealand Maori Arts and Crafts*. Wellington, Seven Seas Publishing Pty Ltd.

Puketapu-Hetet, Erenora. 1989. *Maori Weaving with...* Auckland. Pitman Publishing.

Ryden, S. 1965. 'The Banks Collection: an Episode in 18th Century Anglo-Swedish Relations'. Monograph Series no. 8. Ethnographic Museum of Sweden. Stockholm.

Scheele, S and Walls, G. 1994. *Harakeke, The Rene Orchiston Collection*. Lincoln. Manaaki Whenua Press

Smith, J.R. 1975. *Taaniko Maori Hand Weaving*. London, Octopus Books.

Te Kanawa, D. R. 1992. *Weaving a Kakahu*. Wellington. Bridget Williams Books Limited in association with Aotearoa Moananui a Kiwa Weavers.

Te Rangihiroa (Sir Peter Buck). 1911. 'On the Maori Art of Weaving Cloaks, Capes and Kilts'. *Dominion Museum Bulletin*, no. 3. Wellington.

— 1921. 'Maori Decorative Art (Tukutuku)'. *Transactions of the New Zealand Institute*, vol. 53. Wellington.

— 1923. 'Maori Plaited Basketry and Plaitwork. Part 1.' *Transactions of the New Zealand Institute*, vol. 54. Wellington.

— 1924a. 'Maori Plaited Basketry and Plaitwork. Part 2.' *Transactions of the New Zealand Institute*, vol. 55. Wellington.

— 1924b. 'Review of "The Maori Mantle" by H. Ling Roth.' *Journal of the Polynesian Society*, vol. 33. Wellington.

— 1926a. 'The Maori Craft of Netting.' *Transactions of the New Zealand Institute*, vol. 56. Wellington.

— 1926b. 'The Evolution of Maori Clothing'. *Memoirs of the Polynesian Society*. vols. 34–35. Wellington.

— 1949. *The Coming of the Maori*. Christchurch, Whitcombe & Tombs Ltd.

van de Klundert, J. 1996. *Te Kono Naku, Raranga Harakeke*. Rotorua, Nga Puna Waihanga.